'Although this book is focussed on Australia the content should be of interest to readers around the world. Multigenerational Family Living is a world-wide phenomenon – normal in some countries but a more recent development in some western societies (if you ignore housing history) where housing shortages have forced families to house multiple generations. The book explores those housing market contexts but it also rightly focusses on the lived reality of multigenerational living and the impact this has on the nature of families. The editors have brought the 11 chapters together into an important volume which provides real insights into worlds which many researchers now have only a modest understanding.'

Peter Williams, Department of Land Economy,
University of Cambridge, UK

'Finally a book that takes seriously the fact that one in five Australians live in multigenerational households. *Multigenerational Family Living* is a comprehensive theoretical and empirical exploration of this complex and diverse form of family living. It shatters common assumptions and stereotypes. Most importantly, it demonstrates why the study of mutigenerational family living matters.'

Ann Dupuis, Associate Professor of Sociology,
Massey University

Multigenerational Family Living

Multigenerational living – where more than one generation of related adults cohabit in the same dwelling – is recognized as a common arrangement amongst many Asian, Middle Eastern and Southern European cultures, but this arrangement is becoming increasingly familiar in many Western societies. Much Western research on multigenerational households has highlighted young adults' delayed first home leaving, the result of difficult economic prospects and the prolonged adolescence of generation Y. This book shows that the causes and results of this phenomenon are more complex.

The book sheds fresh light on a range of structural and social drivers that have led multigenerational families to cohabit and the ways in which families negotiate the dynamic interactions amongst these drivers in their everyday lives. It critically examines factors such as demographics, the environment, culture and family considerations of identity, health, care and well-being, revealing how such factors reflect (and are reflected by) a retracting welfare state and changing understandings of families in an increasingly mobile world.

Based on a series of qualitative and quantitative research projects conducted in Australia, the book provides an interdisciplinary examination of intergenerational cohabitation that explores a variety of concerns and experiences. It will appeal to scholars across the social sciences with interests in housing, demographics and the sociology of the family.

Edgar Liu is a Research Fellow at the City Futures Research Centre, Faculty of Built Environment, UNSW Australia (University of New South Wales).

Hazel Easthope is an Australian Research Council Future Fellow and Senior Research Fellow at City Futures Research Centre, Faculty of Built Environment, UNSW Australia.

Routledge Advances in Sociology

For a full list of titles in this series, please visit www.routledge.com/series/SE0511

Multigenerational Family Living

Evidence and Policy Implications from Australia

Edited by Edgar Liu and Hazel Easthope

Routledge
Taylor & Francis Group

LONDON AND NEW YORK

First published 2017
by Routledge
2 Park Square, Milton Park, Abingdon, Oxon OX14 4RN

and by Routledge
711 Third Avenue, New York, NY 10017

Routledge is an imprint of the Taylor & Francis Group, an informa business

© 2017 selection and editorial material, Edgar Liu and Hazel Easthope; individual chapters, the contributors

British Library Cataloguing in Publication Data
A catalogue record for this book is available from the British Library

Library of Congress Cataloging-in-Publication Data
The LOC Data has been applied for.

ISBN: 978-1-4724-7669-2 (hbk)
ISBN: 978-1-315-59626-6 (ebk)

Typeset in Times New Roman
by Apex CoVantage, LLC

Contents

Tables

Figures

Notes on contributors

Erin Borger is a public servant with the Australian Federal Government. She completed a First Class Honours project at the University of Wollongong in 2010. Her research focused on multigenerational households. Erin is a self-confessed 'kidult', with personal experience of returning to the parental home due to high living costs.

Ian Burnley is an Emeritus Professor at UNSW Australia's City Futures Research Centre. He is a human geographer and demographer whose research activities have focused on international migration to Australia. His work is renowned within Australia and internationally, most recently recognized by his election as a Fellow to the Academy of the Social Sciences in Australia in 2010.

Lyn Craig is a Professor and Australian Research Council Queen Elizabeth II Fellow at the Social Policy Research Centre, UNSW Australia. Her research interests include the intersections between the family and the economy, gender equity, work-family balance and comparative family and social policy. She is also an Associate of the Centre for Time Use Research, St Hugh's College, Oxford, a member of the Australian Bureau of Statistics' Gender Statistics Advisory Board and an Executive Member of the International Association of Time Use Researchers.

Hazel Easthope is an Australian Research Council Future Fellow and Senior Research Fellow at UNSW Australia's City Futures Research Centre. With a background in sociology and human geography, she has built up a strong research track record in urban studies. She has particular research interest in residential decision-making and the intersections among mobility, identity and home.

Bianca Fileborn is a Research Officer at the Australian Centre in Sex, Health and Society, La Trobe University. Her research interests include the intersections of space, identity and violence, sexuality and ageing, and gay, lesbian, bisexual, transgender, intersex and queer (GLBTIQ) people's experiences and understandings of sexual violence.

Chris Gibson is a Professor of Human Geography and Director of the interdisciplinary Global Challenges research program at the University of Wollongong, Australia. His research interests include a wide range of cultural geography topics including cultural economy, critical research on creative industries, household sustainability and material responses to volatility. He has published widely on these topics, including several books.

Tiffany Jones is a Senior Lecturer in the University of New England's School of Education. Jones researches and publishes on GLBTIQ issues in education, education policy, youth issues and well-being. She has liaised with UNESCO, and various international and local/state governments and non-government organizations, on policy development around GLBTIQ issues. She has published widely on GLBTIQ issues, including a number of books.

Bruce Judd is the Director of the Australian School of Architecture and Design at UNSW Australia. With a background in architecture, Judd's research interests include housing design and human behaviour, medium-density housing, public housing estate renewal, urban renewal and ageing and the built environment. He has published widely across these topics.

Natascha Klocker is Senior Lecturer in Human Geography in the School of Geography and Sustainable Communities at the University of Wollongong, Australia. Klocker's research interests include ethnic diversity and environmental sustainability, geographies of children and young people, and inter-ethnic intimacy and racism.

Edgar Liu is a Research Fellow at City Futures Research Centre, UNSW Australia. He has background in cultural and human geography, with research interests spanning a number of sub-disciplines within the social sciences: family forms, public policy changes, social impacts of urban renewal and access to housing.

Michael I. MacEntee is a Professor Emeritus of Prosthodontics and Dental Geriatrics at the Faculty of Dentistry, University of British Columbia. His research addresses oral health and quality of life in old age, with a particular focus on frailty and the psychosocial impact of oral prostheses. He has been awarded the Distinguished Scientist Award from the International Association of Dental Research and is an elected Fellow of the Canadian Academy of Health Sciences.

Rodrigo Mariño is an Associate Professor and Principal Research Fellow at the Oral Health Cooperative Research Centre (OH-CRC), Melbourne Dental School, at the University of Melbourne. His research activities target four main areas in health research: inequalities in health status, health in migrant groups, health workforce and economic evaluation in health. He has published widely in public dental health.

Victor Minichiello is an Emeritus Professor in Public Health at the University of New England, a Conjoint Professor in the School of Medicine and Public Health, the University of Newcastle, and Adjunct Professor at the Australian Centre in Sex, Health and Society, La Trobe University. He is an internationally recognized gerontologist and public health researcher with interests in ageing, health care, sexual health and men's health.

Abigail Powell is a Senior Research Fellow at the Centre for Social Impact, UNSW Australia and an Australian Research Council Discovery Early Career Researcher Fellow. Her research interests are in gender, diversity, work-life balance, young people and social policy.

Stephen Whelan is an Associate Professor at the University of Sydney with a background in economics. His research interest is in social policies and their impact on labour market outcomes as well as the effects of housing assistance measures on labour market behaviour. He has published across these topics from the economics and housing perspectives.

Acknowledgements

First, we would like to thank the Australian Research Council (DP120100956) and the other funding bodies that made the research reported in this book possible.

Second, we would like to thank the staff at the City Futures Research Centre and the Faculty of Built Environment at UNSW Australia, where we are both based. Your assistance and support are very much appreciated.

Third, we would like to acknowledge the contribution of Adjunct Professor Jane Marceau, who provided us with much guidance during the funding application stage; and Emeritus Professor Ian Burnley and Professor Bruce Judd, our co-researchers on the *Living Together* project. Your contributions to the intellectual discussions and the research process were motivating, interesting and enjoyable.

Fourth, to all the participants of the *Living Together* project, and the participants of the other research reported in this book. Thank you for telling us your stories, and in turn, allowing us to tell yours.

Finally, to our own families who – in more ways than one can image – encouraged, guided and supported us through our childhood, adolescence and adulthood. We have lived through some of the benefits and challenges that are described in some of the chapters of this book, and we thank you for being part of that experience.

1 Living with the family in Australian cities

Edgar Liu and Hazel Easthope

Introduction

This book is about multiple generations of families living together in Australian cities.

Like many social scientists, we embarked on this study out of curiosity. Having worked in Australian universities for a number of years, we noticed that more and more of the young adults who came through our doors seemed to be living at home with their parents instead of 'slumming it' in share houses as so famously portrayed in the UK television series, *The Young Ones*, or more recently the US television series, *Felicity*. Other studies have also found that the proportion of young adults (aged 20–34 years) living at home in Australia has steadily increased since the mid-1980s (Pink 2009), a trend also reported in several studies conducted in other Western societies (e.g. ONS 2012; Fry and Passel 2014). Indeed, when we first started looking into this household form, we thought that households with young adults living at home with their parents while completing their university education would comprise the bulk of multigenerational households in Australia. As we found out, that was only part of a much more complex story.

In 2011, 4.3 million Australians lived in multigenerational households; that is, one in every five people. This statistic is more than twice as many people than those who lived by themselves in lone person households (1.9 million), and only a fraction of them are university students still living at home. This finding in itself is remarkable, but even more striking is that the overall proportion of Australians living in multigenerational households has remained steady for the bulk of the 1980s, 1990s and 2000s at around 20 per cent of the total population. Apparently, multigenerational living in Australia has been commonplace for decades. Yet, it is only recently that multigenerational households have received much academic interest, with most of this interest riding on the back of concerns about the phenomenon of so-called kippers (kids in parents' pockets eroding retirement savings). We were also guilty of this focus when we embarked on our research, but we soon realized that multigenerational households take many forms, that people live in them for many reasons and that their experiences of multigenerational living are both rich and varied.

The many forms of multigenerational living

Multigenerational households might include mums and dads and their adult children living under one roof, middle-aged couples who took in one or both sets of parents, three- or even four-generation households and skipped generation households where grandparents and grandchildren live together without the middle generation. All of these combinations feature in the research reported in this book, each scenario reflecting different personal pathways to living together.

In their article, Cohen and Casper (2002:1) state that 'conceptually, standard practices for identifying multigenerational living arrangements and their implications remain elusive'. Indeed, having reviewed numerous publications on multigenerational living in the last handful of years, we have yet to find any consensus on how a multigenerational household should be defined.

Few statistics bureaus provide official definitions of multigenerational households; few also collate and publish statistics on multigenerational households. This factor has contributed to multigenerational households being regularly overlooked in the development of policies because no one knows how many there are, or where and how they live. This has particularly important implications for the development of policies relating to the family, including those affecting child and elderly care and housing. The US Census Bureau is one notable exception. Its definition of a multigenerational household, however, is decidedly narrow: 'family households consisting of three or more generations' (Lofquist 2012:1). Research by Bengtson et al. (2002) on how families still matter and the 'practical guide to successful multigenerational living' by Niederhaus and Graham (2013) also follow this definition.

Limiting multigenerational households to those with three or more generations of related people excludes a large number of families. A study by Fry and Passel (2014:1), for example, understands the meaning of 'multi' as 'more than one', and defines multigenerational households as including 'at least two adult generations, such as a parent and an adult child aged 25 or older'. Several other studies in the United States also define multigenerational households as including two or more adult generations (e.g. Kahn et al. 2013).

In research focused on the delayed first home leaving of young adults (a noted cause of multigenerational living), there are also differences in who are considered 'young adults'. For Gee et al. (2003) in Canada, young adults were those between 19 and 35 years old, while the United Kingdom's Office of National Statistics (2014, on young adults who live with their parents rather than multigenerational households as such) views young adults as those between 20 and 34 years old – the same definition as used in Pink's (2009) reflections on changes to young people's living arrangements in Australia. Also in Australia, Cobb-Clark and her colleagues (Cobb-Clark et al. 2009; 2012) in discussing parents' economic support of young adult children used survey data conducted with young adults when they were 18 and 20.

Many other studies that discuss multigenerational households do not define them clearly, especially when intergenerational bonds (such as Chui 2008; Izuhara 2010) are the main focus of discussion. Therefore, no matter whether they are writing specifically of multigenerational households or the delayed first home leaving of young adults, few studies agree on a definition for multigenerational households or young adults, which makes international, or cross-study, comparison difficult.

We wanted to use a definition that encapsulates as many different forms of multigenerational households as possible so as not to miss anyone's stories. Having considered all these differences, in this book we define multigenerational households as follows:

> Households where two or more generations of related adults live in the same dwelling, with the oldest of the youngest generation aged 18 years or older.

This definition is in line with Fry and Passel's (2014) definition, although with the age limit of young adults lowered from 25 to 18. Defining young adults as 18 or older broadens the number of households that fall within our definition. At different conferences where we have presented our findings, we have often been asked to justify this decision, with the comment made that for many of the households included in our statistics, it is simply 'business as usual' for them as the young adult children continue to live in the family home after they turn 18. There are several reasons why we settled on this definition:

1   In order to include 'parents with adult children' and 'skipped generation households', the definition must be broadened to include two-generation households rather than just three or more generations as in Bengtson et al. (2002), Lofquist (2012) and Niederhaus and Graham (2013).
2   We follow the definition of adults as individuals aged 18 or older, the legal age across most societies worldwide.
3   We wanted to do a time-series analysis of census data, and following advice from the Australian Bureau of Statistics (which administers the Australian census), 18 was decided as the lower age limit for 'young adult'.

In gathering our census data, we built in flexibility to minimize the potential skew of young adults still living at home while studying and have included a narrower definition for comparison:

> Households where two or more generations of related adults live in the same dwelling, with the oldest of the youngest generation aged 25 years or older.

Data collated using both of these definitions are presented in the book where appropriate.

There are, however, notable multigenerational household types excluded from both of these definitions. Three- or four-generation households where none of the (great) grandchildren generation has turned 18 (or, in the latter case, 25) are not included in the figures reported in this book. As such, our figures might provide an underestimation of multigenerational households, rather than an overestimation.

Reasons for multigenerational living

Multigenerational living is most often recognized as a common living arrangement among Asian, Middle Eastern and Southern European cultures, as reflected in most of the existing literature on this household form. This literature, however, often describes a relatively narrow range of household forms (namely middle-aged parents with adult children or three-generation households), with strong family values entrenched in cultural traditions often cited as the main reason for multiple generations to live together. However, there are other important drivers of multigenerational living besides cultural tradition. These drivers include structural changes (notably ageing populations, changing employment structures), public policy decisions (notably regarding housing provision and areas of family significance such as child and elderly care and higher education) and changing social norms regarding the role of the family, which may be influenced by the changing cultural make-up of cities, but are not necessarily the direct result of them.

Multigenerational living as cultural tradition

Most literature on multigenerational living in Eastern and Middle Eastern societies identifies cultural tradition as the main reason people live in this household form. These cultural traditions are frequently described as upholding filial piety or carrying out a generational contract.

Filial piety is a Confucian philosophy, which is often understood as the virtue of respecting (and, in many cases, taking care of) one's elders. It is most commonly associated with Eastern cultures. Chui (2008) explains that younger generations within Chinese traditions are often expected to take care of older family members out of respect for filial piety, and multigenerational living is a common means to achieving this respect, despite the often cramped living quarters of many Chinese cities (e.g. Chui's 2008 study of multigenerational living in Hong Kong and Izuhara's 2010 study of Shanghai). In what she describes as a generational contract, Izuhara (2010) explains that caring for older family members is often because of an expectation that the younger generations must reciprocate the care they received when they were younger. While Confucian ideologies including filial piety were openly criticized by the Chinese Communist revolution during the 1940s, Izuhara (2010: 78) reports that the duty of adult offspring to care for their ageing parents remains strong today, so much so that it was legislated under Criminal (1979) and Marriage Laws (1980) as well as the Chinese Constitution (1982).

In writing about Kuwait in the 1990s, Shah et al. (2002) find similarities to Chui's explanation for the stronger prevalence of multigenerational living in Middle Eastern societies. They found that the majority of older people in Kuwait (70 per cent) live with their adult offspring and that the proportions are higher if they are elderly, widowed or divorced (94 per cent of men and 89 per cent of women). These arrangements can arise out of both preference (in respecting filial piety) but also, in many cases, need. Mehio-Sibai, Beydoun and Tohme (2009) note that many women of older generations were unable to support themselves when they became widowed or divorced because of their lower workforce participation once married, and thus their adult offspring were expected to take them in and care for them. At the same time, these women are providing important support in caring for their grandchildren as their daughters and daughters-in-law are increasingly in full-time employment.

The influence of family plays a significant role on Southern Europeans' propensity to live in multigenerational households. A study by Manacorda and Moretti (2002) find that the parents' willingness to have their adult children living at home (and some even working harder to provide the adult children a higher standard of living) was one particular driver for multigenerational cohabitation in Italy. Alessie et al. (2005: 3) also find that financial benefits, especially an ability to save on expenses, were a driver for what they term 'composite households', or 'households where grown children live with their parents'.

When multigenerational households are discussed in Western societies, a distinction is often drawn between households of different cultural backgrounds. In their Canadian study, Gee et al. (2003) note that young Canadians of Asian and Indian backgrounds are more likely to leave the parental home at a later stage than their Anglo counterparts and are therefore more likely to live in multigenerational households. In the United States, Fry and Passel (2014) note the proportional increase in multigenerational households coincides with increased immigration since the 1970s. Asian Americans, Hispanics and African Americans are more likely to live in multigenerational households than non-Hispanic Caucasian Americans. Similarly, in Australia, Pink (2009: 28) highlights that cultural background plays a role in the propensity of young adults to live with their parents, finding that second-generation Australians with Asian ancestry have 'a greater tendency than people of other ancestries to be living with their parents'.

Although these studies indicate that cultural expectations and traditions are strong influences of a propensity for multigenerational living, cultural background alone does not dictate the uptake of such a living arrangement. Other factors also increase the likelihood of multiple generations of a family living together.

Multigenerational living in the context of structural changes and policy decisions

House prices increased rapidly around the world in the 1980s, 1990s and early 2000s (Girouard et al. 2006; Yates and Gabriel 2006; Del Negro and Otrok 2007). In many cases, increases in house prices outstripped increases in income, and this was certainly the case in Australia (PC 2004). Economists and others have speculated that the increase in house prices has been a contributing factor to young adults leaving home at a later stage (Cobb-Clark 2008). Indeed, Australian research by Burke et al. (2007) shows that many young Australians have what they term 'blocked aspirations', where the Australian dream of owner-occupation of a suburban detached house (Apps 1976) has in recent decades turned into an unaffordable nightmare (Yu 2005). By the turn of the twenty-first century, the proportion of all home purchasers who were first-home buyers was merely a fraction of what it was in the 1990s, thanks in part to a significant upsurge of investor-owners flooding the housing market (PC 2004: 21).

In their analysis of the Household, Income and Labour Dynamics in Australia (HILDA) longitudinal dataset, Cobb-Clark and Ribar (2009) identify that rapidly increasing housing costs have a major influence on living arrangement decisions of young Australians, including their propensity to live in multigenerational households. Cobb-Clark (2008) explains that the inability of young Australians to afford independent living as homeowners or private renters is amplified by the persistent retraction of welfare assistance. Although the retractions have not solely targeted young people but rather the population in general, asset-poor young people are often more harshly impacted. Since the 1980s, the retractions in Australia have included, but are not limited to, the end of free tertiary education, reduction in the types of welfare benefits available and welfare benefit payments not keeping up with inflation. Some of these retractions have also been seen across other Western societies (e.g. Prideaux 2001 on the United Kingdom and the United States). Furthermore, Cobb-Clark (2008) in Australia and Mitchell and Lovegreen (2009) in Canada both explain that uncertain economic conditions since the 1990s – a result of the casualization of the workforce, shorter-term employment contracts and de-industrialization, among others – have destabilized young adults' ability to afford (and maintain) independent living for extended periods.

In the United States, Fry and Passel (2014) found that since the late 2000s global financial crisis (GFC), the number of Americans who live in multigenerational households has increased significantly. While the onset of the GFC in the late 2000s stalled or even reduced house prices in many societies worldwide, (Claessens et al. 2010), Fry and Passel (2014: 6) explain that through 'declining employment and wages of less-educated young adults' they are also less able to afford living independently of their parents. By 2012, the number of Americans who lived in multigenerational households was more than twice the 1980 level. The proportion of Americans who live in multigenerational households has also increased from 12.1 per cent in 1980 to 18.1 per cent in 2012, but most rapidly since the GFC (Fry and Passel 2014: 4). Furthermore, they note that the annual rate of increase in multigenerational population in the United States doubled immediately following the GFC, from 1.3 per cent during 2006–2007 to 2.7 per cent in 2007–2008, a level that was maintained until 2010–2011 when economic recovery became more promising. Meanwhile in Australia, where the impact of the GFC on the economy was less severe than in many other developed countries, house prices have continued to increase, especially in major cities where house prices increased on average by 6.8 per cent from December 2013–2014 (ABS 2015). In Sydney, the largest city in Australia, house price growth increased by an extreme 12.2 per cent over the same period (ABS 2015).

With uncertain economic futures, many young adults turn to their families for financial assistance or for shelter, or when it comes time for establishing their own households. Cobb-Clark (2008), Olsberg and Winters (2005) and Barrett et al. (2015) have commented on intergenerational wealth transfers in the Australian context, especially those from older to younger generations, as an increasingly common practice for parents to help their adult children in taking a foothold in the housing market. Albertini et al. (2007) resonate this situation in their European study, and further explain that the frequency and amount of intergenerational wealth transfer strongly correlate with each country's welfare regime. In states renowned for welfare provision, such as Scandinavian countries, parental assistance is more frequent though of much smaller amounts than in countries that are less generous with their welfare payouts. The pattern, however, is different in Central and Southern European countries, and provision of social support (which includes 'personal care, practical household help, and help with paperwork') is more prominent than among the Scandinavian states (Albertini et al. 2007: 321, 324). While they did not investigate the correlation between welfare policies and living arrangements, it is clear that welfare policies influence how families and their extended relations make decisions on how to financially and socially support each other. From the research reported in this book, it is clear that welfare and other public policies also influence decisions about household forms.

Multigenerational living reflecting changing social norms

With cultural traditions and structural constraints considered, some literature has now begun acknowledging the prevalence of multigenerational living – especially in 'non-traditional' places like Australia – as a reflection of changing social norms. Pink (2009: 24) acknowledges that the increase in the proportion of young adults (aged 20–34 years) who live at home with their parents (from 19 per cent in 1986 to 23 per cent in 2006) is 'related to the trend toward partnering at a later age', with partnership being a life stage when young adults would traditionally leave home and establish their own households. Pink (2009: 26) also notes that it is now common for young adults to boomerang and return to live with their parents after having left for some time, with almost half (46 per cent) of the young adults who have ever left returning by age 35. He speculates that changes in circumstance (such as relationship breakdown) and saving to buy their own home as the main catalysts for young adults to return, and the findings reported in this book confirm that.

Although many researchers have recognized a link between cultural background and the propensity to live in a multigenerational household (e.g. Gee et al. 2003 in Canada; Pink 2009 in Australia; Fry and Passel 2014 in the United States), in countries where multigenerational living has not been traditional, the increase of migrants from countries where it has cannot singularly explain these broader social trends. Following a statistical analysis of the HILDA longitudinal dataset in Australia, Flatau et al. (2007) argue that while education, family background and ethnicity play strong roles in young people's parental home-leaving decisions, there has been a gradual increase in first home-leaving age for young Australians since World War II. Their statistical analysis shows that 'birth cohort effects on parental home leaving remain significant once the roles of other determinants [such as education, family background and ethnicity] are taken into account' (Flatau et al. 2007: 67). They conclude by stating that the data 'suggests an important role for changing mores and values, not easily encapsulated in measured effects, in influencing parental home leaving outcomes' (Flatau et al. 2007: 67), with these mores and values having persistent influences on people's propensity to live in multigenerational households.

Experiences of multigenerational living

Most existing literature on multigenerational households, whether in the Eastern or Western worlds, has focused on the reasons for their formation and continuation. Although some acknowledge the outcomes of this living arrangement (e.g. Klocker et al. 2012) on the environmental and economic benefits of resource sharing within multigenerational homes, few discuss in detail the experiences of the people who live in multigenerational households or the short- and longer-term impacts of this household form on care provision, cultural hegemony, family relationships, housing use, resource sharing and social acceptability. In this book, we explore these topics in detail in the Australian context.

Structure of the book

All of the research presented in this book focuses on multigenerational households in Australian cities. The questions of who lives in multigenerational households, why, and how they experience these living arrangements could be asked in any national or geographical context, but we think that our focus on Australia, and on cities, is particularly interesting.

Most Western research on multigenerational households to date has focused on North America and the United Kingdom. This research has often highlighted young adults' delayed first home leaving – precipitated by tough economic prospects, retracting social welfare and the prolonged adolescence of generation Y as the main catalysts for increases in multigenerational living (e.g. Settersten, Furstenberg and Rumbaut 2005; Keene and Batson 2010; Waters et al. 2011; ONS 2012). While Australia has also experienced similar structural and cultural changes as North America and the United Kingdom, our research has found that the causes (and, correspondingly, the outcomes) are more complex than generation Y's unwillingness or inability to leave the parental home. As such, the Australian case provides alternate insights into the phenomenon of multigenerational living in a Western context.

Like Canada, the United Kingdom and the United States, Australia provides an interesting case study for examining multigenerational living because it is also a culturally diverse country. Many migrants to Australia have moved here from countries and regions where multigenerational living is commonplace. Therefore, Australia provides an excellent location from which to explore the extent to which multigenerational living is influenced by cultural norms about the form and function of families.

Our focus on cities is important because not only are cities the locations in which the majority of the population live (UN 2010) and where the majority of new migrants settle (Dobson et al. 2001; Jupp 2002), they are also centres of economic productivity and the locations with the most serious housing affordability pressures. As such, a focus on cities provides a wide range of structural factors that can potentially affect the formation and form of multigenerational households and the experiences of the people who live in them.

We set out to explain the different drivers that motivate different generations of families to live together and what the outcomes might be. Much of the book reflects the findings of a three-year research project funded by the Australian Research Council that examined the cultural, economic, political and social drivers for families to consider multigenerational living in which we spoke to people who live in multigenerational households about the everyday and longer-term outcomes of living together. We also draw on other contemporary Australian research that looked at the benefits and drawbacks of multigenerational living to provide a fuller portrayal of the challenges and pleasures they face in terms of culture, economics, the environment, health and well-being, housing, identity and social relations. As a collection, this book reflects on these factors from the disciplinary perspectives of demography, human geography, sociology, economics, architecture, planning, health and environmental science.

The book's three sections reflect our research focus: who lives in multigenerational households; why they live together; and their experiences of this living arrangement. The majority of the chapters address the third question, because it has received the least attention in international literature to date.

Who lives in multigenerational households?

In Chapter 2, Ian Burnley provides a time-series analysis of demographic and socioeconomic changes in multigenerational households in Australia between 1986 and 2011 and discusses long-term trends in multigenerational living in Australia in relation to demographic and population theories and migration patterns.

Why do multigenerational households live together?

In Chapter 3, Hazel Easthope describes the reasons people live in multigenerational households in Australia. This chapter draws on findings from a survey with multigenerational household members in Sydney and Brisbane, analysis of diaries they kept as well as follow-up interviews describing how they came to live together. The chapter also discusses the impact of wider structural changes, policy changes and changing views about family. These findings are complemented by analysis undertaken by Stephen Whelan of data from the HILDA dataset to examine how resources are shared among family members in multigenerational households in Chapter 4. Through this analysis, Whelan documents the nature and extent of transfers of both money and time within multigenerational households for over a decade (2001–2013) and explores how these transfers have evolved over time as the household members and their circumstances changed.

How do multigenerational households live together?

Chapter 5 describes the experiences of people living in multigenerational households. In this chapter, Edgar Liu draws on the results of a survey, diaries and interviews with multigenerational household members to discuss what people most like and dislike about multigenerational living, understood within the context of relationships among family members.

The three chapters that follow each focus on a particular aspect of the experience of multigenerational living. Lyn Craig and Abigail Powell further discuss relationships among multigenerational household members through their examination of domestic housework, intergenerational dependency and challenges to traditional gender roles in Chapter 6. In Chapter 7, Rodrigo Mariño and colleagues challenge the common assumption that cultural traditions strongly influence individual desire for multigenerational living. Through their case study of older China-born migrants living in Melbourne, they discuss how cultural traditions may not be as influential when transported to a different social setting. In Chapter 8, Bianca Fileborn and colleagues discuss the experiences of LGBT people and the challenges they face – regarding their identity, sexuality, family relationships and stigma – in leading them to live (or not) in multigenerational households.

The final two chapters examine the impact that the dwelling, and its use, can have on the experiences of multigenerational household members. In Chapter 9, Bruce Judd discusses the impact of dwelling design on experiences of multigenerational living. He focuses, in particular, on how concerns about lack of privacy and inadequate space, which can have adverse impacts on relationships among family members, might be addressed through more appropriate dwelling design and the implications for the housing industry and public policy. In Chapter 10, Natascha Klocker and colleagues discuss the potential benefits of multigenerational living in regard to resource consumption and waste production, describing how the frugal practices and skills of older generations and intentional environmental actions of younger generations have coalesced, with profound implications for everyday domestic life.

Recognizing multigenerational households

The book concludes with a brief discussion (Chapter 11) of the role of multigenerational households within the context of structural changes in society, changes in public policy and shifting social and cultural views about the family. These are tied in with findings from interviews we conducted with stakeholders (advocacy groups, state planners and housing developers) on how and what forms of policy solutions may facilitate individuals and households in choosing the appropriate living arrangements for their needs, be it in a multigenerational household or elsewhere.

This book is a call to recognize the importance of multigenerational households. This call is not only to recognize this common household form and the needs and experiences of the people who live in it but also to recognize what it represents more broadly: the importance of family in modern society.

References

ABS 2015, *Residential Property Price Indexes: Eight Capital Cities, December 2014*, Cat. No. 6416.0, Australian Bureau of Statistics, Canberra.

Albertini, M, Kohli, M and Vogel, C 2007, 'Intergenerational transfers of time and money in European families: Common patterns – Different regimes?' *Journal of European Social Policy*, vol. 17, pp. 319–334.

Alessie, R, Brugiavini, A and Weber, G 2005, *Saving and Cohabitation: The Economic Consequences of Living with One's Parents in Italy and the Netherlands*, NBER Working Paper, National Bureau of Economic Research.

Apps, P 1976, 'Home ownership – The Australian dream', *The Australian Quarterly*, vol. 48, pp. 64–75.

Barrett, G, Cigdem, M, Whelan, S and Wood, G 2015, *The Relationship Between Intergenerational Transfers, Housing and Economic Outcomes*, Final Report No. 250, Australian Housing and Urban Research Institute, Melbourne.

Bengtson, VL, Biblarz, TJ and Roberts, RE 2002, *How Families Still Matter: A Longitudinal Study of Youth in Two Generations*, Cambridge University Press, Cambridge, UK.

Burke, T, Pinnegar, S, Phibbs, P, Neske, C, Gabriel, M, Ralston, L and Ruming, K 2007, *Experiencing the Housing Affordability Problem: Blocked Aspirations, Trade-Offs and Financial Hardships*, National Research Venture 3: Housing affordability for lower income Australians Research Paper, Australian Housing and Urban Research Institute, Melbourne.

Chui, EWT 2008, 'Ageing in place in Hong Kong – Challenges and opportunities in a capitalist Chinese city', *Ageing International*, vol. 32, pp. 167–182.

Claessens, S, Dell'Ariccia, G, Igan, D and Laeven, L 2010, 'Cross-country experiences and policy implications from the global financial crisis', *Economic Policy*, vol. 25, pp. 267–293.

Cobb-Clark, DA 2008, 'Leaving home: What economics has to say about the living arrangements of young Australians', *The Australian Economic Review*, vol. 41, pp. 160–176.

Cobb-Clark, DA and Gørgens, T 2012, *Parents' Economic Support of Young-Adult Children: Do Socioeconomic Circumstances Matter?* Melbourne Institute Working Paper Series, Melbourne Institute of Applied Economics and Social Research.

Cobb-Clark, DA and Ribar, DC 2009, *Financial Stress, Family Conflict, and Youths' Successful Transition to Adult Roles*, Discussion Paper, Centre for Economic Policy Research, Australian National University, Canberra.

Cohen, PN and Casper, LM 2002, 'In whose home? Multigenerational families in the United States, 1998–2000', *Sociological Perspectives*, vol. 45, pp. 1–20.

Del Negro, M and Otrok, C 2007, '99 luftballons: Monetary policy and the house price boom across U.S. States', *Journal of Monetary Economics*, vol. 54, pp. 1962–1985.

Dobson, J, Koser, K, Mclaughlan, G and Salt, J 2001, *International Migration and the United Kingdom: Recent Patterns and Trends*, RDS Occasional Paper, Home Office Research, Development and Statistics Directorate.

Flatau, P, James, I, Watson, R, Wood, G and Hendershott, PH 2007, 'Leaving the parental home in Australia over the generations: Evidence from the household, income and labour dynamics in Australia (Hilda) survey', *Journal of Population Research*, vol. 24, pp. 51–71.

Fry, RA and Passel, JS 2014, *In Post-Recession Era, Young Adults Drive Continuing Rise in Multi-Generational Living*, Pew Research Center, Social and Demographic Trends Project, Washington, DC.

Gee, EM, Mitchell, BA and Wister, AV 2003, 'Home leaving trajectories in Canada: Exploring cultural and gendered dimensions', *Canadian Studies in Population*, vol. 30, pp. 245–270.

Girouard, N, Kennedy, M, van den Noord, P and André, C 2006, *Recent House Price Developments: The Role of Fundamentals*, OECD Publishing, Paris.

Izuhara, M 2010, 'Housing wealth and family reciprocity in East Asia', in M Izuhara (ed.), *Ageing and Intergenerational Relations: Family Reciprocity from a Global Perspective*, Policy Press, Bristol, pp. 77–94.

Jupp, J 2002, *From White Australia to Woomera: The Story of Australian Immigration*, Cambridge University Press, Cambridge.

Kahn, JR, Goldscheider, F and García-Manglano, J 2013, 'Growing parental economic power in parent–adult child households: Coresidence and financial dependency in the United States, 1960–2010', *Demography*, vol. 50, pp. 1449–1475.

Keene, JR and Batson, CD 2010, 'Under one roof: A review of research on intergenerational coresidence and multigenerational households in the United States', *Sociology Compass*, vol. 4, pp. 642–657.

Klocker, N, Gibson, C and Borger, E 2012, 'Living together but apart: Material geographies of everyday sustainability in extended family households', *Environment and Planning A*, vol. 44, pp. 2240–2259.

Lofquist, DA 2012, *Multigenerational Households: 2009–2011*, American Community Survey Briefs, US Census Bureau.

Manacorda, M and Moretti, E 2002, *Intergenerational Transfers and Household Structure: Why Do Most Italian Youths Live With Their Parents?* CEP Discussion paper, Centre for Economic Performance, London School of Economic and Political Science.

Mitchell, BA and Lovegreen, LD 2009, 'The empty nest syndrome in midlife families: A multimethod exploration of parental gender differences and cultural dynamics', *Journal of Family Issues*, vol. 30, pp. 1651–1670.

Niederhaus, SG and Graham, JL 2013, *All in the Family: A Practical Guide to Successful Multigenerational Living*, Taylor Trade Publishing, Lanham.

Olsberg, D and Winters, M 2005, *Ageing in Place: Intergenerational and Intrafamilial Housing Transfers and Shifts in Later Life*, Final Report No. 88, Australian Housing and Urban Research Institute, Melbourne.

ONS 2012, *Young Adults Living with Parents in the UK – 2011*, Population, UK Office for National Statistics.

PC 2004, *First Home Ownership: Inquiry Report*, Productivity Commission Inquiry Report, Productivity Commission.

Pink, B 2009, *Australian Social Trends, June 2009*, Cat. No. 4102.0, Australian Bureau of Statistics, Canberra.

Prideaux, S 2001, 'New labour, old functionalism: The underlying contradictions of welfare reform in the US and the UK', *Social Policy and Administration*, vol. 35, pp. 85–115.

Settersten, RA, Furstenberg, FF, Jr. and Rumbaut, RG 2005, *On the Frontier of Adulthood: Theory, Research, and Public Policy*, University of Chicago Press, Chicago.

Shah, NM, Yount, KM, Shah, MA and Menon, I 2002, 'Living arrangements of older women and men in Kuwait', *Journal of Cross-Cultural Gerontology*, vol. 17, pp. 337–355.

UN 2010, *World Urbanisation Prospects: The 2009 Revision.* United Nations, Department of Economic and Social Affairs, Population Division, Population Estimates and Projections Section.

Waters, MC, Carr, PJ, Kefalas, MJ and Holdaway, J 2011, *Coming of Age in America: The Transition to Adulthood in the Twenty-First Century*, University of California Press, Berkeley.

Yates, J and Gabriel, M 2006, *Housing Affordability in Australia*, National Research Venture 3: Housing Affordability for Lower Income Australians Research Paper, Australian Housing and Urban Research Institute, Melbourne.

Yu, X 2005, ' "The great Australian dream" busted on a Brick wall: Housing issues in Sydney', *Cities*, vol. 22, pp. 436–445.

2 Demographic characteristics of multigenerational households in Australia

Ian Burnley

Introduction

Across Australia, one-quarter of all family households were multigenerational households in 2011 (ABS 2012c; 2013a), where a multigenerational household is defined as one that is composed of at least two interrelated adult generations and at least one member of the youngest generation is 18 or older. In Sydney, one-third of all family households were multigenerational.

Using metropolitan Sydney and Brisbane as case studies, this chapter highlights the demographic and socioeconomic characteristics of multigenerational households in Australia, and describes how these have changed between 1986 and 2011. Metropolitan Sydney and Brisbane were chosen because they have different employment and housing markets and different patterns of internal and international migration. While Sydney had the largest numerical population increase of people living in multigenerational households of any city in Australia, Brisbane the highest rate of increase between 1986 and 2011.

Multigenerational living, of course, is not necessarily a new phenomenon in Australia. As noted in Chapter 1, the proportion of Australians who lived in multigenerational households remained relatively constant throughout 1986–2011, at around one-fifth of the total population. This is despite rapid national population growth (38 per cent), especially in the cities, thanks to an upward trend in international immigration that began in the 1950s. Australia, and Sydney in particular, has been strongly impacted by migration from regions where multigenerational households have been culturally or economically embedded, notably Southern Europe and the Middle East (e.g. Mehio-Sibai et al. 2009), but also from areas in Southeast and Northeast Asia where intergenerational obligations were traditionally strong (Hugo 2001; Izuhara 2010).

It is important to note here the sequencing of the migration waves because the outcomes of these waves are reflected in how prevalent multigenerational living is within specific cultural groups. Migration in the 1950s and 1960s was dominated by Southern and Eastern Europeans, alongside significant movements from Northwest Europe. In the 1970s, the dismantling of the 'White Australia' policy and international events saw the beginnings of large-scale immigration from Southeast Asia and the Middle East (Burnley 2000). By the 1980s, changing migration policies resulted in skilled and family reunion movements from Northeast Asia and continuing family reunion migration from North Africa and the Middle East (Burnley 2000). The strong multigenerational traditions of some migrant origin communities in Australia have occurred in the context of the dominance of the nuclear family type there and in Northwest Europe and North America. However, there is growing recognition of diversities within families in academic discussions concerning Western countries (Widmer 2010).

Data and methodology

This chapter utilizes data from the six most recent Australian Censuses of Population and Housing from 1986 to 2011 to present an overview of the sociocultural and economic characteristics of multigenerational households in Australia, and how these characteristics have changed since the mid-1980s. As such, it is a largely descriptive, census-based analysis interjected by references to major Australian events and policy changes to provide context. The 1986 census was taken as the baseline because earlier cross-tabulations could not be matched with post-1986 data. In consultation with the Australian Bureau of Statistics (ABS), cross-tabulations were devised for Australia as a whole, and Sydney and Brisbane metropolitan boundaries as at the 2006 census.[1] The data provided were by individuals who lived in multigenerational households (broad age group, major world region of birth, educational qualifications, occupation and employment status) as well as of the dwellings in which the multigenerational households resided (household size, tenure, dwelling structure, dwelling size and housing cost by quintiles). Where relevant, differences in sociocultural and economic characteristics between multigenerational households where a member of the youngest generation is at least age 18 and where a member of the youngest generation is at least age 25 are highlighted.

Unlike the United Kingdom, the United States and Canada, the Australian census is conducted every five years instead of every ten. However, for reasons of clarity, the data presented in this chapter is at ten-year intervals from 1986 until 2006, with the latest census (2011) included for up-to-date comparison. Data analysis for Sydney and Brisbane is undertaken mostly at the metropolitan level, and supplemented by analysis at the statistical subdivision (SSD) level, which are major geographic subdivisions typically of 100,000–300,000 residents (or 30,000–100,000 households), when spatial distribution is discussed.

Age distributions of people in multigenerational households

Table 2.1 shows the age distributions of persons in multigenerational households where at least one person of the youngest adult generation is aged 18 or older and Table 2.2 where that person is aged 25 or older. In 2011, more than one million people in Sydney (and nearly 400,000 people in Brisbane) lived in multigenerational households where at least one person in the youngest adult generation is aged 18 or older. Between 1986 and 2011, there was a gradual shift in the age

Table 2.1 Percentage shares of persons by age group in multigenerational households in which the youngest adult generation members were aged 18 or older, Sydney and Brisbane, 1986–2011

	Age group	1986	1996	2006	2011	Total population (2011)
Sydney SD	0–17	15%	13%	13%	13%	23%
	18–24	26%	26%	24%	24%	10%
	25–34	8%	10%	10%	11%	15%
	35–44	11%	10%	8%	7%	15%
	45–54	21%	24%	23%	22%	14%
	55–64	13%	11%	14%	15%	11%
	65 or older	6%	7%	8%	9%	13%
	Total persons	718,236	830,484	973,617	1,083,213	4,391,672

	Age group	1986	1996	2006	2011	Total population (2011)
Brisbane SD	0–17	16%	14%	14%	14%	24%
	18–24	26%	26%	25%	25%	10%
	25–34	7%	8%	8%	9%	15%
	35–44	12%	11%	9%	8%	15%
	45–54	20%	25%	24%	23%	13%
	55–64	12%	9%	12%	13%	11%
	65 or older	6%	7%	7%	7%	12%
	Total persons	230,444	277,107	340,971	385,311	2,065,997

Source: Customized tables from ABS (2013)

structure of multigenerational households to the older age groups, so that by 2011 lesser shares of multigenerational household members were represented in the younger age groups of 0–17 and 18–24, with increasing shares especially in the middle age group of 25–34 and older age groups of 55–64 and 65 or older for both Sydney and Brisbane. This ageing structure of multigenerational households is especially stark when only households where at least one person in the youngest adult generation is aged 25 or older are considered. These households doubled (or in Brisbane's case, more than doubled) in numbers between 1986 and 2011, a much more rapid rate than multigenerational households where the youngest adult generation person is aged 18 or older. In multigenerational households where the youngest adult generation person is aged 25 or older, there were also larger shares of household members in the 25–34, 55–64 and 65 or older age groups.

The age structure of multigenerational household members (whether defined by one person in the youngest adult generation being at least 18 or 25) is different from that of the general population. For the general population, the age structures of both cities are more trapezoidal – with a larger share of people in the younger age groups before gradually declining to smaller shares in the older age groups. In the case of Brisbane general population, the 65 or older age group

Table 2.2 Percentage shares of persons by age group in multigenerational households in which the youngest adult generation member was aged 25 or older, Sydney and Brisbane, 1986–2011

	Age group	1986	1996	2006	2011	Total population (2011)
Sydney SD	0–17	6%	4%	5%	5%	23%
	18–24	10%	9%	8%	8%	10%
	25–34	25%	26%	25%	25%	15%
	35–44	7%	8%	8%	8%	15%
	45–54	15%	17%	16%	14%	14%
	55–64	21%	19%	22%	22%	11%
	65 or older	16%	17%	17%	18%	13%
	Total persons	247,045	323,559	382,271	448,948	4,391,672

	Age group	1986	1996	2006	2011	Total population (2011)
Brisbane SD	0–17	6%	4%	5%	5%	24%
	18–24	8%	7%	7%	7%	10%
	25–34	23%	25%	23%	23%	15%
	35–44	8%	8%	9%	9%	15%
	45–54	15%	18%	17%	15%	13%
	55–64	21%	19%	22%	23%	11%
	65 or older	19%	19%	18%	18%	12%
	Total persons	70,302	88,922	112,390	130,723	2,065,997

Source: Customized tables from ABS (2013)

is half that of the 0–17 age group. However, for multigenerational households, the distribution is bimodal, with two notable peaks in the young adult (18–24 and 25–34) and middle-aged age groups (45–54). This reflects the most common household formation of multigenerational households: middle-aged parents and their young adult offspring. There are several reasons for this formation.

For both Sydney and Brisbane, one-third of all households in 2011 were composed of couple families with children (around 30 per cent). Couples without children (around 23 per cent); single persons (around 20 per cent) and single-parent families (around 10 per cent) also represented notable shares of the respective populations. Households that included young children (couple families and single parents), therefore, accounted for more than two-fifths of the total population, a significant base in influencing the trapezoidal age structure of the general populations of these cities. In contrast, multigenerational households more likely composed young adults and their middle-aged parents, for example, resulting from delayed home leaving of the young adults (e.g. Cobb-Clark 2008). Using nondependent children[2] as a proxy, we examine the composition of families in Sydney and Brisbane in Table 2.3. Among multigenerational households (family households where nondependent children are present) in 2011, high shares

Table 2.3 Composition of family households, Sydney and Brisbane, 2011

	Greater Sydney	Greater Brisbane
Multigenerational households		
Couple family with nondependent children only	43%	40%
. . . and with children under 15	6%	7%
. . . and with dependent students	13%	12%
. . . and with children under 15 and dependent students	4%	4%
Single-parent family with nondependent children only	27%	28%
. . . and with children under 15	3%	3%
. . . and with dependent students	3%	3%
. . . and with children under 15 and dependent students	1%	1%
Subtotal	249,781	100,853
Other family households		
Couple family		
. . . with children under 15 only	57%	56%
. . . with dependent students only	10%	8%
. . . with children under 15 and dependent students	11%	10%
Single-parent family		
. . . with children under 15 only	12%	15%
. . . with dependent students only	4%	3%
. . . with children under 15 and dependent students	2%	2%
Other family	4%	4%
Subtotal	517,058	244,905

Source: ABS (2013b)

(59 per cent in Sydney and 55 per cent in Brisbane) were households without young children under age 15. In contrast, low shares of all other family households (18 per cent in Sydney and 17 per cent in Brisbane, including 'other family') did not have young children present in the household. This result further highlights the contrasting family composition of multigenerational and other family households.

Incidences of home-leavers returning to the family home (or boomeranging) are also noted to have increased (Parker 2012; Power 2012). The myriad reasons for returning home include relationship breakdown and increasing travel for study and work. This return reflects greater population transience and may be related to greater temporary mobility among some overseas-born populations and their Australian-born second generations; it may also reflect the growing contract nature of employment. In addition, a form of intergenerational reciprocity may be reflected in older adult generations tending to share homes more, possibly underscored in Sydney's case by housing affordability (Liu et al. 2015).

Many multigenerational households are composed mostly of older members (e.g. middle-aged couples and a parent-in-law). This includes people from the large cohort of baby boomers born from the late 1940s. Increased incidences of divorce, especially for middle-aged people (ABS 2014), have also contributed to the formation of older multigenerational households. In some cases, single-parent families may have moved back with older parents. Increasing life expectancy is also likely to have played a role, and the continued retraction of subsidized elderly care services has resulted in larger numbers of older Australians relying on their families for support (ABS 2014a). The higher shares of 55–64 and 65 or older in multigenerational households with at least one person in the youngest adult generation aged 25 or older reflect this older household composition of middle-aged persons caring for an elderly family member. These household proportions continued to increase between 1986 and 2011.

Changes in the age structure and distribution of multigenerational households were coupled with a retracting average household size. The average Australian household size declined between 1986 and 2011, from 2.9 to 2.5 people. Likewise, the average size of multigenerational households decreased, although less dramatically. For multigenerational households where a member of the youngest adult generation is 18 or older, the average household sizes for Sydney and Brisbane declined from 3.9 and 3.8 respectively in 1986 to 3.7 and 3.6 in 2011; for multigenerational households where a member of the youngest adult generation is 25 or older, the average household size for Sydney remained steady, 3.4 people in both 1986 and 2011 despite a slight decline (to 3.3) in 1996 and 2006, while the decline for Brisbane was also moderate, from 3.3 in 1986 to 3.2 in 2011. The decline in average household size more generally reflects the total fertility rate decline, from 3.5 children per woman in 1965 at the end of the post-war baby boom to 1.7 in the late 1970s and 1980s, rising only to 1.9 in the late 2000s (Hugo 2001; ABS 2014a). Changing migration phases and differences in cultural origins and their demographics can also affect average household sizes more generally. These issues are explored in detail in the next section.

Cultural compositions of multigenerational households in Australian cities

International research highlights cultural differences in propensity to multigenerational living (e.g. Mehio-Sibai et al. 2009; Izuhara 2010), with some cultural backgrounds – mostly Southern European, Middle Eastern and Asian – traditionally more inclined to engage in this living arrangement than others. These migrant backgrounds have featured prominently throughout Australia's migration history, with large numbers of Southern Europeans arriving in the post–World War II period, followed by Asian and Middle Eastern migrants since the 1970s, and most recently in the 2000s with large intakes of Chinese and Indian migrants. By 2011, 30 per cent of the Australian population was born overseas; the percentage of overseas-born residents was higher still in Sydney (40 per cent), which is one of the main migrant-settling areas of Australia, along with Melbourne (ABS 2012e).

In order to investigate the cultural compositions of multigenerational households in Australian cities, the regions of birth of multigenerational household members are presented in Table 2.4. For space reasons, major world regions are used as birthplace categories in this chapter, with the Oceania region including Australia, New Zealand and Southwest Pacific-born, which also includes second- and later-generation descendants of overseas-born migrants (ABS 2013a). The columns of Table 2.4 represent:

- The percentage share of each city's multigenerational household by the region of birth, and;
- The percentage of all people born in each region who lived in a multigenerational household in 2011. This category is further differentiated by whether a member of the youngest adult generation was 18 or older or 25 or older.

As shown in Table 2.4, the majority of Sydney and Brisbane's multigenerational household members were born in Oceania, predominantly in Australia. Of those born overseas, there were strong representations of Southeast Asia–born, Northeast Asia–born and North Africa and Middle East–born in Sydney, and Northwest Europe–born in Brisbane. The latter observation is especially noteworthy: while Northwest Europe (especially the United Kingdom) has long been

Table 2.4 Region of birth of multigenerational household residents and the percentage share from each region living in multigenerational households, Sydney and Brisbane, 2011

Region of birth	Percentage shares of multigenerational household of Sydney SD by region of birth		Percentage of each region of birth population who live in multigenerational households	
	Youngest adult aged 18 or older	*Youngest adult aged 25 or older*	*Youngest adult aged 18 or older*	*Youngest adult aged 25 or older*
Oceania	64%	58%	25%	9%
Northwest Europe	4%	4%	17%	7%
Southern and Eastern Europe	5%	8%	31%	20%
North Africa and the Middle East	6%	7%	40%	20%
Southeast Asia	7%	8%	32%	16%
Northeast Asia	6%	7%	27%	12%
Southern and Central Asia	3%	3%	20%	8%
Americas	1%	2%	21%	10%
Sub-Saharan Africa	1%	1%	25%	9%
Inadequately described	0%	0%	25%	12%
Not stated	2%	2%	7%	3%
Total	100%	100%	25%	10%

Region of birth	Percentage shares of multigenerational household of Brisbane SD by region of birth		Percentage of each region of birth population who live in multigenerational households	
	Youngest adult aged 18 or older	Youngest adult aged 25 or older	Youngest adult aged 18 or older	Youngest adult aged 25 or older
Oceania	79%	76%	19%	6%
Northwest Europe	6%	7%	16%	6%
Southern and Eastern Europe	2%	3%	25%	13%
North Africa and the Middle East	1%	1%	23%	7%
Southeast Asia	4%	5%	26%	11%
Northeast Asia	3%	3%	20%	8%
Southern and Central Asia	1%	1%	14%	5%
Americas	1%	1%	16%	6%
Sub-Saharan Africa	2%	2%	25%	6%
Inadequately described	0%	0%	19%	5%
Not stated	1%	2%	5%	2%
Total	100%	100%	19%	6%

Source: Customized tables from ABS (2013)

a traditional migrant source for Australia, particularly during the pre–World War II and White Australia periods, cultures from this region are not known to have strong multigenerational living traditions (Daly 2005; Cohen et al. 2007). This is clear when the figures are expressed as percentages of total persons born in that same region, with only 16 per cent (at least one person of the youngest adult generation aged 18 or older, or 6 per cent of at least one member of youngest adult generation aged 25 or older) living in multigenerational households, the second lowest among the nine birthplace groups. In Sydney, persons born in North Africa and the Middle East and Southern and Eastern Europe were most likely to live in multigenerational households; in Brisbane, persons born in Southeast Asia and Southern and Eastern Europe were most likely to. We offer some insights on these cultural concentrations of multigenerational living next.

Broadly, overseas-born persons were overrepresented in multigenerational households. The elevated shares among those from Southern and Eastern Europe living in multigenerational households (especially with a member of the youngest adult generation aged 25 or older) reflects their main migrations in the 1950s and 1960s. Studies of Italian, Greek and Macedonian societies indicated that up to 30 per cent of the population was living in multigenerational families in the 1960s (Freidl 1962) so that the possible survival of such patterns among persons of these origins in Australian cities could partly reflect the persistence of intergenerational expectations. To an extent, the same applies with those born in Southeast Asia, North Africa and Middle East, whose main migrations began in the 1970s.

In Sydney and Brisbane, the Oceania-born share of the total population living in multigenerational family households fell between 1986 and 2011, although the percentage of all Oceania-born people living in multigenerational families increased moderately. This increase may have been partly influenced by the second and later generations of immigrant origin that were included in the Oceania-born figures. In metropolitan Sydney, the Oceania-born share of persons in multigenerational households fell from 71 per cent to 64 per cent, in line with a relatively stronger immigration focus on Sydney. Some major immigrant groups with elevated multigenerational living shares disproportionately settled in Sydney. In the 2011 census, 68 per cent of all arrivals to Australia from North Africa and the Middle East who came after 1991 settled in Sydney (ABS 2012e). Likewise, arrivals from Southeast and Northeast Asia were more represented among the multigenerational household population in Sydney than in Brisbane (see Table 2.4).

Meanwhile, while the number of people living in multigenerational households who were of Southern and Eastern European birth was still elevated in 2011, their share of all persons in multigenerational families was lower in 2011 than in 1986 in Sydney, having about halved. A factor in the elevated shares from Southern and Eastern Europe remaining in 2011 was that they had been in Australia long enough to have children and grandchildren. Of particular note is the higher shares of people born in Southern and Eastern Europe in multigenerational households with a member of the youngest adult generation aged 25 or older, despite that some of the earlier migrants will have now died or returned to their country of origin. Some migration of people born in Southeast Asia to Brisbane has comprised internal migration from southern Australian states (Hugo 1998), possibly resulting in lower multigenerational shares among this group in Brisbane. In this case, some household members, rather than the whole family, may have moved.

To summarize, the shares of several major immigrant populations have become more elevated in Sydney than in Brisbane in terms of likelihood of multigenerational living, partly due to their concentration in these cities, especially with Sydney being one of Australia's major migrant settlement areas. It may also be associated with the relatively higher housing costs of these two cities compared with most other regions in Australia, which may have influenced some multigenerational households in these cities to live together to save costs. The latter point is discussed in further detail in the section titled Housing characteristics of multigenerational households.

Labour force and employment status of people in multigenerational households

This section describes the labour force participation and nature of employment of all people living in multigenerational households in Sydney and Brisbane, with a view to providing insights into the socioeconomic characteristics of these households. Reference to differences between populations where a member of the youngest adult generation was aged 18 or older and 25 or older are made. Persons under age 15 and persons with age not stated are excluded from the calculations (ABS 2013a).

In 2011, the labour force status of multigenerational household members differed slightly from the general population, with slightly higher shares in the labour force, especially those employed in part-time positions. This statistic might reflect two observations:

1   As explained earlier, there are relatively larger shares of young adults aged 18–24 (and to a lesser extent those aged 25–34) living in multigenerational households, large shares of whom may still be undertaking their education (e.g. university studies) and may have limited ability to take on full-time employment.
2   There are also elevated shares of people in the preretirement age group of 55–64 (and to a lesser extent the age group of 65 or older) living in multigenerational households, some members of whom may have transitioned to part-time work as a means of providing the care some other household members require while still assisting in financially supporting the household.

The significant increases in the share of multigenerational household members employed part-time also reflect the wider trend of workforce casualization, especially in the 2000s, a trend also observed in the Sydney and Brisbane populations more generally. In Sydney, the proportion of multigenerational household members (at least one youngest adult generation member aged 18 or older) who were employed full-time declined from 69 per cent in 1986 to 57 per cent in 2011 (expressed as a proportion of the total labour force of multigenerational households), while those employed part-time increased from 16 per cent to 30 per cent over the same period. The number of those employed full-time decreased by 18,100, while those employed part-time increased by 129,042. In Brisbane, the proportion of multigenerational household members who were employed full-time declined from 66 per cent in 1986 to 54 per cent in 2011, while those employed part-time increased from 16 per cent to 32 per cent (ABS 2013a). The number of full-time employed increased, despite an overall proportional decline, while those part-time employed increased 34,668, a more than twofold increase. The latter reflect net internal migration gains in Brisbane, resulting in more rapid population growth, compared with net losses in Sydney (Hugo 1998; ABS 2015).

These changes were not accompanied by wider changes to the level of labour force participation of multigenerational household members. Around 70 per cent of multigenerational household members aged 15 or older participated in the workforce, roughly the same as the general population, and a proportion that was largely maintained since 1986. For Brisbane, the share of multigenerational household members not in the labour force declined from 33 per cent in 1986 to

27 per cent in 2011 (below the 30 per cent level of the Brisbane general population), while for Sydney the share only declined moderately from 33 per cent to 32 per cent, the same as Sydney's general population.

In 2011, one-fifth of Sydney and Brisbane's multigenerational household members (at least one youngest adult generation member aged 18 or older) were employed in intermediate clerical, sales and services work, the largest shares among all occupational groups under the Australian Standard Classification of Occupations (ABS 2013a). For both Sydney and Brisbane, these shares increased from 13 per cent in 1986 to 21 per cent in 2011. In comparison, the shares of multigenerational household members employed in professional occupations increased from 11 per cent in 1986 (for both Sydney and Brisbane) to 19 per cent (in Sydney) and 17 per cent (in Brisbane) in 2011. Representations in trade and labouring occupations declined, while the share of those in managerial positions remained stable.

This casualization of the workforce, as reflected in larger shares being employed part-time and especially in intermediate clerical, sales and service occupations, potentially significantly limited the ability of these individuals to afford independent living. This scenario is particularly the case for major Australian cities like Sydney and Brisbane, notably the former, where housing costs are high (Worthington and Higgs 2013). We explore this factor in the next section.

Housing characteristics of multigenerational households

Dwelling size and structure

With comparatively larger households, larger shares of multigenerational households in Sydney and Brisbane lived in larger properties (with three bedrooms or more) compared with the general population. For multigenerational households where at least one member of the youngest adult generation was 18 or older, 82 per cent in Sydney and 89 per cent in Brisbane lived in dwellings with three or more bedrooms in 1986; this increased to 89 per cent in Sydney and 93 per cent in Brisbane by 2006. For multigenerational households where at least one member of the youngest adult generation was 25 or older, 73 per cent in Sydney and 82 per cent in Brisbane lived in dwellings with three or more bedrooms in 1986, which increased to 86 per cent in Sydney and 91 per cent in Brisbane by 2006. Of note especially are the shares that lived in dwellings with four or more bedrooms. In Sydney, the shares doubled from 21 per cent in households where at least one youngest adult generation member was aged 25 or older (29 per cent for households where at least one youngest adult generation member was aged 18 or older) in 1986 to 42 per cent by 2006 (49 per cent for households where at least one youngest adult generation member was aged 18 or older). In Brisbane, similarly rapid increases were noted, increasing from 23 per cent in 1986 in households where at least one youngest adult generation member was aged 25 or older (32 per cent for households where at least one youngest adult generation member was aged 18 or older) to 44 per cent in 2011 (49 per cent for households where at least one youngest adult generation member was aged 18 or older) (ABS 2013a).

The majority of multigenerational households lived in separate houses, shares that were higher than the respective general population of these cities. In 2011, 80 per cent of multigenerational households (whether at least one youngest adult generation member was aged 18 or older or 25 or older in Sydney) lived in separate houses, compared with 59 per cent of the general population. For Brisbane, the shares were 93 per cent (at least one youngest adult generation member was aged 18 or older) and 92 per cent (at least one youngest adult generation member was aged 25 or older) compared with 77 per cent of the general population (see Table 2.5). These observations partly reflect that the majority of larger dwellings (those with three bedrooms or more) are more commonly separate houses than apartments. The different figures between the cities are due to the housing stock that is available locally, with Brisbane having a higher proportion of housing stock being separate houses than in Sydney.

However, the trend since 1986 is that more multigenerational households in Sydney and Brisbane have come to live in semi-detached dwellings. In Sydney, the proportions that lived in semi/row/town houses increased from 4 per cent in 1986 to 10 per cent in 2011 for multigenerational households where at least one youngest adult generation member was aged 18 or older (and also for those where at least one youngest adult generation member was age 25 or older). In Brisbane, the share of multigenerational households living in semi-detached dwellings increased from 0 per cent in 1986 to 4 per cent in 2011. These highlight the wider availability of larger semi-detached dwellings that have come onto the market during this twenty-five-year period, which may be a more affordable option for multigenerational households with a need (or desire) to live in denser or better connected areas (see later subsection for discussion on housing costs and locations).

Throughout the twenty-five-year period, the share of multigenerational households in Sydney and Brisbane that lived in apartments remained stable, so that by 2011 these are comparable to those who live in semi-detached dwellings, when in 1986 shares of apartment-dwelling multigenerational households were three to six percentage points higher than those in semi-detached dwellings. One explanation may be that while both Sydney and Brisbane are strongly promoting compact city agendas, and therefore the building of apartment blocks, most include large amounts of smaller, one- and two-bedroom apartments, with larger apartments (three or more bedrooms) comprising small shares of new apartment developments. In Sydney in 2011, only 14 per cent of apartments had three or more bedrooms, thus comprising only 3.5 per cent of all dwelling units (ABS 2012e).

Tenure

In 2011, around four-fifths of multigenerational households in Sydney and Brisbane (at least one youngest adult generation member was aged 18 or older)

Table 2.5 Dwelling structures occupied by multigenerational households in Sydney and Brisbane, 1986–2011

Sydney SD	Age group	1986	1996	2006	2011	All households (2011)
Youngest adult aged 18 or older	Separate house	85%	84%	82%	80%	59%
	Semi/row/ town house	4%	6%	8%	10%	13%
	Apartments	10%	8%	9%	9%	28%
	Other/not stated	2%	2%	0%	0%	1%
	Total dwellings	204,162	240,789	265,066	293,270	1,723,056
Youngest adult aged 25 or older	Separate house	82%	82%	82%	80%	
	Semi/row/ town house	4%	7%	8%	10%	
	Apartments	12%	9%	9%	10%	
	Other/not stated	2%	2%	0%	0%	
	Total dwellings	72,457	96,766	114,952	132,412	

Brisbane SD	Age group	1986	1996	2006	2011	All households (2011)
Youngest adult aged 18 or older	Separate house	95%	94%	93%	93%	77%
	Semi/row/ town house	0%	2%	3%	4%	9%
	Apartments	3%	2%	3%	3%	13%
	Other/not stated	1%	2%	0%	0%	1%
	Total dwellings	65,280	80,716	94,490	106,097	822,176
Youngest adult aged 25 or older	Separate house	94%	93%	93%	92%	
	Semi/row/ town house	0%	2%	4%	4%	
	Apartments	4%	3%	3%	4%	
	Other/not stated	1%	2%	0%	0%	
	Total dwellings	21,428	28,303	35,658	40,881	

Notes: 'Other/not stated' dwellings less than one per cent in 2011. Total numbers include 'other/ not stated' dwellings. Customized tables from ABS (2013)

lived in owner-occupied dwellings, compared with just over half of the general populations of these cities. Such stark contrast was maintained since the mid-1980s, so that multigenerational households in general had a higher likelihood to be owner-occupiers than other household types. How multigenerational households own their homes, however, has changed between 1986 and 2011, with a dramatic shift from larger shares of outright owners in 1986 in both cities to a larger share of mortgagors in Brisbane by 2011 and roughly the same share of outright owners and mortgagors in Sydney. This change in ownership pattern was less significant among multigenerational households where at least one of the youngest adult generation members was 25 or older. In Sydney, the share of outright ownership declined from 61 per cent in 1986 to 51 per cent in 2011, while the share of mortgagors increased from 20 per cent to 29 per cent (see Table 2.6); in Brisbane, the share of outright ownership retracted from 64 per cent to 48 per cent, while the mortgagor share increased from 21 per cent to 30 per cent.

One explanation of this shift in ownership patterns of multigenerational households is the increase in Australian housing prices during this period. Australian house prices, particularly in Sydney, increased significantly – both absolutely and relative to household income – since the mid-1980s (Burke et al. 2014). For households that purchased their property more recently, this increase has meant both larger monthly mortgage payments as well as longer repayment periods. These house price increases have affected all purchasing households, not only multigenerational households. The outcome is reflected in a transition from high levels of outright ownership achieved at the end of the post–World War II long economic boom periods. Indeed, the share of Sydney households with a mortgage increased from 32 per cent in 1986 to 45 per cent in 2011, and for Brisbane, from 33 per cent to 47 per cent (ABS 1987; 2013b). The rapidly increasing house prices would also mean that more households now enter homeownership later in life, whether by staying in private rental for longer or cohabiting with other family members in a multigenerational household situation. The increased shares of multigenerational households in rental dwellings are reflected in Table 2.6.

Housing costs

Monthly mortgage repayments of multigenerational households in Sydney and Brisbane were acquired as part of the customized tables described previously. For each census, these monthly repayments of multigenerational households were categorized to align with the quintiles of all owner-occupied households with a mortgage in their respective city. The comparisons of the mortgage payments of multigenerational households to all households with mortgages between 1986 and 2011 are displayed in Figure 2.1.

As Figure 2.1 shows, the monthly mortgage payments of multigenerational households were far lower in 1986 compared with all households with mortgages

Table 2.6 Dwelling tenure of multigenerational households in Sydney and Brisbane, 1986–2011

Sydney SD	Age group	1986	1996	2006	2011	All households (2011)
Youngest adult aged 18 or older	Fully owned	51%	59%	43%	38%	27%
	Owned with mortgage	29%	22%	37%	39%	31%
	Rented	16%	16%	18%	20%	28%
	Other/not stated	3%	3%	3%	2%	15%
	Total households	204,162	240,789	265,066	293,270	1,723,058
Youngest adult aged 25 or older	Fully owned	61%	69%	57%	51%	
	Owned with mortgage	20%	14%	25%	29%	
	Rented	16%	15%	15%	17%	
	Other/not stated	3%	3%	3%	3%	
	Total households	72,457	96,766	114,592	132,412	

Brisbane SD	Age group	1986	1996	2006	2011	All households (2011)
Youngest adult aged 18 or older	Fully owned	51%	53%	39%	34%	25%
	Owned with mortgage	33%	30%	40%	42%	33%
	Rented	13%	15%	19%	22%	29%
	Other/not stated	3%	2%	2%	2%	14%
	Total households	65,280	80,716	94,490	106,097	822,174
Youngest adult aged 25 or older	Fully owned	64%	67%	54%	48%	
	Owned with mortgage	21%	18%	27%	30%	
	Rented	12%	13%	17%	19%	
	Other/not stated	3%	3%	3%	3%	
	Total households	21,428	28,303	35,658	40,881	

Note: 'Other/not stated' were between 2–3 per cent in 2011 and included in the total persons figures. Customized table from ABS (2013).

across both Sydney and Brisbane. Almost half of multigenerational households (at least one youngest adult generation member was aged 25 or older) in Sydney and Brisbane had monthly mortgage payments in the lowest quintile; for multigenerational households with at least one youngest adult generation member aged 18 or older, more than one-third had monthly mortgage payments in the lowest quintiles. As such, comparatively low shares had mortgage payments in the higher quintiles, despite their propensity to live in larger dwellings as

Sydney SD

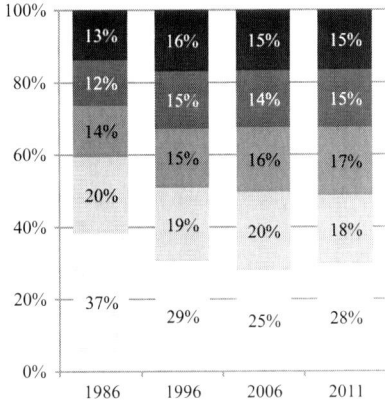

Youngest adults aged 18 or older

Brisbane SD

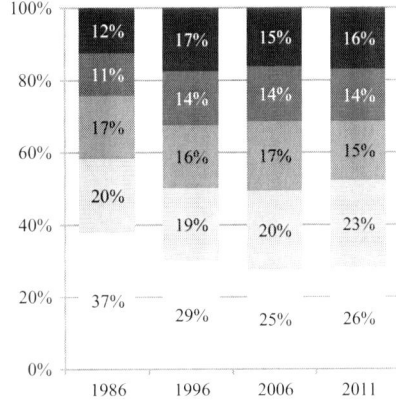

Youngest adults aged 18 or older

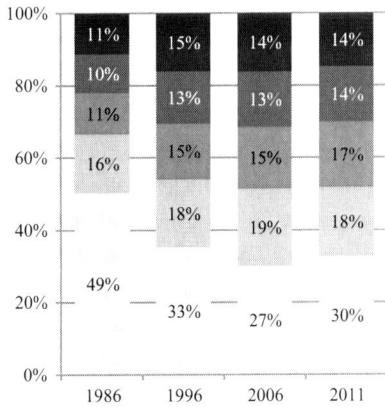

Youngest adults aged 25 or older

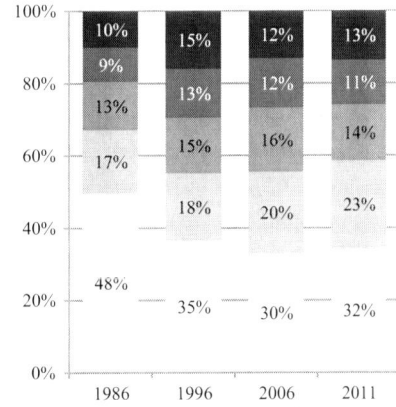

Youngest adults aged 25 or older

Legend

■ Highest quintile ■ Fourth quintile ■ Third quintile Second quintile Lowest quintile

Figure 2.1 Monthly mortgage repayments by quintiles of multigenerational households in Sydney and Brisbane, 1986–2011

discussed in an earlier subsection, which usually cost more to purchase (and therefore attract a higher mortgage repayment) than smaller properties in the same area. Therefore, multigenerational households in larger properties may have been living in lower-cost areas such as the middle and outer suburbs of Sydney and Brisbane.

Over time, however, the shares of multigenerational households with relatively low mortgage payments have declined. By 2011, less than one-third of multigenerational households (at least one youngest adult generation member was aged 18 or older) had mortgage payments in the lowest quintile of their respective city; the shares were around one-quarter for multigenerational households with at least one youngest adult generation member aged 25 or older. The corresponding increases in the highest quintiles, however, were not observed, with only marginal increases in shares between 1986 and 2011.

This is despite the significant increases in house prices that were observed in Sydney and Brisbane since the 1980s as discussed in the previous section. The main increases have been in the second and third lowest quintiles. This again suggests that multigenerational households have purchased their homes in lower-housing cost areas.

Figure 2.2 shows the percentage change in the number of multigenerational households (at least one youngest adult generation member was aged 18 or older) at the SSD level between 1986 and 2011. The lightest shade indicates an absolute decline during this period in the number of multigenerational households that lived in this SSD, while the darkest shade indicates the number of multigenerational households that lived in this SSD had more than doubled. As can be seen in Figure 2.2, the SSDs where absolute decline occurred between 1986 and 2011 were the inner city areas of Sydney and Brisbane; areas with more than doubled growth are the outer suburban SSDs of these two cities. There are several explanations for this outward shift of multigenerational households.

First, there were relatively few households (including multigenerational households) living in the outer suburban areas of Sydney and Brisbane in the mid-1980s. As such, the base populations on which these percentage changes were calculated were relatively small (e.g. there were only 6,569 multigenerational households living in Caboolture Shire in 1986, compared with 58,611 in Northwest Outer Brisbane). Relatively small absolute increases may translate to large percentage increases, as in the case of Caboolture Shire, where the number of multigenerational households increased absolutely by 21,753 (equivalent to a 331 per cent growth), compared with the 16,251 increase in Northwest Outer Brisbane (equivalent to 28 per cent growth).

Second, the outer suburban location of detached houses was a strong factor in the evolving distributions of multigenerational households in Sydney and Brisbane. For both cities, the strongest growth in multigenerational households corresponds with major areas of Greenfield developments of these cities, with much of the new housing stock delivered being larger detached houses, which are more suitable to the needs of multigenerational households.

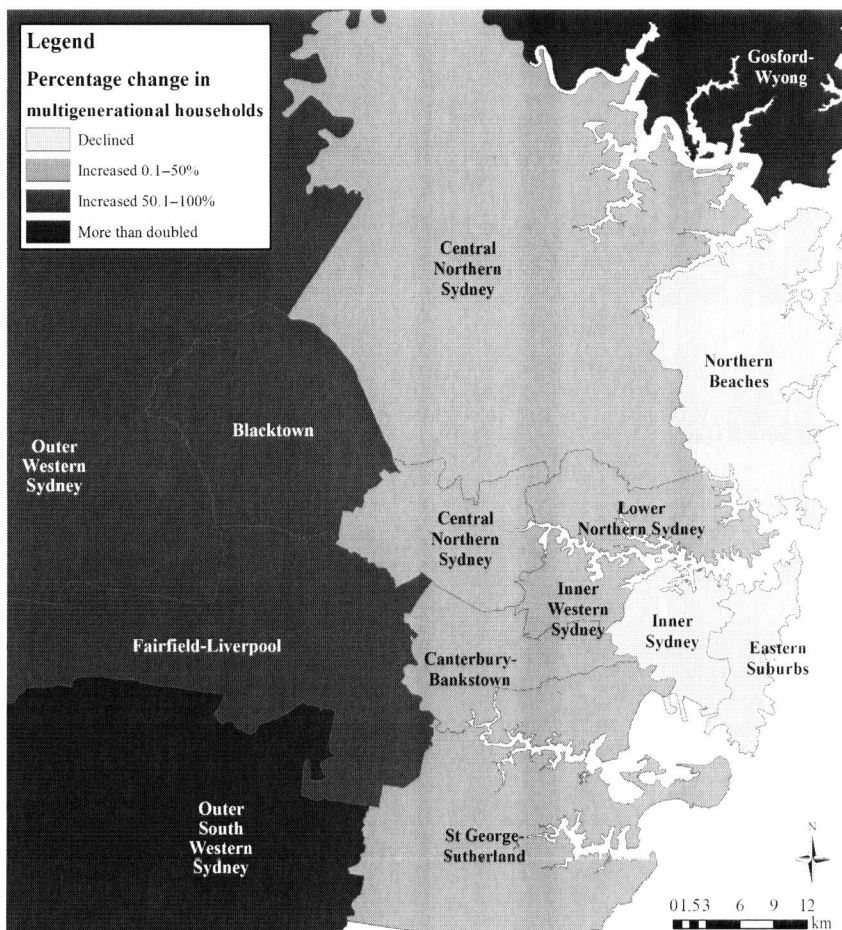

Figure 2.2 Percentage change in multigenerational households in metropolitan Sydney and Brisbane, 1986–2011

Note: Youngest adults aged 18 or older. Sourced from ABS (2013) customized tables.

Third, the decline in the number of multigenerational households in inner city Sydney and Brisbane may be partly attributed to the few larger dwellings being built in these areas, with most new housing stock delivered (especially since the 2000s) being higher density apartment blocks (ABS 1987; 2012a; 2012b). In addition, of the existing larger housing stock in these areas (most likely detached and semi-detached), these units have become sought-after with

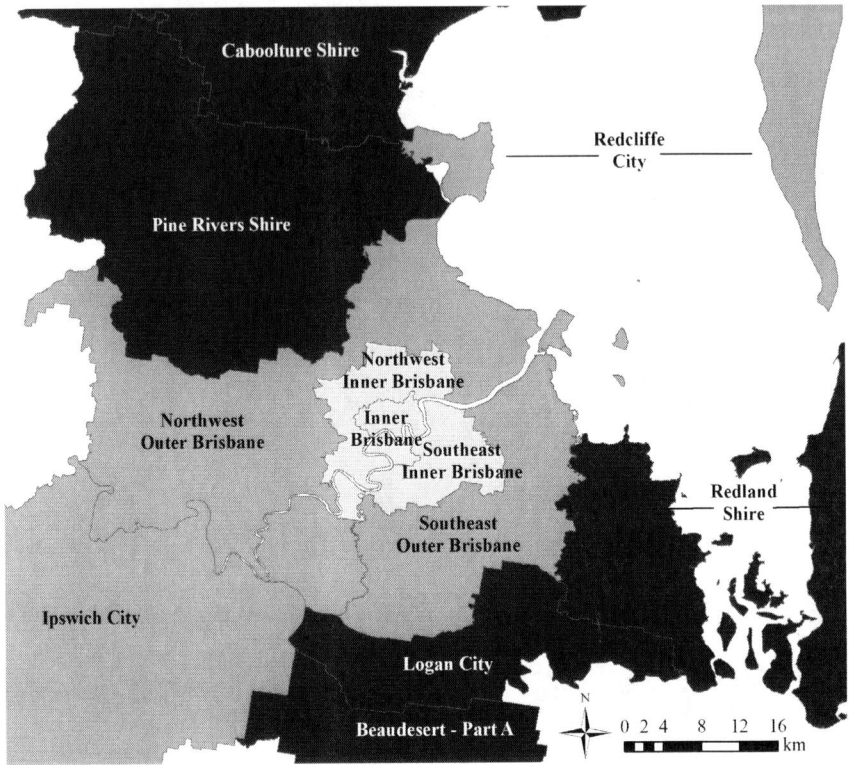

Figure 2.2 Continued

gentrification and access influences, putting the prices of these properties out of reach for many families including multigenerational households (Rofe 2009; Hu 2014). In Sydney's main areas of gentrification (the Inner, Eastern, Inner Western and Canterbury-Bankstown SSDs), for example, the share of multi-generational household increase between 1986 and 2011 was only 14 per cent compared with the total population increase of 29 per cent (ABS 1987; 2012a; 2013). This lack of growth occurred despite Canterbury-Bankstown having a relatively large immigrant population, especially those of East Asian and Middle Eastern backgrounds which, as discussed earlier, have higher tendencies to multigenerational living.

Fourth, the shift in concentration of multigenerational households to middle and outer suburban Sydney and Brisbane might also be influenced by a change in migration patterns after the 1980s. There are, for example, a notable concentration of Vietnamese migrants in the Fairfield–Liverpool area of Sydney since the 1970s, and more recently North African and Filipino settlements in Blacktown since the 1990s. In Brisbane, there are strong Indian representations in Logan City and Redland Shire; Logan City is also a common settlement area for migrants from Asia. The emergence of these middle and outer suburban areas as areas of concentration of multigenerational households may be the result of family reunion, or the children of migrant families who settled earlier having turned 18 but continued to live in the family home for cultural or other reasons. For a more detailed discussion of the change in spatial distribution of multigenerational households in Sydney, see Burnley et al. (2015).

Summary

Over the quarter century, multigenerational family households maintained their share of all households in the rapidly increasing population of Australia, while in Sydney they increased their share significantly. The change was caused by the rapid increase in populations in multigenerational households where at least one youngest adult generation member was 25 or older, with corresponding rapid growth in the 55–64 age group, while the share of older household members aged 65 or older increased as well. The population with at least one youngest adult generation member aged 18 or older remained the larger of the two, but its share declined. In this group, there were relatively few children under age 15, and with both groups, children were underrepresented relative to the general population. Households were diverse, and some of this diversity overlapped with particular regions of origin birthplaces – notably people from North Africa and the Middle East and Southeast Asia, and to an extent, Northeast Asia – particularly in Sydney. Although populations from Southern and Eastern Europe had decreased since 1986, persons in multigenerational households, which were above the metropolitan levels, almost certainly reflected first- and second-generations living together, the latter included in the Australian-born figures presented earlier.

Some variations in growth patterns of the two populations in Sydney and Brisbane (i.e. with at least one youngest adult generation member aged 18 or older or aged 25 or older) were most likely the result of migration differentials: net internal migration gains in Brisbane over time, notably from southern states, and in Sydney, net internal migration losses and relatively stronger levels of immigration from overseas, particularly from regions such as East Asia where multigenerational family living, or at least intergenerational social obligations, are more traditional (Izuhara 2010). The stronger Sydney focus of immigrants from societies where multigenerational living was more traditional occurred both in the post–World War II era and later periods.

It is important to note the growth, compared with the general population, of adults aged 25–44 in multigenerational family households. These adults are mostly beyond the age of professional and tertiary study (although households with dependent adult students clearly grew). It is likely that increasingly more people were staying at home to save for housing deposits (see Liu et al. 2015 and Chapter 3).

In line with general population trends across Australia, but accentuated in Sydney, was an increase in the part-time workforce among people in multigenerational households. Total workforce participation increased, more so in Sydney. Labour force participation, although increasing over time, was several percentage points lower than among the general population in Sydney in 2011.

The greater growth in part-time employment among multigenerational household members has likely been compounded by casualization of the workforce, which certainly would have affected the young adult age groups more so than others. Another contributing factor may have been the role of carers. Some middle-aged adults may have chosen to work fewer hours in order to care for elderly parents in the same household. The choice could also reflect the cost of home care elsewhere, so that multigenerational living represents the preferred option (Vincente and Sousa 2009).

The occupational status change of employed individuals was broadly in line with those of the wider population with the notable exception of a significantly lower share of persons in managerial and administrative occupations by 2011. The implication for housing affordability was that such persons commonly have higher incomes. Given that managers are usually older than the rest of the workforce (ABS 2012d) and may have more time-consuming work responsibilities, they may not be able to give sufficient time to a caring role when this is a factor in multigenerational household formation. Declining rates of full-time employment, despite increases in labour force participation, may also have constrained the housing that multigenerational family households could afford. The substantial growth of these households in outer, more affordable, areas of Sydney and Brisbane might be the result.

There was a markedly high tendency for owner-occupancy of dwellings among multigenerational households when compared with all households. However, the share owning outright, albeit relatively high, fell over time as shares holding mortgages increased. Although many multigenerational households still held mortgages smaller than for other households, this share has declined over time, with more paying mortgages in the medium ranges. The share renting remained relatively low, a little more than half compared to all households. Associated with these trends was the strong persistence in separate house living, although in Sydney in particular, residence in semi-detached or row housing increased significantly. Occupation of apartments remained low, despite urban consolidation initiatives and strong increases in prices for detached houses, particularly in Sydney. A factor in apartment avoidance might have been the smaller number of bedrooms in the majority of apartments compared with detached houses. Multigenerational households would almost certainly require more bedrooms than the average households of families with children or couples, given their relatively higher average household size.

This study, being census-based, may understate multigenerational household living in close proximity because secondary dwellings on the same lot are classified as separate dwellings and the persons in them as separate households, even if related to persons in the primary dwelling. Such dwelling construction, particularly in Sydney, has become an integral part of urban consolidation initiatives.

After 1986, however, average household sizes declined although in Sydney there was a pause in total household size decline between 1996 and 2011. Multigenerational household growth, plus a recovery in the Total Fertility Rate from 1.7 to 1.9, almost certainly contributed to this growth. Thus, there are strong implications for the demand and supply of dwellings with three or more bedrooms and perhaps more living spaces, particularly in detached or semi-detached homes, but also in apartment configurations. Therefore, more nuanced housing policies are required, which are addressed in Chapter 11.

Notes

1 Statistical boundaries for Australia were updated significantly between the 2006 and 2011 censuses. Census analysis for the *Living Together* project was taken at the 2006 boundaries because of their higher comparability with the earlier censuses. Data from the 2011 census was adjusted to reflect the 2006 boundaries.
2 Defined by the ABS (2011) as 'a person aged 15 years or more, who is a natural, adopted, step, or foster child of a couple or lone parent usually resident in the same household, who is not a full-time student aged 15–24 years, and who has no identified partner or child of his/her own usually resident in the household.'

References

Australian Bureau of Statistics 1987, *1986 Census of Population and Housing, Time Series Profile*, Cat. no. 2003.0, Australian Bureau of Statistics, Canberra.
Australian Bureau of Statistics 2012a, *2011 Census of Population and Housing*, 'Table T08. Country of Birth of Person by Sex', times series spreadsheet, Cat. no. 2003.0, Australian Bureau of Statistics, Canberra.
Australian Bureau of Statistics 2012b, *2011 Census of Population and Housing*, 'Table T15. Dwelling Structure by Number of Persons Usually Resident', times series spreadsheet, Cat. no. 2003.0, Australian Bureau of Statistics, Canberra.
Australian Bureau of Statistics 2012c, *2011 Census of Population and Housing*, 'Table T27. Family Composition and Social Marital Status by Number of Dependent Children', times series spreadsheet, Cat. no. 2003.0, Australian Bureau of Statistics, Canberra.
Australian Bureau of Statistics 2012d, *2011 Census of Population and Housing*, 'Table T34. Occupation by Sex', times series spreadsheet, Cat. no. 2003.0, Australian Bureau of Statistics, Canberra.
Australian Bureau of Statistics 2012e, *2011 Census of Population and Housing*, 'Table X03. Country of Birth (Minor Group) of Person by Year of Arrival in Australia', expanded community profile, Cat. no. 2005.0, Australian Bureau of Statistics, Canberra.
Australian Bureau of Statistics 2013a, *Australian Census of Population and Housing, 1986, 1996, 2006, 2011*, Australian Bureau of Statistics, Canberra.

Australian Bureau of Statistics 2013b, *TableBuilder Pro*, Australian Bureau of Statistics, Canberra.

Australian Bureau of Statistics 2014a, *Australian Social Trends*, Cat. no. 4102.0, Australian Bureau of Statistics, Canberra.

Australian Bureau of Statistics 2015, *Regional Internal Migration Estimates by Region 2006–7 to 2014*, Cat. no. 3412.0, Australian Bureau of Statistics, Canberra.

Burke, T, Stone, W and Ralston, L 2014, *Generational Change in Home Purchase Opportunity*, Final Report No. 232, Australia Housing and Urban Research Institute, Melbourne.

Burnley, IH 2000, *The Impact of Immigration on Australia. Demographic Approaches*, Oxford University Press, Melbourne.

Burnley, I, Liu, E and Easthope, H 2015, 'Geographies of adult multigenerational family households in metropolitan Sydney,' Geographical Research, Online first version.

Cobb-Clark, DA 2008, 'Leaving home: What economics has to say about the living arrangements of young Australians', *The Australian Economic Review*, vol. 41, pp. 160–176.

Cohen, S, Crawford, K, Giullari, S, Michailidou, M, Mouriki, A, Spyrou, S, Taylor, F and Walker, J 2007, *Family Diversity: A Guide to Teachers*, Theor. Press Ltd, Nicosia, Cyprus.

Daly, M 2005, 'Changing family life in Europe: Significance for state and society', *European Societies*, vol. 7, no. 3, pp. 379–398.

Freidl, E 1962, *Vasilika: A Village in Modern Greece*, Holt, Reinhart and Wilson, New York.

Hu, R 2014, 'Remaking of central Sydney: Evidence from floorspace and employment surveys in 1991–2006', *International Planning Studies*, vol. 14, no. 1, pp. 1–24.

Hugo, GJ 1998, *Internal Migration of the Overseas-born in Australia*, Bureau of Immigration and Population Research, Melbourne.

Hugo, GJ 2001, *A Century of Population Change in Australia*, Australian Bureau of Statistics, Canberra.

Izuhara, M 2010, 'New patterns of family reciprocity? Policy changes in ageing societies', in M Izuhara (ed.), *Ageing and International Relations: Family Reciprocity from a Global Perspective*, Policy Press, Bristol, pp. 149–159.

Liu, E, Easthope, H, Judd, B and Burnley, I 2015, 'Housing multigenerational households in Australian cities: Evidence from Sydney and Brisbane at the turn of the 21st century', in R Dufty-Jones and D Rogers (eds), *Housing in 21st-Century Australia: People, Practices and Policies*, Ashgate, Farnham, 21–37.

Mehio-Sibai, A, Beydoun, M and Tohme, R 2009, 'Living arrangements of ever-married Lebanese women: Is living with married children advantageous?' *Journal of Cross-Cultural Gerontology*, vol. 24, no. 1, pp. 5–17.

Parker, K 2012, 'The boomerang generation: Feeling OK about living with mom and dad', *Social and Demographic Trends*, Pew Research Center, Washington, DC.

Power, J 2012, 'Boomerang kids: Are babyboomers stuck with babygloomers?' *Sydney Morning Herald*, 28 August.

Rofe, MW 2009, 'Globalisation, gentrification and spatial hierarchies in and beyond New South Wales: The local/global nexus', *Geographical Research*, vol. 47, no. 3, pp. 292–305.

Vincente, H and Sousa, L 2009, 'The multigenerational family and the elderly: A mutual or parasitical symbiotic relationship?' in A Sousa (ed.), *Families in Later Life: Emerging Themes and Challenges*, New Science Publishers, New York, pp. 27–48.

Widmer, E 2010, *Family Configurations: A Structural Approach to Family Diversity*, Ashgate, Farnham.
Worthington, A and Higgs, H 2013, 'Macro drivers of Australian housing affordability, 1985–2010: An autoregressive distributed lag approach', *Studies in Economics and Finance*, vol. 30, no. 4, pp. 347–369.

3   The drivers of multigenerational households in Australia

Hazel Easthope

Introduction

One in five people in Australia live in multigenerational households. In order to understand this significant and yet largely overlooked household form, we need to understand the drivers behind multigenerational living in Australia. This chapter (and book) draws on research undertaken as part of the Australian Research Council Discovery Project *Living Together: The Rise of Multigenerational Households in Australian Cities* (hereafter *Living Together*), including findings from a survey with 392 multigenerational household members in Sydney and Brisbane, analysis of 21 diaries and 21 follow-up interviews with multigenerational household members. This chapter focuses on their descriptions of how they came to live together.

The chapter begins with a description of the research and the research methods employed in this study, which is followed by a summary of the reasons for living in a multigenerational household given by respondents to the survey. These findings demonstrate a complex interplay between choice and constraint in people's decisions to live in multigenerational households. The following sections discuss the influence of wider structural changes, policy changes and changing views about the family on people's decisions to live in multigenerational households, by drawing on the survey findings in conjunction with information collected through diaries and interviews. The chapter concludes with a discussion of the major drivers of multigenerational living within the context of modern Australian cities.

Research methods

A mixed methods approach was taken in the *Living Together* project, including the use of an online survey, solicited diaries and follow-up interviews. The two cities of Sydney and Brisbane were chosen as case studies. These cities were chosen because of their contrasting demographic and housing stock mixes as well as housing demands and constraints. The cities were also chosen because they represented extremes in relation to multigenerational living. Since the 1980s, Sydney has had the highest percentage share of its population living in multigenerational households among all Australian state capitals, while Brisbane had the most rapid proportional growth of multigenerational households over this period. Thus, the results reported in this chapter reflect the views of individuals who live in multi-generational households in these two cities rather than Australia more generally.

An online survey was conducted with members of multigenerational households living in Greater Sydney and Brisbane between August 2012 and July 2013. Hosted on the online portal KeySurvey, the survey focused on three aspects of multigenerational living:

1   the dwelling in which these households lived at the time of the survey;
2   the living arrangement – including the reasons why they live together – and how it affects their personal and family lives;
3   their personal thoughts on multigenerational living and their likelihood of continuing with this arrangement.

The survey included both closed and open questions in which participants could write responses, which were later back-coded by a member of the research team.

Multiple adult members of the same households were encouraged to complete the third section (in confidence) to provide multiple perspectives, and in ten households two members of the same household completed the survey. A total of 392 valid surveys were received from 382 multigenerational households in Greater Sydney and Brisbane. The cultural and household make-up, dwelling structure and tenure profiles of participants matched closely with the customized data we received from the Australian Bureau of Statistics based on 2011 census data. The confidence interval for the survey is 4.95 at 95 per cent confidence, calculated based on individuals living in multigenerational households in these two cities.

Of the survey respondents, 66 per cent ($n = 259$) lived in Sydney and 34 per cent in Brisbane ($n = 133$). Many more women (78 per cent) than men (22 per cent) completed the survey. A large proportion of respondents were aged 24 or under (39 per cent), 26 per cent were aged 25–44, 31 per cent were aged 45–64 and just 4 per cent were over 65. Just over half (55 per cent) of survey respondents lived in households with between four and six family members, an additional 42 per cent had two or three household members, and only 4 per cent had seven or more members. The majority lived in owner-occupied properties, with 39 per cent living in a property owned outright and 45 per cent in a property owned with a mortgage. An additional 14 per cent rented privately and 2 per cent rented public or community housing. When asked to identify their ancestry, the most common response by respondents was 'Australian' (44 per cent) followed by East Asian (13 per cent), Western European (12 per cent), Southeast Asian (7 per cent) and South Asian (6 per cent). A smaller proportion of respondents (less than 5 per cent each) chose their primary ancestry as Eastern European, Southern European, Middle Eastern, North American, African, Latin American, New Zealander, Indigenous Australian and mixed ancestries.

Of particular note, two-thirds (64 per cent) of our survey sample lived in households with two generations of adults where the youngest adult generation had a member under age 34 (hence, the 'two-generation younger' households). This reflects the make-up of multigenerational households in these two cities as a whole. According to custom tables we ordered from the Australian Bureau of Statistics based on 2011 census data, 94 per cent of all multigenerational households in Sydney and Brisbane combined are two-generation households and 37 per cent of people living in multigenerational households are under age 24, with an additional 10 per cent aged 25–34. These figures combined indicate that two-generation younger multigenerational household make up the bulk of all multigenerational households in these cities. The survey sample also included two-generation older households (where the youngest generation was 35 or older) as well as some three- and four-generation households.

People who completed the survey were asked whether they would continue with the study to complete a diary and participate in an interview about their experiences of multigenerational living. Twenty-one people subsequently completed a diary and twenty-one completed an interview. These research methods are described in more detail in Chapter 5.

Deciding to live in a multigenerational household

Results from the survey of multigenerational household members provide an indication of the breadth and importance of different reasons for living in a multigenerational household. The survey included a question that asked: 'What are the reasons that prompted multiple generations of your family to live together?' People were asked to write a response to this question, and their responses were then back-coded by the research team. Of the 303 survey respondents who answered this question, more than half (55 per cent) provided two or more reasons for living in a multigenerational household. Figure 3.1 provides a summary of the most

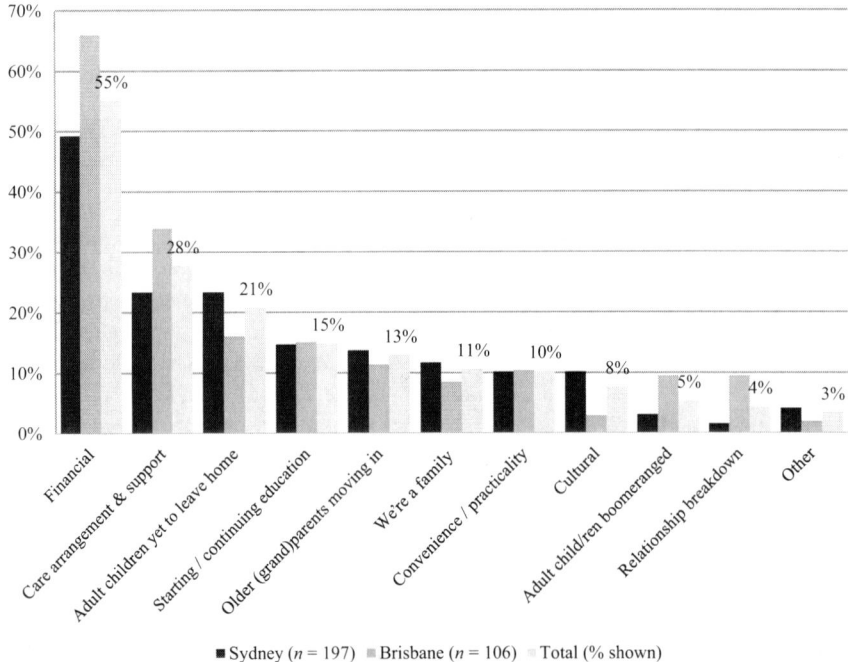

Figure 3.1 Reasons for living together, results by city

common responses to this question by city. Financial reasons were the most commonly cited reasons for living in a multigenerational household across the survey respondents, followed by care arrangements and support.

The next two most common responses – 'adult children yet to leave home' and 'starting or continuing education' – likely reflect the high proportion of our survey sample who were living in households that included an adult student. Almost two-thirds (64 per cent) of the households who completed the survey had an adult student living in the household. Figure 3.2 presents the reasons given for living in a multigenerational household for those households that include one or more adult students and those that do not. As can be seen from this figure, financial considerations remained the most important reason for living together for both groups. However, care arrangements and support and older (grand)parents moving in appear to be relatively more important for households without adult students. In contrast, adult children yet to leave home, starting or continuing education and feeling that they are a family and it makes sense to live together are reasons more commonly given by households with adult students in them.

Differences in reasons given for living together can also be seen when we compare the results for different types of households. Figure 3.3 demonstrates that the most common reasons for living in a multigenerational household differed for different household types. Particularly notable is that two-generation households in which the youngest generation was older (35 or older) noted care arrangement and support, followed by older parents or grandparents moving in as the most important reasons for multiple generations to live together. This contrasted with both younger two-generation households ($n = 226$) and three- and four-generation households

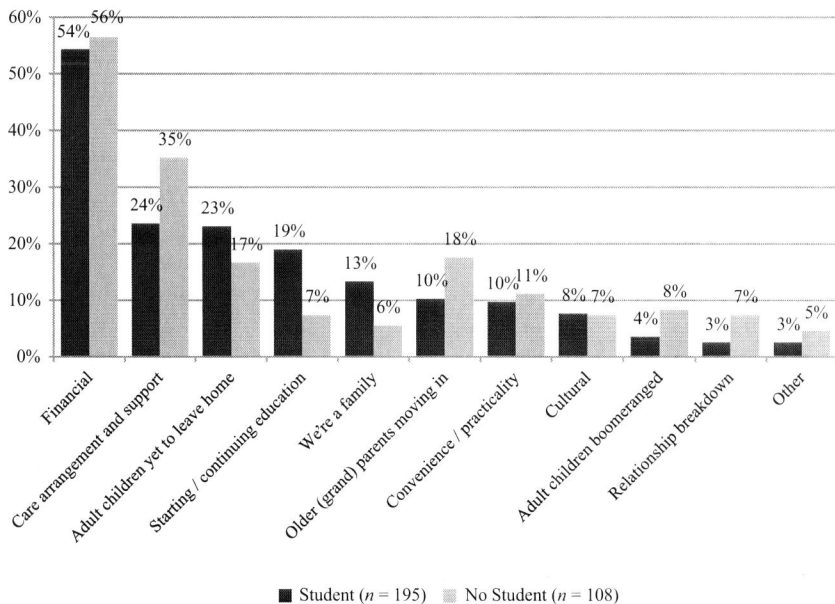

Figure 3.2 Reasons for living together, families with and without students

42 *Hazel Easthope*

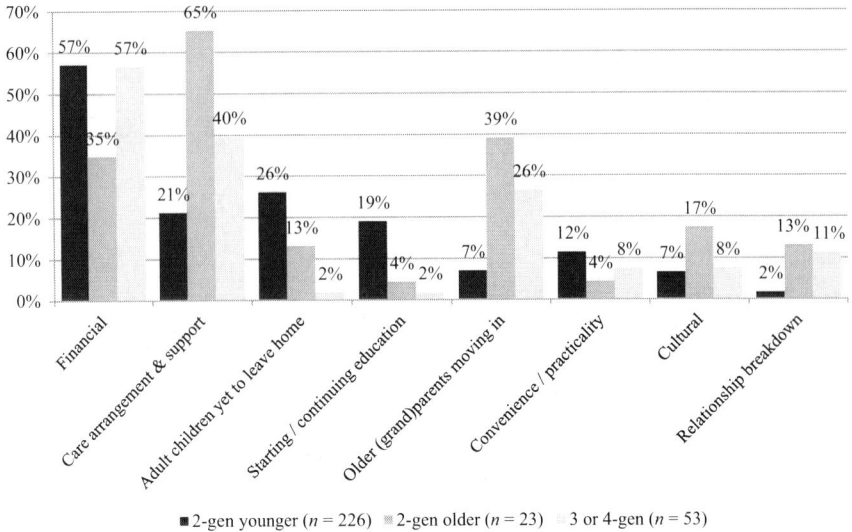

Figure 3.3 Reasons for living together, different household types

($n = 53$), which were both more likely to list financial considerations as drivers of multigenerational living. Only twenty-three households of the two-generation older household type completed the survey and answered this question, as a result we cannot be confident that these findings represent this subgroup as a whole. However, these findings demonstrate that multigenerational households are diverse, and that this diversity is likely to be reflected in their reasons for living together.

In addition to the open question asking people to chose the reasons for which they live in a multigenerational household, survey participants were also asked to what extent they agreed with a series of statements designed to test whether a list of hypothesized reasons for multigenerational living identified by the research team played a role in their decisions to live together. These included financial, cultural and practical reasons for multigenerational living. Figure 3.4 presents the results. Notably, financial considerations (it being more affordable to share housing costs and adult children being unable to afford to move out) were the statements most commonly agreed with by survey respondents, reflecting the findings to the open question that financial considerations were important for most participants. However, while family and cultural reasons were only mentioned by a relatively small proportion of survey respondents in the open question, 41 per cent of the survey respondents agreed that it was traditional for their family to live in a multigenerational household arrangement and 39 per cent agreed that it was traditional for people of their family's cultural background to live in this type of household.

Social and cultural views about the family, and about multigenerational living as an acceptable living arrangement, thus also seem to have played a role in the decision of many of our research participants to live in a multigenerational

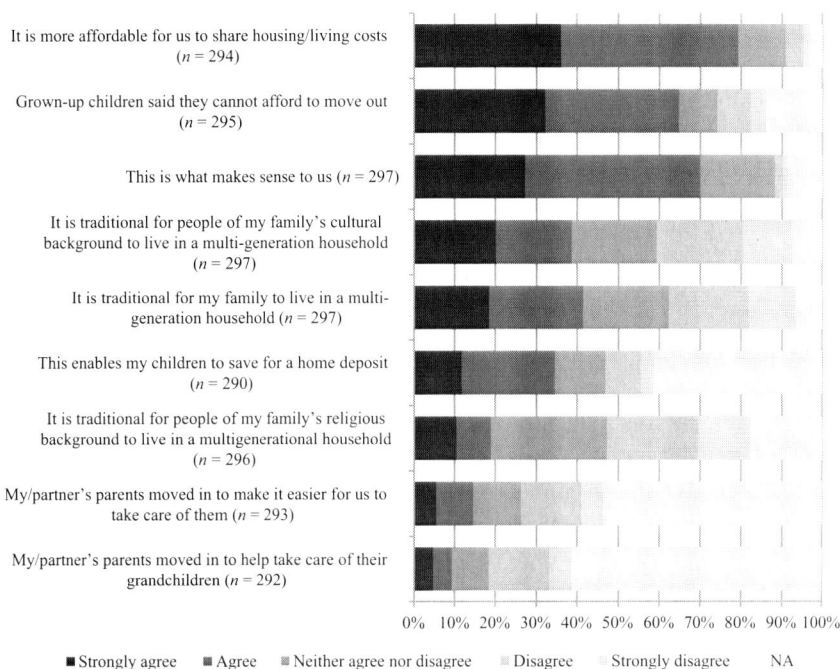

It is more affordable for us to share housing/living costs (*n* = 294)

Grown-up children said they cannot afford to move out (*n* = 295)

This is what makes sense to us (*n* = 297)

It is traditional for people of my family's cultural background to live in a multi-generation household (*n* = 297)

It is traditional for my family to live in a multi-generation household (*n* = 297)

This enables my children to save for a home deposit (*n* = 290)

It is traditional for people of my family's religious background to live in a multigenerational household (*n* = 296)

My/partner's parents moved in to make it easier for us to take care of them (*n* = 293)

My/partner's parents moved in to help take care of their grandchildren (*n* = 292)

0% 10% 20% 30% 40% 50% 60% 70% 80% 90% 100%

■ Strongly agree   ■ Agree   ■ Neither agree nor disagree   ░ Disagree   ░ Strongly disagree   NA

Figure 3.4 Reasons for living together, pre-coded question

household. This finding is supported by the analysis of Australian census data on multigenerational households reported in Chapter 2 of this book, which demonstrates that people from particular cultural backgrounds are more likely to live in a multigenerational household. These findings also reflect studies undertaken in Australia (Pink 2009) and other Western societies (Gee et al. 2003 in Canada and Fry and Passel 2014 in the United States) that have demonstrated a relationship between cultural background and the propensity to live in a multigenerational household.

Choice and constraint

The findings of the survey demonstrate that the decision to live in a multigenerational household can be complex, with many people providing multiple reasons for living in this household form. These findings also suggest that these decisions are made both through active choice and in response to constraints on the individual and the family.

The line between choice and constraint is often blurred. For example, the nomination of financial considerations as an important reason for multigenerational living among the survey respondents represents a complex set of considerations being made by members of multigenerational households, reflecting both active choice by members of these households, as well as financial constraints. In their responses to this question, survey participants talked about sharing household running costs, supporting adult children while they studied and/or worked part-time, supporting older parents or grandparents and responding in the best way they could to the constraints imposed by unaffordable housing markets:

> To help with the cost of living, to have a better quality of life, to support/help each other.
>
> [Survey]

> My eldest daughter is working part-time and going to university.
>
> [Survey]

> My mother did not have enough savings or pension to live alone.
>
> [Survey]

> The fact that my parents are pretty much close to retiring, and the mortgage has yet to be paid off so it's possible that I will have to take over repaying it and be the main financial head of the household thus meaning I will never be able to leave home again and have an independent life, because all other options just can't work. It feels like a trap that I may never be able to leave.
>
> [Survey]

Similarly, the provision of care and support to family members in many cases was a choice made within the context of practical constraints as demonstrated in the following quotes:

> Second-born daughter is still finding her feet, has had significant mental health issues and is not yet financially independent.
>
> [Survey]

> The cost of living is too high for myself. I am divorced and studying full time. My father assists me with baby sitting and picking up the kids from school. He also helps to pay my mortgage.
>
> [Survey]

The choice to live in a multigenerational household is often made in the context not only of practical constraints, such as the need to finance everyday living expenses and to provide care to family members, but is also often made in the context of social and cultural constraints. As indicated in Figure 3.4, for many of our research participants, multigenerational living was a tradition within their family or among people from their cultural background. In some cases, this meant that people felt they had no choice other than to live in a multigenerational household to provide the support required by other family members.

My mother did not have enough savings or pension to live alone. Culturally, having her live by herself was unacceptable to me.

[Survey]

I think that it's just expected that you look after your children until they're ready to fly the coop, as it were, and then they'll look after you when you're in your old age. It's kind of a trade.

[Interview]

It is our belief that we should 'give back' or contribute to the older generation who sacrificed much to provide with our upbringing. It is important to provide that respect and acknowledgement of the older generation.

[Diary]

While some participants might have seen this duty to family as a difficult but necessary requirement, the taken-for-granted duty to and connection with family was also often seen in a positive light by research participants:

The main reason is we cannot live without each other. We are bonded strongly to each other as in family.

[Survey]

We're a family – it makes sense for us to live together.

[Survey]

The influence of broader social change

The research findings outlined above demonstrate that the reasons for living in a multigenerational household are many and varied, that they are often different for households in different circumstances and that people make active choices to live in multigenerational households within the context of broader practical, social and cultural constraints. This section explores these constraints in more detail, considering the impacts that structural changes, public policy decisions and social and cultural views about the family can have on the decision to live in a multigenerational household.

Structural changes

One of the most important considerations for many of our research participants in both Sydney and Brisbane was the high price of housing to both rent and own in these cities. As noted by Worthington (2012), housing affordability has worsened over the past twenty-five years and Australia is now among the world's most unaffordable housing markets as a result of strong economic and population growth driving demand, the availability of cheaper and more accessible mortgage finance and tax incentives for property ownership. Housing affordability constraints are particularly acute in the major cities, including Sydney and Brisbane. Cobb-Clark and Ribar (2009) have demonstrated a direct relationship between increasing house prices and rent in Australia and the propensity of young Australians to live in multigenerational households. For many people, multigenerational living allows for a more efficient use of housing resources and finances than members of the household moving into their own properties. In some cases, people explained that while they would like to live in a separate property, housing unaffordability in their area made this option out of reach:

> My daughter, her partner and two children have been unable to secure a suitable rental property.
>
> [Survey]

For others, the only properties they could secure had poorer amenities than their multigenerational home and thus they had decided to live in a multigenerational arrangement as a trade-off:

> I can't afford to rent in areas that provide reliable access to the CBD. Areas I possibly could afford are too far for daily commuting and are poorly serviced by public transport.
>
> [Survey]

For yet others, a period of multigenerational living was enabling them to save money with a view to purchasing a property in the future:

> Saving money to buy a place.
>
> [Survey]

In some cases, these constraints to living independently in a separate property resulted not only from constrained housing affordability in these cities but also from the insecure or low incomes of family members resulting from changing structures of employment in modern cities as well as changing expectations regarding the need for higher education to obtain well-paid and secure employment (Evans 2012). As Cobb-Clark and Gørgens (2012: 1) note, 'A young person's life chances are shaped in large part by the investments in education, training and career development that he or she makes early in adulthood. These investments now take substantially longer than they once did and young people are increasingly turning to their families to help'.

As noted by Woodman (2012: 1074) in Australia, 'Young people increasingly mix study with variable hours of employment in a precarious youth labour market'. Many of our research participants discussed how this situation affected them:

> Son has been a full-time student until recently and now looking for full-time employment in his chosen profession. Can't afford to live anywhere else.
>
> [Survey]

My two oldest adult children cannot afford to move out of home. My oldest has a university degree but works in retail part time and cannot find full-time work. My second child has worked but could not afford to move out and now is a full-time student again.

[Survey]

The effects of the structural changes outlined above have been in many cases further exacerbated by public policy decisions made over the past few decades, notably public policy decisions regarding costs of higher education and care for children, the elderly and people with mental and physical disabilities.

Public policy decisions

The past few decades in Australia have seen, in common with many other Western societies, the promulgation of neo-liberal ideas in public policy decisions (Davis 2014). Notably, at the same time as higher education has been increasingly considered as a prerequisite for stable and well-paid jobs, government support for higher education costs have been reduced. During the period 1974–1989, domestic students enjoyed free education, but in 1989, the Federal Government set up the Higher Education Contribution Scheme (HECS), which required students to take out loans to pay for fees for attending university. Changes to the HECS system in 1996 to a tiered fee structure, followed by the deregulation of university fees in 2005, have seen the costs of university fees continually increase (Parliament of Australia 2015). The result has been that more young adults are attending university while accruing debt that must be paid off once they start working. At the same time, while the Commonwealth Government provides some income support for students to cover living expenses, this support is means tested and students are considered 'dependent' on their parents for the purposes of this means test until age 25. As a result of the difficulties in qualifying for this support, as well as the limited amount of financial support offered, the Australian university sector peak body Universities Australia (2015) stated that 'too many students are dependent on other means of income to the extent that the quality of their studies is threatened'. Therefore, many young people are trying to cover their living costs by working part-time while studying, by living with their parents, or both, as this parent explains:

It's really different from when I was young . . . I actually left home when I was 18 . . . but then we had a student allowance . . . I didn't have to work when I was studying. So it was really a different kind of situation. Now they've got HECS debt and . . . they're trying to work and they're trying to do all these things. It's really a very different situation. So I think it's financially, things are just not the same. Because of that, society has to change as well to accommodate that.

[Interview]

As well as increasing the burden of care for young adults as they complete their studies, changes to public policy regarding care for the elderly, children and people with disabilities have also increased the burden of care on families, with some families choosing to live in a multigenerational household to manage these needs. The most significant public policy changes have been the deinstitutionalization of care and a reduction in government support for people with a disability (Wiesel and Bigby 2015) and a policy shift toward 'ageing in place' for older people in the context of an ageing population (Olsberg and Winters 2005), with both resulting in a move toward supporting families to care for family members within the family home rather than in a specialist facility. These changes have had an influence on the creation of multigenerational households in Australia, as reflected in the fact that after financial considerations, providing care and support was the second most common reason given by survey respondents for living in a multigenerational household.

> Save money. Cultural reason to care for elderly parents.
>
> [Survey]

> My mother and step-father need care for many chronic health issues, so they chose to move in with me.
>
> [Survey]

Many of our research participants expressed a preference for their family members to age at home:

> It [a multigenerational living arrangement] keeps the aged people from going into villages and nursing homes and wherever they go, because they've got these children to keep them happy and active and their pets, everything. It keeps them young at heart really, whereas I've worked in a nursing home and it's very – there are a lot of elderly people who just want to see a child, they want to see a child or a dog or a cat or something to relate to.
>
> [Interview]

> In my family and my extended family living in aged care is one of the worst things that you can do to your parents unless they need . . . I mean if they have dementia or something where they really . . . living with you or living alone is not going to work out; but it's about putting somebody who can live outside aged care, if you put them in there then it's just really mean in our family.
>
> [Interview]

Public policy changes over the past few decades have increased the reliance of people who need some form of care or support, either physical or financial, on other members of their family, which has no doubt had an impact on the decisions of many people to live in a multigenerational household. However, this is not necessarily seen in a negative light by members of multigenerational households, with some expressing a desire to support their family members in the family home rather than relying on institutions.

Views about the family

As demonstrated in Chapter 2, people from certain cultural backgrounds have a greater propensity to live in multigenerational households in Australia. We might expect then to see changing views about the family in Australian cities because of changes in the cultural make-up of those cities. However, there is also evidence of a broader shift in the way in which the family is understood, even after changes in cultural make-up are taken into consideration. For example, research by Flatau et al. (2007) drawing on data from the Household, Income and Labour Dynamics in Australia survey found that level of education, family background and ethnicity strongly influence the home-leaving decisions of young adults; however, they also found that after controlling for these factors, there has still been a gradual increase in the age of adult children when they first leave the parental home in Australia. As such, they suggest that broader changes in norms and values about the family have influenced these changing household outcomes (Flatau et al. 2007). The findings of the *Living Together* project also indicate there has been a social shift in the acceptability of multigenerational living and it appears that this shift has been influenced by the structural changes and public policy decisions discussed in the previous sections of this chapter.

The interviews and diaries undertaken as part of the study included many reflections from research participants on the extent to which multigenerational living was an accepted practice in Australia. Among those people who felt that multigenerational living was more widely accepted, some said that they felt this was the case because of the difficulties faced by younger people in affording independent living, especially if they were still studying:

> Well, incomes aren't proportionate to the price to buy a house. You can't do it. You cannot live on an income and pay a mortgage, it doesn't balance out and I have every expectation that my girls will never leave home because it's too expensive and they won't be able to afford to leave home. I'm alright with that. I think it's more common, a lot more common especially at Uni. They're mostly young. They're all living at home, no one cares, no one's oh my God I can't believe you're still living at home. It's just expected, normal.
>
> [Interview]

> I think it's not feasible for most families to move their children out straight away especially if they're not going into the workforce full time. If they're doing any sort of study whether it's an apprenticeship or like tertiary education it's way too expensive.
>
> [Interview]

However, not all research participants agreed that multigenerational living was necessarily more accepted because of these pressures:

> I think the majority of society, in Brisbane/Australia, has a set perception of adults who live with their parents/remain in the family home, and that this

hasn't become more acceptable, even if it seems to be more widely practiced. I often get comments like 'aren't you lucky' and 'wish I still lived at home and didn't have to do anything' which I find pretty hurtful and offensive . . . It's frustrating and I doubt that the widely held views mentioned above are likely to die out until after the baby-boomer generation or even gen-x have moved on.

[Diary]

Other participants said that they thought that multigenerational living was more accepted but only in certain circumstances. In the case of young adults living with their parents, acceptability of multigenerational living was often seen to hinge on the life stages during which it was socially acceptable for adults to remain financially dependent on their parents:

When you're still studying, it's okay to live at home still. But once you're earning – once you're working full time and earning your wage, I think that's when you start looking at, okay, I need to move, I need to purchase property, I need to actually get on with my life now.

[Interview]

Others noted that the assumption that because they were living with their parents, young adults were financially dependent on them was frustrating, as this was not always the case. Many young adults who participated in our research made financial contributions to the household and in some cases had sole or joint responsibility for maintaining the mortgage on the family home:

People who jump to conclusions about what 'living at home' means don't seem to realize how many different situations that descriptor covers.

[Diary]

I find the biggest drawbacks or negative aspect of living in a multigenerational household are actually external to the household/family. Specifically, other people's perceptions . . . I find that when I tell people – of all different ages or backgrounds – that I 'live at home' or with my mum, they immediately presume that what I mean is that I live off my parent's charity and everything is done for me, that I'm some kind of adult-sized child. It's super irritating, considering that my family home has evolved into more of a share house/flat style of living arrangement with shared/divided household duties, dinners, and purchases. What is especially annoying is that it's rude and inappropriate to explain that actually I own more of the house than mum, have put more money into up-grading and maintaining it – like with kitchen renovations and a new hot water cylinder being paid for by me – and I have paid all the rates so far.

[Diary]

Thus, some of our research participants were experiencing what Niederhaus and Graham (2013: 240) have termed 'the cultural stigma of "dependence"' associated with multigenerational living.

Similarly, among older multigenerational families, where an older parent was living with their middle-aged son or daughter and their family, research participants noted their frustration at this situation being seen as not socially acceptable by others:

> My friends or people I work with ask me 'do your in-laws live with you?' I said 'yeah they do' and there's a shocked look on their face like 'really, how do you cope with that?' I say, 'well we just get on with it.'
>
> [Interview]

This situation occurs particularly where there were no clear, or what are deemed 'legitimate', reasons for the older person to be living with them such as illness or some other form of dependence:

> I think if there was an obvious medical reason like yeah mum has to live with us because she's got diabetes or something that would be just really obvious. But I think . . . it's just not within their sphere of recognition or whatever . . . you can't just want to, you've got to have a clear-cut reason for it and then it's acceptable.
>
> [Interview]

These findings indicate that there has been a social shift in Australian cities regarding the acceptability of multigenerational living. However, this has been a qualified shift, with multigenerational living as a response to structural changes (such as precarious employment and increased higher education participation) and public policy changes (around care for children, the elderly and the disabled, for example) becoming more acceptable. The reasons for multigenerational living in these circumstances appear to be socially acceptable and justifiable as they necessitate one or more members of the family being dependent financially or in terms of care on other household members. However, in those cases where members of the family do not need to rely on others for financial or care support, it appears that multigenerational living is still not entirely accepted.

The influence that these changing social norms regarding multigenerational living might have on the choices people make about whether to live in a multigenerational household in the future are hard to predict. However, these findings suggest that while choosing to live in a multigenerational household for reasons of financial support and care provision might become an easier proposition for people concerned about the social stigma associated with multigenerational living, for those households where the decision to live in a multigenerational household is not only about parents supporting their children financially as they study, or people providing care to their elderly parents, it seems that members of these households are still likely to experience some social stigma as a result of living together.

Conclusion

There are many different types of multigenerational households and there are many different drivers of multigenerational living. This chapter has explored some of the most common reasons for families choosing to live together, while considering these reasons within their broader social context. The decision to live in a multigenerational household can be a complex one and our research participants spoke about multiple reasons influencing their decision to live together. These decisions are made through both active choices and in response to constraints affecting individuals and their families.

The most commonly discussed drivers of multigenerational living related to financial considerations and providing care and support for family members. However, many other reasons for multigenerational living were also discussed, including family and cultural traditions. The decisions about multigenerational living are not made in a vacuum, and this chapter demonstrates that broader social changes have affected both the drivers of multigenerational cohabitation and the life experiences of those people living in these households. Notably, structural changes including housing affordability constraints, a rise in precarious employment among young adults and an increased demand for higher education qualifications have had important impacts on the decisions made by multigenerational households, especially households with young adult members. Public policy decisions affecting the costs of higher education, as well as care for the elderly and people with disabilities, have also influenced the decisions of people to live in multigenerational households.

These significant social shifts also appear to have had some impact on the acceptability of multigenerational living in Australia. However, the shift toward greater acceptability of multigenerational living has been a qualified one, with multigenerational living as a response to structural changes and public policy decisions having become more acceptable in those situations where a family member is dependent on others (students dependent on their parents and frail elderly dependent on their children), while multigenerational living for other reasons appears to be less socially acceptable.

References

Cobb-Clark, DA and Gørgens, T 2012, *Parents' Economic Support of Young-Adult Children: Do Socioeconomic Circumstances Matter?* Melbourne Institute Working Paper no 4/12, Melbourne Institute of Applied Economic and Social Research, Melbourne.

Cobb-Clark, DA and Ribar, DC 2009, *Financial Stress, Family Conflict, and Youths' Successful Transition to Adult Roles*, Discussion paper, Centre for Economic Policy Research, ANU, Canberra.

Davis, M 2014, 'Neoliberalism, the culture wars and public policy', in C Miller and L Orchard (eds), *Australian Public Policy: Progressive Ideas in the Neoliberal Ascendency*, Policy Press, Bristol, pp. 27–44.

Evans, A 2012, 'Generational change in leaving the parental home', in A Evans and J Baxter (eds), *Negotiating the Life Course: Stability and Change in Life Pathways*, Springer, Dordrecht, pp. 53–67.

Flatau, P, Hendershott, P, James, I, Watson, R and Wood, G 2007, 'Leaving the parental home in Australia over the generations: Evidence from the household, income and labour dynamics in Australia (HILDA) Survey', *Journal of Population Research*, vol. 24, no. 1, pp. 51–71.

Fry, RA and Passel, JS 2014, *In Post-Recession Era, Young Adults Drive Continuing Rise in Multi-Generational Living*, Pew Research Center, Social and Demographic Trends Project, Washington, DC.

Gee, EM, Mitchell, BA and Wister, AV 2003, 'Home leaving trajectories in Canada: Exploring cultural and gendered dimensions', *Canadian Studies in Population*, vol. 30, pp. 245–270.

Niederhaus, SG and Graham, JL 2013, *All in the Family: A Practical Guide to Successful Multigenerational Living*, Taylor Trade Publishing, Lanham.

Olsberg, D and Winters, M 2005, *Ageing in Place: Intergenerational and Intrafamilial Housing Transfers and Shifts in Later Life*, Final Report No. 88, Australian Housing and Urban Research Institute, Melbourne.

Parliament of Australia 2015, *The Higher Education Contribution Scheme*, accessed 11 September 2015, www.aph.gov.au/About_Parliament/Parliamentary_Departments/Parliamentary_Library/Publications_Archive/archive/hecs

Pink, B 2009, *Australian Social Trends*, June 2009, Australian Bureau of Statistics, Canberra.

Universities Australia 2015, *Student Fees and Income Support*, accessed 11 September 2015, www.universitiesaustralia.edu.au/uni-participation-quality/students/Student-Fees-and-Income-Support#.Vfl92VWqpBc

Wiesel, I and Bigby, C 2015, 'Movement on shifting sands: Deinstitutionalisation and people with intellectual disability in Australia, 1974–2014', *Urban Policy and Research*, vol. 33, no. 2, pp. 178–194.

Worthington, A 2012, 'The quarter century record on housing affordability, affordability drivers and government policy responses in Australia', *International Journal of Housing Markets and Analysis*, vol. 5, no. 3, pp. 235–252.

Woodman, D 2012, 'Life out of Synch: How new patterns of further education and the rise of precarious employment are reshaping young people's relationships', *Sociology*, vol. 46, no. 6, pp. 1074–1090.

4 Multigenerational households

Economic considerations

Stephen Whelan

Introduction

The increase in the number of multigenerational households in Australia has been attributed to a range of social, demographic and economic factors (Cobb-Clark 2008). The discussion in this chapter considers the *economic* reasons behind the proliferation of such households and the implications for policy. Central to the discussion is the notion that multigenerational households facilitate and encourage the sharing and transfer of resources. By focusing on the resource implications of households that span more than one generation of adults, it is possible to identify how the growth of multigenerational households has been influenced by economic forces, and how a range of policies have shaped, and can respond to, this development.

The discussion begins by presenting a framework, namely the economic model of the household, and highlights the economic incentives associated with multigenerational living arrangements. Next, data from the Household Income and Labour Dynamics in Australia (HILDA) dataset is used to provide evidence around the growth of multigenerational households in Australia over the past decade, focusing on the economic drivers behind this development at the household level. Next, the behaviours and outcomes experienced by members of multigenerational households are set out. The focus of this discussion is the nature of transfers that are associated with, and facilitated by, multigenerational households. Finally, the implications of the rise of multigenerational households for policy are explored. While such developments clearly have important implications for housing-related policies, it is argued that childcare, elderly care and redistributive policies are also impacted by the proliferation of multigenerational households.

A definitional note

The definition of the multigenerational household adopted for this book, namely 'households where two or more generations of related adults live in the same dwelling, with the oldest of the youngest generation aged 18 years or older', represents the starting point for the discussion in this chapter. However, from an economic perspective, such households can be viewed as consisting of two distinct types of households: namely two- and three-generation households. The former generally consists of parents and their adult children. This type of household has attracted an increasing amount of attention in the face of rapid social and economic changes that have seen the departure of children from the family home delayed (Flatau et al. 2007) or the return of nondependent children following major life events such as relationship dissolution (Wood et al. 2013). The increase in the number of such households is usually inextricably linked to developments in the housing market, education and social norms around the age of marriage which have occurred in Australia and other countries (Cobb-Clark 2008).

The second type of multigenerational household is the 'three-generation household', consisting of households where at least three distinct generations co-reside.[1] Although numerically smaller in number, they have grown substantially from a small base in some countries such as the United States and have also become increasingly common in Australia (Williams 2011; Brandon 2012). The discussion below considers both types of multigenerational households as they have distinct but nonetheless significant implications when viewed from an economic perspective.

The economic model of the household

The economic approach focuses on the notion that economic agents generally maximize utility subject to a set of constraints, such as those relating to financial or time limitations. In other words, agents make the best possible choice given the alternatives available to them. A key advantage of formulating problems in this way is that attention is focused on the costs and benefits of alternative choices. Consider the following description of the household formation problem by Ermisch (1999). In particular, consider the choice of a young adult or child to form a household independently of the parents. The utility or well-being of the parent (p) depends on consumption of goods and services along with the utility of their children (c). In a mathematical sense, the parent's utility can be expressed as:

$$U^p\left(x_p, h_p, U^c\left(x_c, h_c, i\right), i\right) \tag{1}$$

Where x_p and h_p represent non-housing and housing consumption of the parent respectively, and where x_c and h_c represent non-housing and housing consumption of the child. In general, utility is increasing in consumption of goods and services. The utility of the young adult or child is shown by (U^c). The utility of both parent and young adult depends on whether they co-reside $(i = r)$ or live apart $(i = a)$. Note that the utility of the child enters into the utility function of the parent in part because of altruistic concerns of parents for their offspring.

The decision to co-reside or live apart will be shaped in part by the financial constraints that parents and children face. Assuming that a dwelling provides an equal level of housing services for all residents, if co-residency occurs or a multigenerational household is maintained then the amount of housing consumed for both the child and parent are equal, so that $h_p = h_c$. In turn, the constraints faced by parents and child are shown as the following:

$$M = x_p + p_h h_p + T_r \tag{a}$$

$$y + T_r = x_c \tag{b}$$

$$T_r \geq 0 \tag{c}$$

Where M is parental income, T_r is financial transfers to the young adult, p_h is the price of housing and y is the child's income. Effectively, the constraint (a) requires that the income of the parent must equal the amount spent on housing, consumption of other goods and transfers to children. Similarly for the child, constraint (b) requires that the value of their total consumption (x_c) must not exceed the value of income and parental transfers. Note that by co-residing, parents and children can share housing costs.

Rather than co-residing, children could choose to live independently $(i = a)$ in forming their own household. In this case, the constraints become:

$$M = x_p + p_h h_p + T_a \tag{a'}$$

$$y + T_a = x_c + k p_h h_c \tag{b'}$$

$$T_a \geq 0 \tag{c'}$$

where T_a is financial transfers to the young adult and k is the share of housing costs incurred by the child. For example, if the child lives alone (shares accommodation with others), then $k = 1 (k < 1)$. In the event that the child lives independently, housing costs are incurred for the parent *and* the child so that total housing costs are likely to be higher.

The economic approach posits that individuals (parents and children) maximize utility subject to their budget constraints. That is, they choose co-residency or independent living through a comparison of the utility levels available under each alternative subject to the constraints faced. How those decisions are made varies across models reflecting underlying assumptions about the nature of decision making within a 'household'.[2] Central to this economic approach is the notion that agents maximize their utility by choosing the best possible outcome from among the set of feasible alternatives. If an economic variable such as the price of housing or income changes, the set of alternatives available will also change, and a different choice can be made. What is pivotal in economic models such as these is that they highlight how the formation of households, including multigenerational households, is driven by economic considerations as encapsulated in the preferences of parents and their children, and the budget constraints which are faced. The framework is general in nature and can be formulated in a variety of ways to capture different assumptions about the nature of the relationship between parents and their children, such as the degree of altruism exhibited by parents toward their children (Laferrère and Wolff 2006).

It is useful to consider some of the key features of household formation into which the economic approach provides insight. The most obvious feature is that if the child remains co-resident, housing is shared and additional housing costs for the separate household are avoided $\left(h_p = h_c = h_i\right)$. It is also true that other savings are available when co-residency is maintained, owing to the nature of many housing-related goods being 'public' in nature. That is, they can be consumed by a number of individuals jointly without diminishing the level of enjoyment experienced by individuals. Within a household, services such as heating can be consumed by all occupants and little or no additional cost is incurred if another individual joins the household (Felkey 2013). It is also the case that larger households generate economies of scale. A large refrigerator will generally cost less than two smaller ones that are required if a separate household is formed. Such cost and resource sharing considerations are likely to be important determinants of the decision to form a separate household or to remain part of a multigenerational household, because savings will allow greater consumption of non-housing goods by both adult and child $\left(x_p \ and \ x_c\right)$.

Although the sharing of housing and related costs is generally identified as a key benefit of co-residency, such an arrangement is offset by the reduced privacy and independence that living in a separate household brings. Across individuals, some will place a high value on or derive greater benefits from the privacy associated with independent living. More important, it can be captured in their preferences or utility function. Hence, when parents and children derive greater utility from the privacy and freedom offered by independent living $\left(h_a\right)$, or place a high value on such arrangements, they are more likely to form a separate household, all else being equal. In effect, the higher benefit that some individuals place on the advantages that come from living apart can be incorporated into the model through the utility function.

A second important consideration highlighted by the model is that it makes clear that members of households are often related through more than simply financial or economic transactions. In (1), the utility or welfare of children enters directly into the utility of the parent. This altruism or concern for the child on the part of the parent serves to highlight the familial relationships that underlie multigenerational households. Indeed, such an assumption is captured by the inclusion of parental transfers $\left(T_i\right)$ in the model. The nature of the familial links within households is an important consideration associated with understanding the behaviours of individuals and the nature of transfers that occur within the household unit (Laferrère and Wolff 2006).

The model is highly stylized and does not cover at least two important considerations associated with household formation. First, the model does not examine how time is allocated within a household. Arguably, an important benefit from larger households is that they provide for members to specialize in household and non-household tasks in which they have a comparative advantage. Within the household, there are also potential gains from economies of scale in activities such as washing and cooking (Van Klaveren et al. 2008). Although it is possible to set out models that focus on these issues, the fundamental rationale behind the formation of households and the resource savings available are similar to those described earlier.

The second limitation of the model is its static nature. That is, it does not consider intertemporal considerations associated with decision making over the life cycle. Such a consideration is likely to be important in the context of multigenerational households. Often, the formation of a separate household requires a period of saving or deferred consumption. Such savings may be supplemented by parental transfers that facilitate the formation of a new household. Indeed, in-kind transfers associated with multigenerational households are generally made by forward-looking agents with a concern for the current and future welfare of children and other related parties. Again, it is possible to formulate models with this feature that retain the fundamental characteristics of the economic approach described here (Laferrère and Wolff 2006).

In general, it is important to note that although the model described here is potentially flexible, it is underpinned by a strong set of assumptions that require agents to compare the costs and benefits associated with their decisions. Those costs and benefits are shaped by economic factors such as the price of housing and incomes, along with the nature of preferences. Although the formal nature of the model facilitates analysis of how behaviours change in response to economic factors, it also highlights the model's limitations. Noneconomic considerations, such as social norms around multigenerational living, may be difficult to incorporate into such models.

The framework described here posits the retention of a multigenerational household with a dependent adult child, or the formation of a separate household by that individual. A similar framework can be applied to the formation of a three-generation household in which the grandparents join an existing household or live independently. Although the budget constraints and utility functions will be altered, analogous principles will apply to household formation. Similar savings will be possible from the sharing of housing and similar resources, as well as the potential for care services or time transfers, to be provided within the household. Such services may be upward in nature, with parents looking after elderly grandparents, or downward in nature, with grandparents providing childcare services to grandchildren. These intergenerational transfers may be motivated by a range of considerations related to altruism, exchange motives, demonstration effects or insurance motives (Cox 1987; Laferrère and Wolff 2006).

With this framework in mind, it is possible to consider the characteristics of households in Australia and the behaviour and outcomes experienced by their inhabitants.

Multigenerational household formation, characteristics, behaviours and outcomes

Description of the data

The analysis in this chapter uses the Household Income and Labour Dynamics in Australia (HILDA) dataset.[3] The HILDA dataset is a longitudinal database that contains a rich array of individual and household-level information on key demographics, the labour market and household-related measures. The HILDA data has been collected annually since 2001 and thirteen waves of data are available for analysis with a large top-up sample added in 2011 (Watson 2011). In some waves, additional question modules have been added that cover special topics of interest.

The key advantages of using the HILDA dataset are its longitudinal nature, which allows for dynamics within households to be tracked over time, and the rich set of variables available for analysis purposes. The key disadvantage is that it is a general household survey so that the number of multigenerational households within the data is limited. Notwithstanding this factor, the general nature of the dataset allows for comparison across household types covering a number of dimensions. The discussion that follows provides insight into four broad questions around the economic considerations that drive household formation and the behaviours of individuals within households. In particular:

1   How has the number of multigenerational households changed over time, and what are the characteristics exhibited by multigenerational households compared with other household types?
2   How do the economic behaviours of individuals within multigenerational households compare with those in other household types?
3   What transfers occur within multigenerational households?
4   Why do individuals join multigenerational households?

A comparison of multigenerational households to other household types requires a taxonomy of household types. The challenge in such an undertaking is to capture the heterogeneity exhibited among households in a coherent manner. As noted, two types of multigenerational households are identified separately. In addition, four other household types are identified in the HILDA data:

1   *Multi 2* – Two-generation households containing a parent (or parents) and at least one adult child greater than age 18.
2   *Multi 3* – Three-generation households containing grandparents, parents and grandchildren where the age of at least one grandchild is 18 years.
3   *Couple households* – Households containing a couple with or without dependent children or students less than 18 years of age. Couple households may also contain other nonrelated individuals.
4   *Single households* – Households consisting of a lone person or a lone parent with dependent children or students less than 18 years of age. Such households may also contain other nonrelated individuals.
5   *Lone households* – Households consisting of a lone individual.
6   *Other* – Group households and multifamily households and other unclassified household types.

With this taxonomy in mind, it is now possible to consider each of the questions identified above.

Household characteristics 2001–2013

In Table 4.1, I present the characteristics of each *household* type using the 2013 HILDA data. Note that the characteristics presented are those of the household

Table 4.1 HILDA household characteristics

	Household type						
	Multi_2	Multi_3	Coup_hh	Single_hh	Lone_hh	Other_hh	All
No. h/holds 2013	1,515,772	256,692	4,137,866	509,016	2,127,706	149,909	8,696,961
No. h/holds 2001	1,092,214	179,342	3,505,615	516,971	1,776,459	211,320	7,281,921
% Change 2001–13	38.8	43.1	18.0	−1.5	19.8	−29.1	19.4
Location							
New South Wales	0.329	0.339	0.321	0.292	0.309	0.250	0.317
Victoria	0.289	0.259	0.233	0.214	0.259	0.388	0.251
Queensland	0.174	0.216	0.203	0.236	0.205	0.193	0.200
South Australia	0.076	0.062	0.069	0.101	0.089	0.084	0.077
West Australia	0.101	0.082	0.119	0.101	0.094	0.053	0.106
Tas./ACT/NT	0.032	0.042	0.055	0.055	0.045	0.032	0.048
Sydney	0.217	0.260	0.196	0.177	0.176	0.175	0.195
Melbourne	0.232	0.208	0.167	0.139	0.179	0.174	0.181
Brisbane	0.095	0.126	0.094	0.096	0.086	0.100	0.094
Adelaide	0.066	0.059	0.048	0.077	0.065	0.075	0.058
Perth	0.079	0.072	0.086	0.078	0.066	0.051	0.079
Household equivalized expenditures							
Grocery exp. ($)	2785	2119	3553	4164	5762	2632	3938
Telecomm. exp. ($)	477	388	693	943	1515	520	855
Utilities exp. ($)	495	394	671	768	1262	411	775
Household income & related characteristics							
Household size	3.518	4.854	2.939	2.662	1.000	2.493	2.598
HH total income ($)	148,035	123,413	125,532	66,554	52,814	95,349	107,709
HH inc. per pers ($)	42,079	25,425	42,712	25,002	52,814	38,247	41,458
Wage/salary inc. ($)	121,808	91,236	116,205	55,018	62,223	84,599	102,996
SEIFA10	5.731	4.745	5.781	4.799	5.343	5.483	5.572
Tenure							
Owner	0.811	0.713	0.723	0.342	0.500	0.274	0.653
Renter	0.172	0.249	0.252	0.617	0.440	0.568	0.311
Other	0.013	0.034	0.024	0.040	0.057	0.158	0.033

Note: Author's own calculations using HILDA waves 1 and 13. All means use household weights.

rather than the individuals within the household. The total number of households is presented for both 2001, the first year of the HILDA data collection, and 2013.[4] Extrapolating from the HILDA data, the total number of households in Australia has grown over this period by around 19.4 per cent, from 7.3 million to 8.7 million. Of note, the largest growth has been in the multigenerational households. In particular, the number of two- and three-generation households has grown by approximately 38.8 and 43.1 per cent respectively during this period, significantly higher than other household types. It is important to stress that though the growth of three-generation households has been rapid, they remain relatively small in number. It should be noted that the growth in multigenerational households in recent decades has been noted elsewhere in the literature (Liu and Easthope 2012).

Of particular interest are the characteristics of the households and how they relate to the economic considerations that drive household formation. Perhaps the clearest signal about the importance of economic considerations in the formation of multigenerational households is their location. Extrapolating from the HILDA data, around 60 per cent of multigenerational households are located in New South Wales and Victoria, compared with around 57 per cent of all households being located in these states. This pattern is more pronounced when Sydney and Melbourne are considered. Around 22 per cent of two-generation households and 26 per cent of three-generation households are located in Sydney. In comparison, around 20 per cent of all households are located in that city. Similarly, multigenerational households are 'overrepresented' in Melbourne. A likely reason for this pattern is that Sydney and Melbourne have experienced rapid house price growth over the past decade (ABS 2015). The public nature of housing services provides a means by which the burden imposed by the relatively high cost of housing services can be alleviated through co-residency and the sharing of housing costs among members of intergenerational families (Ermisch 1999). This pattern reflects an important economic consideration that explains in part the tendency for young Australians to remain in the family home for longer periods (Flatau et al. 2007). In addition to providing an opportunity for individuals to benefit from the economies of scale associated with multigenerational households, it provides an important mechanism by which parents can transfer resources to children and facilitate entry into homeownership.

The economic benefits of multigenerational households are clearly demonstrated by considering 'equivalized household expenditures' across household types. The equivalization process provides a means by which households can be compared using a common metric. The approach requires that the number of 'adult equivalents' in a household is measured by assigning weights to each individual in the household.[5] Dividing total household expenditure by the number of adult equivalents then provides a measure of household expenditure for each 'adult' in the household. Table 4.1 reports equivalized expenditures for each type of household across a number of different expenditure items reported in the HILDA data. In each case, the lower costs associated with the larger households, especially multigenerational households, are clear. Consider, for example, the expenditure on groceries. Compared with an average annual expenditure of $3,938 per adult equivalent, the expenditure in two- and three-generation households is substantially lower at $2,785 and $2,119 respectively. Similarly, the expenditure per adult equivalent on utilities such as heating and electricity is $495 and $394 per adult equivalent in multigenerational households, significantly below the overall average of $775. Although it is to be expected that total expenditures on goods such as heating will be higher in larger households, the 'public' nature of such goods provides significantly lower expenditures per 'adult equivalent'. Only 'other household' types, which primarily consist of group households, have similar equivalized expenditures to the multigenerational households.

Consistent with *a priori* expectations, two- and three-generation households tend to be larger than other types of households. Interestingly, total household income in 2013 is similar across the couple and three-generation households, with two-generation households reporting somewhat higher income ($148,000), most likely reflecting the higher proportion of relatively young independent adults in the household. In turn, three-generation households generally exhibit somewhat lower labour market income in the form of wages and salaries ($91,000) when compared with couple households ($116,000).

The relative value of resources available to the household can also be assessed along two other dimensions. First, note that among all household types, two-generation families are the most likely to live in owner-occupied housing (81 per cent), while rates of ownership in couple and three-generation households are similar. This most likely reflects, in a life cycle sense, the relatively mature nature of the households and their members. Second, a measure of the areas in which households are located can be gleaned by using local measures of socioeconomic status derived by the Australian Bureau of Statistics. The Socio-Economic Indexes for Areas (SEIFA) measure reported in Table 4.1 captures the relative socioeconomic advantage and disadvantage of the local area where a household resides. On a scale of 1 to 10, higher numbers indicate that the area in which the household is located contains a higher proportion of families with high incomes and tertiary education. Three-generation households generally occur in somewhat disadvantaged areas, at least relative to couple households and two-generation households. Such a pattern is consistent with the formation of three-generation households in response to more limited resources available to household members (Matsudaira 2016). It is notable, for example, that on a per person basis, household income is lowest in three-generation households and single households, and in both cases is lower than the overall average.

Household member characteristics and behaviours

The HILDA data also provides an opportunity to consider the behaviours of individuals within different types of households. In Table 4.2, data about the behaviours and experiences of individuals aged 18 and over in wave 13 (2013) of the data are presented.

In terms of demographics, it is notable that three-generation households tend to be female dominated with only 39 per cent of members being male. This demographic is in stark contrast to the other types of households and may reflect

Table 4.2 HILDA Wave 13 household member characteristics

	Household type					
	Multi_2	*Multi_3*	*Coup_hh*	*Single_hh*	*Lone_hh*	*Other_hh*
Male	0.497	0.390	0.507	0.360	0.514	0.527
Age < 25 years	0.272	0.159	0.038	0.090	0.067	0.186
Age 25–44 years	0.180	0.294	0.455	0.457	0.290	0.533
Age 45–64 years	0.395	0.321	0.270	0.261	0.283	0.161
Age > 65 years	0.089	0.160	0.183	0.055	0.358	0.111
Number children	0.029	0.126	0.024	0.042	0.000	0.088
Married	0.413	0.470	0.869	0.018	0.036	0.257
Separated	0.089	0.133	0.045	0.335	0.287	0.237
Widowed	0.041	0.087	0.003	0.033	0.242	0.026
Never married	0.456	0.310	0.083	0.612	0.434	0.480
Economic participation						
FT employed	0.413	0.304	0.439	0.324	0.408	0.431
PT employed	0.261	0.164	0.200	0.254	0.116	0.172
Unemployed	0.044	0.085	0.027	0.074	0.024	0.076
Not in the labour force	0.282	0.448	0.333	0.347	0.450	0.255
Education						
University	0.185	0.156	0.319	0.196	0.227	0.311
Diploma	0.078	0.086	0.098	0.080	0.094	0.069
Certificate	0.204	0.218	0.202	0.209	0.189	0.267
High school	0.244	0.176	0.116	0.136	0.152	0.176
Less than high school	0.288	0.364	0.260	0.373	0.336	0.177
Background						
Australian born	0.765	0.567	0.658	0.764	0.722	0.624
Imm. – Eng. speaking	0.072	0.102	0.132	0.085	0.128	0.071
Imm. – NESB	0.163	0.331	0.210	0.151	0.150	0.305
Caring behaviours						
Care of resident parent	0.024	0.079	0.003	0.005	0.000	0.000
Care of non-resident parent	0.021	0.016	0.019	0.021	0.022	0.015
Care child (not own child)	0.062	0.220	0.119	0.080	0.065	0.503
Childcare (hrs)	7.743	15.260	8.670	4.939	9.506	6.279
Satisfaction (means)						
Life	7.893	7.820	8.009	7.535	7.682	7.814
Time	6.800	6.505	6.691	6.356	7.414	6.743
Housing	8.166	7.889	8.023	7.680	7.945	7.925
Financial responsibilities						
Independent adult	0.353	0.153	0.021	0.125	–	–
Board payer	0.150	0.154	0.034	0.045	–	–
Resp. for bills	0.089	0.164	0.019	0.339	–	–

Note: Authors own calculations using HILDA wave 13. All means use appropriate weights.

an important role played by such households in providing care to elderly parents, especially the mother or mother-in-law. Indeed, there is evidence that indicates that daughters are more likely to provide care to elderly parents and in particular their mother (Whelan 2013). Such behaviours can potentially have important implications for other behaviours such as participation in employment (Leigh 2010). The age structure of the alternative household types also reflects the function the household serves and is largely consistent with *a priori* expectations. For example, around 70 per cent of individuals in couple households are between 25 and 65 years old, and less than 15 per cent are over age 65. Within three-generation households, the age distribution is far more uniform with over 15 per cent of individuals being over age 65. As might be expected, the proportion of widowed individuals in three-generation households is relatively high, reflecting the likelihood that such households are formed following the death of a parent, although the proportion of individuals who are married in two-generation households is relatively low. This latter pattern most likely reflects the fact that two-generation households generally contain nondependent adults who are yet to partner.

An important economic consideration is participation in the labour market. In couple households, around 65 per cent of individuals aged 15 and over report being in paid employment, with the proportion being somewhat lower in single households (58 per cent). In two- and three-generation households, the proportion of individuals who report being employed is approximately 67 per cent and 47 per cent respectively. While the proportion of individuals engaged in the labour market is significantly lower in three-generation households, it reflects the presence of the grandparent generation within the household and the much greater tendency for such individuals to be retired or not in the labour force (NILF). Unlike unemployed individuals, retired individuals are classified as NILF because they are not seeking work. It is also noteworthy that individuals in multigenerational households tend to have lower levels of education. Over one-third of those in three-generation households have less than a high school education. This statistic in part reflects the higher age of these individuals as younger cohorts have tended to attain more education.

Although evidence suggests that the formation of multigenerational households is driven by economic considerations, cultural and related considerations are also important. Individuals who reside in three-generation households are substantially less likely to be born in Australia (57 per cent) compared with those in other households. In comparison, over 75 per cent of individuals in single households are born in Australia. It is likely that younger individuals within a household are more likely to be born in Australia, including descendants who live with their overseas-born family in multigenerational households. Nonetheless, multigenerational households are more likely to contain migrants, including those who have a non-English-speaking background (NESB). Therefore, cultural norms, such as those associated with expectations around the provision of care among the extended family, may play an important role in shaping the preferences and decisions of individuals around multigenerational household formation.

Transfer behaviours and life satisfaction

An important role played by a household is that it can facilitate nonmarket economic transactions. These transactions can be thought of as interactions between economic agents that *could* occur in a market setting, but for some reason occur outside such a setting. It may be due to the savings associated with the organization and completion of such a transaction outside of the market, or because of noneconomic motivations such as altruism that drive the behaviour. The HILDA data provides an opportunity to gain insight into such transactions including those that involve the transfer of financial resources or temporal transfers associated with the provision of services and time.

An important function carried out within families and households is the provision of care. Such transfers may be upward or downward in nature and the HILDA data provides insight into both types of care. An upward transfer refers to the care of an older parent or relative by an individual from a younger generation. Table 4.2 reports the proportion of individuals in each type of household who recall providing care for resident and non-resident parents or parents-in-law. For example, in couple households 1.9 per cent of individuals report actively providing care to a non-resident parent or parent-in-law due to a long-term health condition; a much smaller percentage (0.3 per cent) also report caring for a resident parent. In comparison, in two-generation households the corresponding figures are somewhat higher at 2.1 and 2.4 per cent respectively, and in three-generation households at 1.6 and 7.9 per cent. This is consistent with the role of multigenerational households facilitating the care of elderly and less-abled individuals.

Time transfers might also be downward in nature, for example when they are being provided by grandparents to their grandchildren. Table 4.2 shows the proportion of individuals greater than 45 years of age across household types who report providing care to 'other people's children on a regular unpaid basis'. Among those who provide care, the number of hours of care provided on a weekly basis is also reported.[6] Again, multigenerational households represent an important mechanism by which this type of transfer is facilitated. In two-generation and three-generation households, 6.2 and 22.0 per cent of individuals report providing such care to other people's children respectively. In comparison, the corresponding figures for couple and single households is 11.9 and 8.0 respectively. It is noteworthy that the amount of care provided is extensive, with those in three-generation households providing over fifteen hours of childcare on a weekly basis.

The role that multigenerational households play in facilitating intra-family and intra-household transfers has been given increasing attention because of developments in housing markets over the past decade. In particular, there has been increasing anecdotal evidence that individuals are receiving direct and indirect assistance from parents to aid them to enter into homeownership (Barrett et al. 2015). Similarly, there is evidence that familial support is important for individuals who transition out of homeownership due to economic shocks such as the loss of employment or relationship breakdown (Wood et al. 2013). While existing evidence supports the view that financial transfers and bequests have played an important role in facilitating transitions into homeownership, less is known about in-kind transfers such as co-residence. The increase in the number of two-generation households noted previously is indirect evidence that this has become an increasingly important means of intra-family support.

Consider initially the financial responsibility that young adults report in wave 13 of HILDA. For each type of household, individuals between 17 and 30 years of age and identified as 'nondependent children', 'dependent students' and 'other related family members' are termed independent adults. The proportion of 'independent adults' in each household type is reported in Table 4.2 and varies between 35 per cent in two-generation households and 2 per cent in couple households.[7] Among these individuals, it is possible to identify the proportion who share the financial burden associated with housing and related expenditures. For example, in two- and three-generation households, 15.0 and 15.4 per cent of independent adults report making a financial contribution to the household's housing and running costs. This pattern also holds for other housing-related costs, with 8.9 and 16.4 per cent of independent adults in two- and three-generation households respectively identifying as being responsible for paying household utility bills or purchasing groceries.

The economic framework makes clear that there are trade-offs or costs *and* benefits associated with multigenerational living. While there is evidence that the financial constraints on younger individuals less than 30 years of age can be mitigated by living in such arrangements, there is a potential cost associated with the loss of independence and more crowded living arrangements. Some evidence is available in HILDA in the form of life satisfaction questions, which ask individuals how satisfied they are with various aspects of life on a scale of 0 (totally dissatisfied) to 10 (totally satisfied). Overall life satisfaction is similar across individuals in all household types, and satisfaction with the house in which the individual lives is also similar across all household types.

One potentially important role played by co-residence is that it provides opportunities for parents to assist children into homeownership. The role that such

Table 4.3 HILDA homeownership plans

	Multigenerational households	Non-multigenerational households
Age	21.8 years	23.7 years
% plan to purchase house in future	97.0%	96.0%
Age plan to purchase a house	27.9 years	29.1 years
% concerned about ability to do so?		
Very worried	12.1%	12.7%
Somewhat worried	51.9%	56.6%
Not at all	36.1%	30.6%
Deposit		
% started	28.0%	35.0%
Amount saved if started saving	$10,394	$11,355

Note: Author's own calculations using HILDA wave 4. All means use person weights. The sample size for each response differs because questions are asked sequentially and are conditional on previous responses. For the age variable, means reported are based on a sample of 562 respondents in multigenerational households and 943 respondents in non-multigenerational households.

transfers play in facilitating homeownership in this way can be gleaned by examining the responses available to a series of questions posed to adults younger than 30 years of age in wave 4 of the HILDA survey.[8] In particular, individuals were asked questions about actual and proposed homeownership. Results of those responses by young individuals across household types (multigenerational and non-multigenerational) are reported in Table 4.3.

Similar proportions of individuals in multigenerational and non-multigenerational households reported they planned to purchase a property in the future. Among those who plan to purchase a house in the future, those in multigenerational households reported planning to do so at an earlier age (27.9 years) compared with those in non-multigenerational households (29.1 years). Moreover, those in multigenerational households reported being less worried about the prospect of attaining the aim of homeownership at the nominated age. In terms of actual behaviour, fewer individuals in multigenerational households actually report having started saving for a deposit, while among those who have, the amount saved is approximately $1,000 less than the deposit saved by those who do not reside in multigenerational households.

Joiners in multigenerational households

A useful feature of the HILDA dataset is that it is longitudinal in nature, allowing individuals to be followed over time. Since wave 3 it has been possible to identify why individuals who join a household do so (Table 4.4). An important caveat when interpreting the data reported in Table 4.4 relates to the creation of a multigenerational household. It is important to note that when an individual joins a household identified as a multigenerational household, it will not necessarily become multigenerational because of that person joining the household. For example, a two-generation household may become a three-generation household with the arrival of a grandchild. In that case, the household was an existing multigenerational household. In other cases, for example, where grandparents move into a couple household, it will turn into a two-generation household according to the taxonomy used.

Table 4.4 Reasons for joining household

	Household type					
	Multi_2	*Multi_3*	*Coup_hh*	*Single_hh*	*Lone_hh*	*Other_hh*
Marriage/partnering	7.74	3.69	34.71	2.36	–	8.23
New baby	7.48	20.72	42.06	26.34	–	1.25
Share/fin. reasons	6.53	3.72	3.91	16.36	–	67.67
Returned to family h/hold	43.88	28.47	4.95	16.81	–	1.10
Moved with family member	17.16	26.81	8.35	21.6	–	4.04
Care/support	5.02	7.09	1.25	4.64	–	1.40
Other reason	12.20	9.49	4.77	11.89	–	16.32

Note: Author's own calculations using HILDA waves 3–13, enumerated person files. All means use enumerated person weights.

The patterns of joiners differ across household types. Among couple households, the primary reasons for an individual to join a household were because of marriage or the birth of a child, accounting for over 75 per cent of joiners to such households. In the case of single households, the arrival of a baby or an individual returning to the family household are identified as the principal reasons for joining the household. While financial reasons are the main reason that individuals join group households, care and support is more likely to be the reason cited for joining a multigenerational household. Such a pattern is consistent with the patterns described earlier and highlights the economic motivations and rationales behind multigenerational households, namely the financial and in-kind support, that such living arrangements can offer (Pezzin and Schone 1999).

Policy implications

An obvious question to pose is how the economic approach can be used to inform policy. To this point, it is important to note that the discussion previously has been descriptive rather than prescriptive. In both dimensions, the economic approach can provide important policy insights. Consider first the descriptive insights provided by the economic approach.

Recall that the economic framework posits that individuals compare the costs and benefits of alternative tenure arrangements (co-residency versus independent household formation), and are hypothesized to maximize their utility subject to the constraints they face (Ermisch 1999). Intuitively, policy settings will both directly and indirectly affect the constraints that individuals face and the choices they make. Consider, for example, macroeconomic developments such as interest rates and more broadly the tax treatment of owner-occupied housing through measures such as stamp duties. To the extent that policy settings or economic conditions more generally directly affect the cost of housing, the formation of households including multigenerational households is likely to be affected. In the case of Sydney and Melbourne, the relatively high cost of housing provides a likely reason why multigenerational households are more likely to be found in those cities (Table 4.1). Similarly, the real increase in house prices over the past two decades across many parts of Australia (Kohler and van der Merwe 2015) have coincided with a large increase in the number of multigenerational households. It is noteworthy, for example, that the secular decline in household size has stopped over the past decade. Such a pattern is consistent with a higher likelihood that younger Australians remain co-resident with parents in multigenerational households, partly in response to the higher cost of housing. Moreover, there is evidence that the recent economic downturn and higher unemployment associated with the global financial crisis led to a delayed exit from the parental home and a rise in multigenerational living arrangements (Dunne 2012).

In a similar fashion, transfer policies will influence household formation. There is evidence, for example, that increasing rates of educational attainment and limited support for independent living while studying are associated with the increase in multigenerational households (Ermisch and Di Salvo 1997; Andrew 2010). In general, analysis in the United Kingdom has highlighted how transfer and income support policies have an important bearing on the decision to return to the parental home following a major life course event such as unemployment and relationship breakdown (Berrington et al. 2012). Viewed another way, tax and transfer policies that have a direct or indirect effect on the constraints faced by individuals will ultimately affect the formation and persistence of multigenerational households and economics can help quantify the impact of economic variables on household formation.

The increasing importance of multigenerational households also has important implications for a variety of policy settings. Perhaps the clearest example is in the context of caring activities described in this chapter. Clearly, multigenerational households facilitate the transfer of time and services within the household. Such patterns are significant because these transfers are often substitutes for services, such as elderly care and childcare, that would otherwise require subsidies on the part of governments (Pezzin and Schone 1999). Indeed, there is ample evidence that provision of such care is more likely in the event of co-residence (Whelan 2013). When such transfers are provided within the household, governments potentially achieve significant fiscal savings. It is this feature of intra-household transfers that highlight the prescriptive role of the economic approach.

The economic approach argues that individuals assess the relative costs and benefits associated with forming an independent household. These costs and benefits faced by the *individual*, along with their preferences or utility function, are relevant in the decision-making process. A comprehensive approach would take into account all resource costs associated with such a decision rather than simply those that are incurred by the individual. It may be the case, for example, that the total resource costs associated with caring for elderly individuals is minimized by providing care within a multigenerational household. If so, then it may be possible to formulate policies that achieve a more efficient or better outcome. For example, subsidies or transfers could be made available to households where elderly parents reside to reflect the savings in health-related costs that would be incurred if the individuals were to live independently. In this way, economics can inform the development of policy that encourages the formation of multigenerational households in a way that is consistent with the best or most efficient use of resources.

On a more general note, the increasing tendency for younger Australians to reside in the parental home for longer periods potentially has important equity implications. In the absence of government support through the tax and transfer system, households are increasingly required to provide support to younger and older generations through measures such as co-residency. In the United Kingdom, discussion has occurred around 'housing asset-based welfare' in which accumulated housing wealth is used to pay, at least in part, for costs such as elder care (Searle and McCallum 2014). In Australia, proposed changes to income support for unemployed individuals has focused attention on the role that parents may increasingly play in supporting younger generations following economic shocks and as they accumulate human capital through education. It is important to emphasize in this context that an equity issue arises if households have different capacities to provide such support through the sharing of resources. The role of tax and transfer policies then becomes critical. A key challenge then is to put in place policy settings that ensure support is available to those individuals for whom private support is not available, especially in the shape of multigenerational households.

Conclusion

Multigenerational households are not a new phenomenon, although they have become increasingly common as social, demographic and economic trends have brought into focus the resource-sharing benefits available from such arrangements. Economics has provided insight into these developments as data such as the HILDA dataset has become available, and a greater understanding of the decision-making process within households has developed. Nonetheless, challenges remain around identifying and quantifying the causal relationships of interest, and understanding the long-term implications of multigenerational living arrangements.

Notes

1 Households that contain only grandchildren older than 18 years of age and grandparents are treated as two-generation households.
2 Within a household consisting of more than a single individual, decision making may involve 'joint decision making' by members within the household. A variety of models have been developed to account for such situations, reflecting the different nature of relationships within the household and collective decision making by members of the household (Bourguignon and Chiappori 1992).
3 This chapter uses unit record data from the Household, Income and Labour Dynamics in Australia (HILDA) Survey. The HILDA Project was initiated and is funded by the Australian Government Department of Social Services (DSS) and is managed by the Melbourne Institute of Applied Economic and Social Research. The findings and views reported in this chapter, however, are those of the author and should not be attributed to either DSS or the Melbourne Institute.
4 The HILDA data is based on a non-random sample and weights are provided so that a representative picture of households and their inhabitants can be derived. The means and population totals presented in Tables 4.1–4.3 use the relevant cross-sectional weights available in HILDA (Watson and Fry 2002).
5 There are a variety of ways that households can be equivalized. The approach in this chapter uses the modified OECD scale that assigns a value of 1 to the first individual greater than 15 years in the household and a value of 0.5 for each additional person older than 15 years of age (Australian Bureau of Statistics 2013). Individuals younger than 15 years are assigned a weight of 0.3. Hence, a couple household with two adults and two children younger than age 15 has a size of 2.1 ($= 1 + 0.5 + 0.3 + 0.3$) 'equivalized adults'.
6 Although the question in wave 13 of HILDA does not specifically refer to grandchildren, existing analysis suggests that such care is generally provided to grandchildren (Whelan 2013).
7 Lone households and 'other households' by definition do not contain independent adults.

8 Some of the data reported in Table 4.4 is derived from responses to a special 'youth module' in wave 4 of HILDA. To date, the questions in this module have not been asked of respondents again.

References

Andrew, M 2010, 'The changing route to owner occupation: The impact of student debt', *Housing Studies*, vol. 25, no. 1, pp. 39–62.

Australian Bureau of Statistics 2013, *Household Income and Income Distribution*, Cat. no. 6523.0, Australian Bureau of Statistics, Canberra.

Australian Bureau of Statistics 2015, *Residential Property Price Indexes: Eight Capital Cities*, Cat. no. 6416.0, Australian Bureau of Statistics, Canberra.

Barrett, G, Cigdem, M, Whelan, S and Wood, G 2015, *The Relationship Between Intergenerational Transfers, Housing and Economic Outcomes*, AHURI Positioning Paper No. 163, Australian Housing and Urban Research Institute, Melbourne.

Berrington, A, Stone, J and Falkingham, J 2012, *Gender Differences in Returning to the Parental Home in the UK: The Role of Social Policy*, Paper for the 10th European Social Policy Analysis Conference, Edinburgh, 6th–8th September.

Bourguignon, F and Chiappori, PA 1992, 'Collective models of household behaviour: An introduction', *European Economic Review*, vol. 36, no. 2–3, pp. 355–364.

Brandon, PD 2012, 'The rise of three-generation households among households headed by two parents and mothers only in Australia', *Journal of Family and Economic Issues*, vol. 33, no. 3, pp. 376–388.

Cobb-Clark, DA 2008, 'Leaving home: What economics has to say about the living arrangements of young Australians', *The Australian Economic Review*, vol. 41, no. 2, pp. 160–176.

Cox, D 1987, 'Motives for private income transfers', *Journal of Political Economy*, vol. 95, pp. 508–546.

Dunne, T 2012, *Household Formation and the Great Recession*, Economic Commentary Number 2012–12, Federal Reserve of Cleveland, Cleveland.

Ermisch, J 1999, 'Prices, parents, and young people's household formation', *Journal of Urban Economics*, vol. 45, no. 256, pp. 47–71.

Ermisch, J and Di Salvo, P 1997, 'The economic determinants of young people's household formation', *Economica*, vol. 64, pp. 627–644.

Felkey, AJ 2013, 'Husbands, wives and the peculiar economics of household public goods and bads', *European Journal of Development Research*, vol. 25, no. 3, pp. 445–465.

Flatau, P, James, I, Watson, R, Wood, G and Hendershott, P 2007, 'Leaving the parental home in Australia over the generations: Evidence from the Household, Income and Labour Dynamics in Australia (HILDA) Survey', *Journal of Population Research*, vol. 24, no. 1, pp. 51–71.

Kohler, M and van der Merwe, M 2015, *Long-run Trends in Housing Price Growth*, Reserve Bank of Australia Bulletin, September, pp. 21–30.

Laferrère, A and Wolff, FC 2006, 'Microeconomic models of family transfers', *Handbook of the Economics of Giving, Altruism and Reciprocity*, vol. 2, pp. 889–969.

Leigh, A 2010, 'Informal care and labor market participation', *Labour Economics*, vol. 17, no. 1, pp. 140–149.

Liu, E and Easthope, H 2012, *Multigenerational Households in Australian Cities*, AHURI Final Report No. 181, Australian Housing and Urban Research Institute, Melbourne.

Matsudaira, JD 2016, 'Economic conditions and the living arrangements of young adults: 1960 to 2011', *Journal of Population Economics*, vol. 29, no. 1, pp. 1–29.

Pezzin, LE and Schone, BS 1999, 'Intergenerational household formation, female labor supply and informal caregiving: A bargaining approach', *Journal of Human Resources*, vol. 34, no. 3, pp. 475–503.

Searle, BA and McCollum, D 2014, 'Property-based welfare and the search for generational equality', *International Journal of Housing Policy*, vol. 14, no. 4, pp. 325–343.

Van Klaveren, C, Van Praag, BMS and Maassen van den Brink, H 2008, 'A public good version of the collective model: An empirical approach with an application to British household data', *Review of Economics of the Household*, vol. 6, no. 2, pp. 169–191.

Watson, N 2011, *Methodology for the HILDA Top-up Sample*, Technical paper 01/11 Melbourne Institute of Applied Economic and Social Research, Melbourne.

Watson, N and Fry, T 2002, *The Household, Income and Labour Dynamics in Australia (HILDA) Survey: Wave 1 Weighting*, Technical paper 03/02 Melbourne Institute of Applied Economic and Social Research, Melbourne.

Whelan, S 2013, *Work or Care: The Labour Market Activity of Grandparents in Australia*, paper presented to the Econometric Society European Meeting 2013, Gothenburg, Sweden.

Williams, MN 2011, 'The changing roles of grandparents raising grandchildren', *Journal of Human Behavior in the Social Environment*, vol. 21, no. 4, pp. 948–962.

Wood, G, Smith, S, Ong, R and Cigdem, M 2013, *The Edges of Home Ownership*, AHURI Final Report No. 216, Australian Housing and Urban Research Institute, Melbourne.

5 Living with the extended family

Experiences and outcomes of living in multigenerational households

Edgar Liu

Introduction

This chapter reports on findings from the *Living Together* project, focusing especially on the experiences of individuals who lived in multigenerational households in the two Australian cities of Sydney and Brisbane. As noted in the introductory chapter, this is an often neglected area of research into multigenerational living arrangements, which has tended to focus instead on why these households live together. Understanding the experiences of multigenerational household members, however, is important because these experiences reflect the interpersonal relationships among the household members, which affect their overall well-being and satisfaction with their living situation.

Limited existing research has discussed the outcomes of multigenerational living arrangements from the perspective of the household members. Of the few studies that have, the discussions often focused on intergenerational financial transfers, especially the financial subsidies that parents provide their children (such as by charging their children low or no rent; Cobb-Clark and Gørgens 2012). These studies at times portrayed the younger generations of these households as taking advantage of their older relatives, and terms such as 'kippers' (kids in parents' pockets eroding retirement savings) have been commonly used in popular media to describe these younger people's 'failure' to transition into 'proper' adults (e.g. Salt 2013). These media reports suggest that the parental generations in multigenerational households were hard done by. Indeed, as Craig et al. (2014; and also in Chapter 6 in this volume) found, the parental generation not only took on financial burdens but also often shouldered more household duties. International evidence also recognized a growing trend of the 'sandwich' generation, where middle-aged householders were 'beleaguered' by financial, emotional and caring pressures from the adult children and elderly parents in their multigenerational households (Loomis and Booth 1995; Grundy and Henretta 2006).

The results from the *Living Together* project showed, however, that support provided within multigenerational households was not as unidirectional as these previous works had portrayed. Different kinds of support were offered and provided by different household members. Indeed, as one of our participants noted in an interview, one benefit of living in a multigenerational household was that each member brought their own special expertise and therefore contributed to the household their individual strength. As such, each member might contribute to, and experience, their household differently. This chapter highlights these differences in the context of inter-personal relationships both within and outside of the multigenerational household.

Following this introductory section is a brief overview of the methodological approach taken in the *Living Together* project. That overview is followed by a review of the benefits of multigenerational living as recounted by our research participants; these benefits include companionship and support as well as ease in financial pressures. Research participants were also asked to reflect on the challenges of living in a multigenerational household, with a lack of privacy, impacts on the relationship with their families and social circles, and conflicts over household chores standing out as common concerns. This chapter concludes with a reflection on the different experiences that individuals in multigenerational households might face, and how individuals in these households adjust to the impacts that this living arrangement have on their relationships.

Methodology

For the *Living Together* project, a mixed-method approach was taken, including the use of an online survey, solicited diaries and follow-up interviews. The cities of Sydney and Brisbane were chosen as case studies, each with contrasting demographic and housing stock mixes as well as housing demands and constraints. The online survey was conducted with members of multigenerational households living in Greater Sydney and Brisbane between August 2012 and July 2013. For a more detailed discussion of case study choice and the survey, please see Chapter 3 of this volume.

Two qualitative methods – solicited diaries and follow-up interviews – were designed to provide more in-depth data from multigenerational households, especially regarding the day-to-day experiences and interpersonal relationships among multigenerational household members. These participants were recruited via the online survey, where one (or in some cases more than one) household member was nominated to participate in further research. In all, members from nineteen households continued with the qualitative fieldwork, with one household exiting following the diary exercise, and members from five households proceeding directly to the interviews only.

A package containing instructions, a stamped return envelope and two A5 notebooks were provided to each household participating in the diary exercise. The instructions asked each household to complete at least three entries per week over a four-week period, documenting the day-to-day interactions among household members and their personal thoughts regarding their current living arrangement. Again, multiple household members were encouraged to contribute to the diaries, with five households returning two diaries and one household returning three diaries. Some participants included drawings of their home to illustrate their point; some opted to type out their diaries and emailed them directly to the research team. In all, twenty-one completed diaries were returned from fifteen households, with each diary containing between fifteen and thirty (often single-page) entries completed between October 2013 and February 2014.

A follow-up interview with each participating household was arranged to take place two to four weeks following the return of the diaries. The interviews focused on some of the interactions described in each household's diary as well as any questions that arose out of that household's particular situation. Members from three households were interviewed separately because of scheduling difficulty; no participant requested that they be interviewed separately for reasons of confidentiality. The main interviews were completed face to face at the participant's home and supplementary interviews were conducted over the phone. Interviews lasted between twenty minutes and two and a half hours. In all, twenty-one interviews were conducted with eighteen households between November 2013 and March 2014. All interviews were professionally transcribed, and together with the diary entries these transcripts were analyzed using thematic coding.

For more detailed descriptions of each of these methods, see Liu et al. (2015).

The benefits of multigenerational living

Existing literature often portrays the younger members of multigenerational households – especially the young adults who have yet to leave the parental home for independent living – as the main beneficiaries of this living arrangement (Cobb-Clark and Gørgens 2012; Craig et al. 2014). Even in instances where related adult generations do not live together, international evidence still suggests that the older generations are more likely to be 'net donors' of financial and time resources to their younger family members (Attias-Donfut et al. 2005). While this may be the case in some family settings, as our participants reflected, living together could sometimes mean collaborative decision making and physical contribution to the household in what Vicente and Sousa (2009: 35) called 'a setting which provides opportunities for mutual help and support'. Indeed, while finance was noted by survey respondents as one of the main factors that drove multigenerational households to live together, it was only considered a secondary benefit. Overwhelmingly, companionship and support were understood as the main benefits of living together, with four-fifths of our survey respondents thinking so (see Table 5.1). The benefits of companionship and support as well as ease in financial pressures are discussed in detail in the following two subsections.

Table 5.1 What multigenerational household members like most about living together

	No.	*%*
Companionship and support	217	78%
Financial benefits	38	14%
Practicality and convenience	32	12%
Generational contract / intergenerational solidarity	30	11%
Care arrangement	15	5%
Nothing	10	4%
Cultural traditions	4	1%
Total respondents	277	

Source: survey (open question, post-coded responses)

Keeping company and supporting each other

Companionship and support in multigenerational households can come in many forms. For many, simply knowing that someone will be there should they want to have a conversation or help them with a particular situation can be comforting. As one of our survey respondents articulates:

> I am never alone – there is always someone else around. It doesn't mean that we have to be engaged in conversation or anything like that, but it is comforting to know that someone else is around.
>
> [Interview]

This kind of comfort that one has in a multigenerational family situation might be likened to Giddens' (1991: 92) discussion of ontological security, which he defined as 'the confidence that most human beings have in the continuity of their self-identity and the constancy of their social and material environments. Basic to a feeling of ontological security is a sense of the reliability of persons and things.'

The importance of ontological security was previously discussed in conjunction with housing and shelter (Saunders 1990; Dupuis and Thorns 1998). These often highlighted the importance of having a stable housing situation and secure tenure, although less so on how each individual household member might (or might not) get along with each other. Easthope et al. (2015), for example, highlighted that ontological security, especially the feelings of control afforded by homeownership, could significantly affect a household member's feeling of home. This chapter also contends that ontological security is affected by the interpersonal relationships among the household members, and thus their overall sense of well-being.

As discussed in Chapter 3 of this volume, multigenerational households come about through a complex decision-making process informed by a number of drivers, some of which were intentional (such as to provide a better level of care to family members) and others more incidental. One of the more incidental drivers was relationship breakdown, a situation where familial support can be especially valuable. For most multigenerational households in our study that formed because of a relationship breakdown, it was usually the younger generation who moved in with their parents. Although incidental in their formation, the ability to rely on their family was a tremendous source of support to these individuals:

> I couldn't afford to rent as a single parent. Even though I was working at the time, I would not have the income to be able to afford to rent and cover all the bills, so the only alternative I had was to come here.
>
> [Interview]

Some other younger participants had elected to (stay) living in a multigenerational household to support and assist a divorced parent, as in these two cases:

> We are both single so living together gives us both company and someone to share the expenses with.
>
> [Diary]

I don't believe that [Mum being divorced] has directly caused me to want to stay on. But then I suppose – sorry, I'm going to totally contradict myself – but then I feel like I want to make sure that my Mum's okay and that she doesn't feel like she's been abandoned because I feel like she has been looked after and I want to make sure that she's okay and knows that someone loves her.

[Interview]

Structural changes may also influence how we value familial companionship and support. Across many Western societies, there are increasing numbers of policy measures directed at reducing welfare support for families. In Australia, one such form of welfare retraction is the deinstitutionalization of elderly care through the promotion of ageing in place for older people with low care needs (DHA 2009); there is a similar move to deinstitutionalize disability care in favour of home-based care through the introduction of the National Disability Insurance Scheme in 2013 (Australian Government 2014). As such, the responsibility of caring for the elderly or otherwise less physically and mentally abled often rests on the immediate family. Living in a multigenerational household has allowed some carers to receive occasional respite from other family members:

The company of my daughter and grandchildren because my husband is ill and as I am also his carer my daughter and her children offer me some support and respite at times.

[Survey]

Concurrently, increased global mobility means that employment and work patterns are also becoming increasingly complicated. The 2000s mining boom in Australia, for instance, increased the number of fly-in/fly-out workers who spent extended periods of their working life away from their family home (Storey 2010). For these families, having another adult in the household provides an important remedy to what Franklin and Tranter (2011: 1) called a 'disturbing feature of contemporary societies', that of loneliness. As this mother attested, having her adult daughter living in the family home meant that she would not be left on her own for extended periods when her husband was away on the work roster:

Our household comprises my 20-year-old daughter, husband who works a roster away 3 weeks, then home 1 week and myself working full-time, so it is mainly my daughter and myself at home on evenings and weekends. This is a huge benefit to me for both social and logistical reasons as otherwise I would be on my own for 3 weeks at a time and also have the total responsibility of looking after our 2 dogs, house and yard work.

[Diary]

In addition to the benefits of companionship and support this living arrangement could bring, it could also mean a change to the parent-child relationship and family dynamic. For many, this change was positive, allowing a friendship to form beyond that of blood relations. When asked what aspects of multigenerational living she liked, one survey participant responded 'the friendships I have made with my children'. For another, having a friendship with her daughter also meant witnessing her mature:

> With [my daughter who I live with] my relationship, we're adults and we can talk about politics, or we have quite adult discussions about finances and life in general and stuff. Whereas with my other daughter [who left home straight after high school], it's . . . you're still just the mum. She never got to be that adult at home and seeing me as another adult.
>
> [Interview]

This quote also presents contrary evidence to what many media reports and academic literature described as the failed transition to adulthood of contemporary young adults (e.g. Goldscheider and Goldscheider 1999), and suggests that living in the parental home need not necessarily be interpreted as being dependent on one's parents.

While many of our survey participants said that they only expected their multigenerational living to be an intermediate arrangement, that 'ideally' it would last no longer than five years, sometimes the changed family dynamic could have a much longer-lasting impact than this intermediary period. This participant, a grandmother whose daughter and granddaughters moved in with her and her husband following the daughter's divorce, noted in her diary that things going back to the way they were might no longer be the ideal that she once imagined:

> I am a neat freak and no one else is. So I have learnt to let go – up to a point – and accept that we must have things lying around because there is no more room to put things away. When all is neat again they will be gone, and I will be very sad.
>
> [Diary]

Affording a better lifestyle

Many of our respondents enjoyed some form of financial benefit from their living arrangement. The most common benefit was the ability to share expenses. As some literature reported (e.g. Cobb-Clark and Gørgens 2012), the younger members of multigenerational households were more likely to be the recipients of financial subsidies from the older generations, as this participant articulated:

> Sure my dependency on them was greater when I was younger, although now I am earning my own money some things have changed. Nevertheless, they still do help out a lot.
>
> [Diary]

Like companionship and support, financial benefits of multigenerational living could also come in many forms. For a number of our participants, lifestyle was a big driver, and this could mean several things. For this survey participant, living in a multigenerational household and having lower living costs meant that she could afford to spend on other aspects that would better her children's lives: 'I can afford to give my children a better lifestyle because it is more affordable to live in a multi-generational household.' Multigenerational living might also drive a change in lifestyle and life plans. For one family, who recounted similar experiences of changed life plans of their contemporaries, entering a multigenerational living arrangement meant that they were able to afford a change in career as well as a return to study:

Mother:	I've now talked to a number of families here in Brisbane, and one of the things that they find quite beneficial – maybe not necessarily beneficial – but one of the things that often happened is that it allowed them to change their plans somehow. Maybe [daughter's] change of career or [son-in-law] going back to study.
Daughter:	You [husband] probably wouldn't be doing your Bachelor of Business if we didn't live this way.

[Interview]

Indeed, educational attainment featured prominently in the benefits that many of our respondents appreciated from living in a multigenerational household. For the most part, these benefits were more readily enjoyed by the younger generations, especially in the form of low or no housing and living costs:

> The support my parents give me while I study (food, a place to live, moral support).
>
> [Survey]

> At university I worked part-time and paid my way through university basically. I didn't get any money from my parents but obviously I didn't pay rent or anything and they drove me around and cooked for me, that kind of thing.
>
> [Interview]

For some parents, they also saw this as their way of investing in their children's future, by allowing them to concentrate on their education rather than working while studying. For this mother, as her daughter did not qualify for the Australian tertiary education student loan and discount scheme (Australian Government n.d.), the only way she could see herself assisting her daughter's education was to lessen her need to provide for herself:

> For me I can't help my children pay for university fees, because we're New Zealanders so you have to pay the fees. You can't get HECS, but I can buy the groceries and have petrol in the car and pay the electricity and be able to support them in that way. So they don't have to be out flatting or paying board somewhere or rent. So for me that was the only way I can help them.
>
> [Interview]

Indeed, some parents saw that it was their responsibility to assist and support their children when and however they could to help them lead a more comfortable and less stressful life, both currently and later on. As a result, some younger people living in multigenerational households were able to save up significant sums, with many intending to use that money as a mortgage deposit later on, as these participants elaborated:

> I believe it is the parents' role to assist and support wherever possible their children. To me it was more logical that they stay with me than rent a house or part house at $400/week. I know I saved them $20K or thereabouts.
>
> [Diary]

> I've got to pay the rates and the insurance on the house anyhow, so why have two bedrooms sitting in the back not being used when my daughter's out paying $300-$400 a week in a unit which she can't afford. Move back in here, pay a little bit of money . . . it's how we can help the kids save to go forward or do better.
>
> [Interview]

As the last quote above shows, living in a multigenerational household could also mean making use of rooms and resources that would otherwise sit idle. This scenario relates especially to Australian (Judd et al. 2010) and international arguments (Harding 2007) that older, empty-nest households underutilize the housing stock that they occupied, indirectly increasing the pressure for new stock supplies.

The challenges of multigenerational living

Not all experiences of multigenerational living were positive. As Olsberg and Winters (2005) highlighted, multigenerational living was often not a preferred arrangement for older Australians. Among our survey respondents, only one-fifth (of all age groups) said that this was their ideal arrangement, with moving out for establishing one's own owner-occupied home or having their current home all to themselves (or with a partner) being the preferred options. This section highlights some of the challenges that multigenerational household members faced when living together. Lack of privacy, impacts on their relationship with others, and the unequal sharing of household chores were the issues of most concern (Table 5.2). All of these could have significant impact on how multigenerational household members live with each other, and can affect their overall personal and household well-being.

A time of one's own

While companionship and support were the main reported benefits of multigenerational living, many of our survey respondents found that they were not afforded

Table 5.2 What multigenerational household members dislike most about living together

	No.	*%*
Privacy / interference	162	59%
Impact on intra/interfamilial relationships	52	19%
Chores / not pitching in	38	14%
Space	24	9%
Lack of flexibility / compromises	20	7%
Nothing	16	6%
Financial constraints	10	4%
Noise	7	3%
Generational contract / expectations	6	2%
Stigma of living at home	5	2%
Total respondents	274	

Source: survey (open question, post-coded responses)

much privacy in their living arrangement. It was a contradiction that many multi-generational household members had to contend with, as one of our interviewees articulated:

> There are emotional benefits . . . you always have somebody there, you always have somebody to talk to, you always have different perspectives on situations, you always have that. I think that in itself can be a challenge because you never can be alone, you never can have any privacy, you can never get away from people being there all the time.
>
> [Interview]

Indeed, three-fifths of our survey respondents found a lack of privacy as well as interference from other household members to be the biggest challenges of living together. The lack of privacy in a multigenerational household setting – or, indeed, any other household settings – can affect each household member's sense of home. As Saunders and Williams (1988: 88) discussed, privacy is the 'freedom from surveillance,' situations where 'the need to maintain role performance is relaxed and where one can be oneself'. Sense of privacy can be affected by the design and layout of the house (e.g. Ledbetter et al. 2010; see also Chapter 9 of this volume); sometimes it can also be related to an actual or perceived sense of security (e.g. Sykes 1999). As it relates to surveillance, however, privacy in the home can also relate to the presence and intrusiveness of other household members. As Aronson's (1999) study of same-sex attracted young men in Hanoi showed, the presence of others at home could significantly reduce a person's sense of privacy, so much so for some that a dimly lit bench in a public park might be a more preferred place for enjoying some privacy and intimacy.

As Shehan et al. (1984: 71) highlighted, 'every individual needs periods of solitude.' The lack of privacy, especially because of crowding (which can be the case in some multigenerational households) could also have adverse effects on personal development and life satisfaction. To Shehan et al. (1984: 71), such negative impacts could include 'lack of self-sufficiency, destruction of childhood illusions concerning people, sexual maladjustment, deep emotional fatigue, and lack of objectivity with regard to one's life situation'.

In many cases, the lack of privacy in the multigenerational home was a result of poor communication. In the next example, the lack of privacy that this survey participant felt came from a sense of assumed responsibility of the older members in her household that they should be providing for all members of their household, when in reality it might not be necessary or even welcomed.

> There is little privacy in this situation and I think there is a shared sense of obligation. The older generation feel as though they must always provide, especially in terms of food preparation, when in fact this puts pressure on them in terms of money and time. The middle generation can start to feel a loss of personal independence as important daily tasks such as cooking and shopping are performed by others.
>
> [Survey]

Such assumptions relate to family values that highlight a sense of responsibility to each other (McDonald 1997). For heads of households, or assumed heads of households, there is often the assumption or expectation that they are responsible for providing for other household members, especially those who are younger or less financially and/or physically abled. As Doherty (1992) argued, however, this focus on responsibility in the family is slowly changing to one that encourages satisfaction and flexibility, and with that, the need for privacy may also increase.

Sometimes, lack of privacy resulted from poor housing design, or more precisely, that the 'normal' detached suburban family home was not originally designed with multigenerational living in mind. As a result, there was often a lack of personal space within such households:

> Yeah, there's nowhere to go to sit by yourself.
>
> [Interview]

Often, the only solution was to 'hide' in one's bedroom:

> The beginning was hard because of the space and where do you go to get away and I feel bad because she's in her bedroom but that's all she's got.
>
> [Interview]

Some multigenerational households had come about as a result of boomeranging (Veevers and Mitchell 1998); situations where young adults had previously left home but have since returned. Their boomeranging could be the result of a wide variety of reasons, including relationship breakdown, returning from travelling and/or working overseas, and sometimes even for health reasons (such as following an accident or to care for another household member). Among multigenerational household members who had boomeranged, most seemed to notice a change in the parent-child relationship. As discussed previously, parents who shared their multigenerational home with their adult children often afforded them the opportunity to see their children as adults; but in some cases, this might not be the case, and the boomeranged child might feel constricted:

> Privacy's the biggest one, I think. It's quite hard to be adult in your child-hood home. It's kind of like the relationships that were there 30 years ago or 40 years ago become really rigid.
>
> [Interview]

The presence of other household members can also affect the relationship between spouses:

> Sometimes would like more time alone with my husband.
>
> [Survey]

Among our participants, comments such as this were more common among middle-aged couples who took on the responsibility of caring for an older family member. Emerging evidence increasingly highlights social isolation and feelings of loneliness among older people both in Australia (e.g. Findlay 2003) and in other post-industrial societies (e.g. Cattan et al. 2005), and as such more and more rely on their families for social stimulation. In a multigenerational living situation, cohabiting family members would therefore be the most obvious choices, especially for multigenerational households who live in suburban areas where social outlets for older people are more limited or are difficult to access without adequate public transport options. For example, one older woman who lived in a granny flat with her daughter and son in law in the outer suburbs only had access to the family car once a week for her volunteering commitments and any personal errands that she needed to run. For this older woman, all of her other face-to-face social activities revolved around her own household, or the few neighbouring households that shared their cul-de-sac.

In some three-generation households, the presence of the extended family could also intrude on the life of the nuclear family and have significant impacts on spousal relationships, and perhaps the relationship between parents and their young children.

> Not being able to completely focus on my own nuclear family.
>
> [Survey]

> I think lack of privacy is a big challenge. Lack of any time just with your husband and child because I think it's always perceived that everybody must be included in every activity. So if you want to go away for the weekend then I think [my husband] particularly will feel obliged that he has to invite

everybody to come along, because yes we must all move as one big family unit. There's no scope for just going on a picnic by yourself or whatever.

[Interview]

While many multigenerational household members made do with the lack of privacy by spending time in their own bedrooms, other families went to great lengths to address this issue. With the lack of appropriate space often a cause for the lack of privacy, some of the families in our study considered moving to a larger home, while others considered building their own custom-designed homes. These solutions are only workable for those households where they see this living arrangement as being more than temporary and when they have the financial means to do so. For others with less financial freedom, bettering communications among household members might offer some respite. Failing that, stepping away, going out for a walk or a drive might also temporarily give these household members the personal space that they need.

I mean more often than not I can just sort of say, "Look, just give me some space for a little while." You know we're not one for blowing up at each other too often. It does happen but it certainly doesn't happen very often at all. If it does happen, that's when I'm more inclined to just get in the car and head out somewhere.

[Interview]

Impact on wider familial and social networks

The second most common challenge of multigenerational living was how this arrangement affected personal relationships. Thus far, the focus of this chapter has mainly been on the impacts to people of the same household. This section shifts this focus to relationships with relatives and friends outside of the multigenerational household, a challenge that one in five of our survey respondents identified as a concern.

As highlighted in the previous section, multigenerational living can affect household members' romantic relationships:

Can't bring girls home.

[Survey]

Although some young adults said that their parents were generally 'cool' with them bringing a boyfriend or girlfriend home, it could make for an awkward situation, especially for the parents:

It is really difficult when your adult children are still at home and have boyfriends and want to have sleepovers with them . . . I never expected them to remain virgins but I hate being a parent when it comes to this.

[Diary]

Our research, however, suggested that it was more often multigenerational households where an older person was being cared for that relationships with other non-cohabiting relatives could become strained. This could be because the multigenerational home became the central gathering place for the extended family, limiting personal freedoms on when and how household members could use the space:

> The house acts as a gathering place for wider family so it is often busy and can sometimes be difficult to get other stuff done.
>
> [Survey]

It could also be that non-cohabiting relatives did not see the daily challenges of multigenerational living but only the benefits:

Wife: I have one other sibling. He wouldn't know 5 per cent of the things that I have to get involved in because he doesn't live here. I think it's placed a big strain on the relationship between us as brother and sister because his wife's perception is that it's our problem to look after our parents and that's not her value at all. The relationship definitely has changed and it's changed with other members of the family as well . . . The aunties, my mum's got a lot of sisters and I think they all have this perception too like it's this amazing. . .

Husband: Yeah, we've got this amazing arrangement of having them living with us and having all this babysitting and all this help. They don't see all the emotional challenges that come with it. So it creates a lot of resentment I suppose, especially between [my wife] and the rest of the extended family.

Wife: Definitely, definitely there are massive changes in those relationships and it is through lack of understanding about what it's like too, because none of them have lived in multigenerational households so it's not as easy as it appears. On the surface there are a lot of benefits for sure but on a daily basis there are a lot of issues that you have to deal with that you would never even know about probably in a normal or a generational relationship where you lived separately.

> [Interview]

To outsiders, it could be that they felt a level of comfort that their older relative was being looked after by a family member, and so they did not feel the need to contribute as much (or, in some cases, at all):

> Expectation of other family members that I and my children (her grandchildren) have sole responsibility for my mother's care including physical, emotional and financial.
>
> [Survey]

For one 'boomerang kid', living away from the family home allowed her to gain a better view of the relationships between her parents and siblings, especially (in her own view) the inadequate level of support that her siblings gave to their parents. It prompted her to re-evaluate her own relationship with her parents:

> I could see the relationship between my parents and siblings, and that my parents need support in some ways that my siblings are not giving to them. So when I came back, I felt I really need to contribute more, and each time I feel that so I take on more responsibility around the house or just in emotional support for my mother for example. My mother and I are much, much closer after me having moved away and come back again.
>
> [Interview]

In many instances, the most significant impact multigenerational living had was on social friendships. For many of our participants, whether it was due to a lack of space for socializing, or a lack of privacy, they no longer invited friends over for visits:

> I used to do that. I don't do that at all now, and I don't – I've tried having friends over but I sort of avoid it now, because you just don't get privacy.
>
> [Interview]

> I moved into the house [two years ago] and have very rarely had any visitors – it's too uncomfortable for me and for mum.
>
> [Diary]

For other households, the reliance on other household members meant they spent less time and effort cultivating friendships. For this participant, for example, it was a downside that caught her by surprise:

> I realised today, while ringing around trying to find a trusted friend to help watch the dog on Saturday that my social structure outside my family has really shrunk. I could only think of 4 people I trust that live in Brisbane and that I felt I could ask that type of favour. . . . I think because I can rely so much on my husband and parents I have not had to foster so many external relationships.
>
> [Diary]

The chore war

Most existing literature describes the young adults who live in multigenerational households as non-contributing family members both in the financial sense as well as in contributing to household chores. Craig et al. (2014; and also in Chapter 6 of this volume) highlight that while many young adults in multigenerational households contribute to household chores, these efforts often do not relieve the rest of the household in any significant way. Indeed, many of our participants of the parental or older generations were unhappy with how little the younger generations did to help out:

> When my son-in-law doesn't help.
>
> [Survey]

> I am annoyed that he rarely contributes as a member of this family and that he treats our home like a hotel.
>
> [Diary]

Some parents said they understood the different commitments that younger members of their household had for study or work, or that they should be able to enjoy a social life:

> I guess my feelings are contradictory – I sometimes feel dissatisfied or disappointed that she [daughter] doesn't help me more in the garden or with those tasks other than cooking, but then I don't want her to not go out and do things with friends and colleagues as I want her to have her own strong circle of friends and support group and social life outside of home and our relationship.
>
> [Diary]

Others, however, felt that there was a sense of entitlement, especially when the younger generation was asked to contribute financially, as in this survey participant's situation:

> My daughters thinking that just because they pay board, means they don't have to help out around the house anymore. I do more now than when they were little.
>
> [Survey]

Recognizing individuals in the households

The findings discussed in this chapter thus far have mainly focused on how multigenerational household members feel about their experiences in this living arrangement. Throughout, there were hints of how the benefits and challenges faced by multigenerational households affected their personal relationships. In this section, the discussion shifts to how different individuals acclimated to multigenerational living and their changing roles within these households. This shift refers to Dannefer and Sider's (2012: 289) discussion of changing social structure and family solidarity, particularly that 'families are private entities, and we have little detailed information on the actual dynamics that occur in everyday family life.' Following from this, we (as a research team) had argued that the different experiences of sense of home among individuals living within multigenerational households have been largely unrecognized (Easthope et al. 2015). Likewise, the differences in how each individual acclimated to this living arrangement and their changing roles had received little research attention thus far.

The use of solicited diaries in the *Living Together* study allowed our participants to reflect on their personal relationships. While some parents said that their relationships with their cohabiting adult children had grown and transformed to resemble relationships more akin to friendships, adjusting to this change – and deviating from the more conventional parent-child relationship – might not necessarily be straightforward. Documented evidence on parent-child relationships show how they might change when the child transitions from adolescence to young adulthood (e.g. Aquilino 1997). That is most certainly a part of the story of many multigenerational households. For two of our participants, both of whom were mothers to young adult daughters, in reflecting their parent-child relationships, the conflicting roles of being both mother and friend to their daughters were hard to grapple with:

> Living with your adult child takes a little adjusting as you are still their mother but don't want to be mothering them.
>
> [Diary]

> It's a funny dual thing, where she's [daughter] an adult, so we operate as adults a lot of the time. But then sometimes, she still wants to be a kid. She still wants to be jealous of the other kids, who might be getting more than her. Or – even though she's an adult – she still . . . sometimes she plays the kid's role. Sometimes I have to be mum and sometimes I'm a friend.
>
> [Interview]

The same difficulty in adjusting parent-child roles also existed in three-generation households. In the following cases, the adult daughters (who were in the middle, 'sandwich' generation) both faced difficulties in reconciling their roles as mothers and daughters. Likewise, the grandmother in the second case also had difficulties in juggling the dual roles of mother and grandmother:

> One thing I see as a drawback to our arrangement is I get out less with the girls (my kids) as my Mom believes they are happier at home and I find it easier just to stay home than to justify to my Mom why I am going somewhere.
>
> [Diary]

> The girls [granddaughters] are well-behaved and delightful, but [daughter] as mother and father to them has to keep control. She has to discipline them mostly in our hearing, but we do not comment or interfere as we know it must be done. She knows I hate to see the girls in tears, but I just have to harden up! She says she feels judged, but we are not doing that. She is a great and fair mother.
>
> [Diary]

As Shehan et al. (1984: 70) argued, because multigenerational households (at least within the context of Western societies) had not traditionally been considered as part of the familial norm, there exists no 'time-proven guidelines' on how family members should behave and interact with each other, which may 'produce confusion, frustration, and severe socio-psychological stress for both parents and their children'. The kind of frustration that was brought out by conflicting parent-child roles was clearly demonstrated in the next case of a single mother of two young children who boomeranged to the family home following a relationship breakdown and also to look after an ill mother. These frustrations might partly arise from generational differences, in this case the elderly mother being of the silent generation (those born in the period between World War I and World War II), which was typically characterized as being frugal, cautious and generally risk-averse (Lehto et al. 2008: 239):

> I wanted to buy a cooked free-range chicken (on sale) for dinner/lunch the next day. She [elderly mother] wanted to buy an uncooked chicken. The difference was at most $1-$2 and I was paying. We argued in [supermarket]. It's worth paying it when I'd have to cook it and it's my money.
>
> [Diary]

Aside from the difficulty in reconciling conflicting parent-child roles, one challenge to familial relationship, and perhaps one that was unique to multigenerational households, was that of being the middle person. By 'middle person' we mean the individual who was directly related – whether through blood or marriage – to all other members of the household, and who was also the person most (if not all) other household members felt most comfortable communicating with. As a result, a strain was often put onto this middle person to take on the role of translator (in the case of a mixed-culture household), messenger or even mediator:

> My husband . . . he's the one in the middle that has to translate things. Everyone's whinging onto him about their problems.
>
> [Interview]

> Yes, I guess I'm the person who is connected in both ways and that's incredibly stressful yes, because sometimes they won't go to [my husband] because [he] is not family but he is family, he's not directly related. So it always will have to come through me and so I do a lot of communicating more than the average person would need to.
>
> [Interview]

Conclusion

This chapter highlights some of the benefits and challenges multigenerational households face when living with their extended family. While existing literature often points to finance as the primary reason for multigenerational cohabitation, human and social factors also greatly affect the experiences of these household members. These factors can also often be conflicting, from enjoying the company of other family members to a feeling of being constantly surveilled. These highlight the complications and sometimes contradictions that are familial relationships, which, like the relationships themselves, continuously change over time. There may be an adjustment to the parent-child relationship as the child grows up, facing the reality of an ageing parent and the care and support they require from different household members, differences in generational views, or because of external pressures from study, work, or ability to maintain social relations outside of the household.

Recognizing common positive and negative experiences helps us to understand multigenerational households better, which can aid in considering how they might be helped to have better experiences. This is important because they can affect the health and well-being of the different household members. These factors are especially important because they relate both to the family and to the house as home – two essential and central components of people's lives.

Practical guides are slowly emerging, covering important practical (e.g. in choosing the 'right' dwelling, legal and financial arrangements; Niederhaus and Graham 2013) considerations, while social and interfamilial relationships are often less readily discussed and left to be worked out by the families themselves. From the evidence presented in this chapter, many multigenerational households had to learn these lessons the hard way, whether it was through multiple changes in their household arrangement, learning to walk away from arguments or compromising on their own personal space. Each household and the relationships that exist within it, whether they are multigenerational or not, are unique and present their own set of challenges, so there can be no simple guidelines or best practice to multigenerational living. Setting up basic house rules and drawing up these rules collaboratively, as some of our participants had done, would help in making sure that individual boundaries are respected and multigenerational living more likely to succeed; however, these rules must be revisited from time to time as the individuals and relationships change. The challenge, therefore, is in recognizing and working with the dynamics of families.

References

Aquilino, WS 1997, 'From adolescent to young adult: A prospective study of parent–child relations during the transition to adulthood', *Journal of Marriage and Family*, vol. 59, pp. 670–686.

Aronson, J 1999, "Homosex in Hanoi? Sex, the Public Sphere, and Public Sex" in WL Leap (ed.) *Public Sex/Gay Space*, Columbia University Press, New York, pp. 205–221.

Attias-Donfut, C, Ogg, J and Wolff, FC 2005, 'European patterns of intergenerational financial and time transfers', *European Journal of Ageing*, vol. 2, pp. 161–173.

Australian Government 2014, *National Disability Insurance Scheme Act 2013, C2014C00386*, Canberra.

Australian Government n.d., *HECS-HELP*, accessed 21 August 2015, studyassist.gov.au/sites/studyassist/helppayingmyfees/hecs-help/pages/hecs-help-welcome#WhatIs HECS-HELP

Cattan, M, White, M, Bond, J and Learmouth, A 2005, 'Preventing social isolation and loneliness among older people: A systematic review of health promotion interventions', *Ageing & Society*, vol. 25, pp. 41–67.

Cobb-Clark, DA and Gørgens, T 2012, *Parents' Economic Support of Young Adult Children: Do Socioeconomic Circumstances Matter?*, Melbourne Institute Working Paper Series, Melbourne Institute of Applied Economics and Social Research, Melbourne.

Craig, L, Powell, A and Brown, JE 2015, 'Co-resident parents and young people aged 15–34: Who does what housework?' *Social Indicators Research* 121, 2, pp. 569–588.

Dannefer, D and Siders, RA 2012, 'Social change, social structure, and the cycle of induced solidarity', in M Silverstein and R Giarusso (eds), *Kinship and Cohort in an Aging Society: From Generation to Generation*, John Hopkins University Press, Baltimore, pp. 284–292.

Department of Social Services 2009, *Ageing in Place*, accessed 17 March 2015, www.agedcareaustralia.gov.au/internet/agedcare/Publishing.nsf/Content/ageing+in+place

Doherty, WJ 1992, 'Private lives, public values: The future of the family', *Psychology Today.*

Dupuis, A and Thorns, DC 1998, 'Home, home ownership and the search for ontological security', *The Sociological Review*, vol. 46, pp. 24–47.

Easthope, H, Liu, E, Burnley, I and Judd, B 2015, 'Feeling at home in a multigenerational household: The importance of control', *Housing, Theory and Society*, vol. 32, pp. 151–170.

Findlay, RA 2003, 'Interventions to reduce social isolation amongst older people: Where is the evidence?' *Ageing & Society*, vol. 23, pp. 647–658.

Franklin, A and Tranter, B 2011, *AHURI Essay: Housing, Loneliness and Health*, Final Report, Australian Housing and Urban Research Institute, Melbourne.

Giddens, A 1991, *Modernity and Self Identity: Self and Society in the Late Modern Age*, Polity Press, Cambridge.

Goldscheider, FK and Goldscheider, C 1999, *The Changing Transition to Adulthood: Leaving and Returning Home*, SAGE, Thousand Oaks.

Grundy, E and Henretta, JC 2006, 'Between elderly parents and adult children: A new look at the intergenerational care provided by the "sandwich generation"', *Ageing & Society*, vol. 26, pp. 707–722.

Harding, E 2007, *Older People's Housing and Under-occupancy: A Policy Brief*, International Longevity Centre, United Kingdom.

Judd, B, Olsberg, D, Quinn, J, Groenhart, L and Demirbilek, O 2010, *Dwelling, Land and Neighbourhood Use by Older Home Owners*, Final Report, Australian Housing and Urban Research Institute, Melbourne.

Ledbetter, AM, Heiss, S, Sibal, K, Lev, E, Battle-Fisher, M and Shubert, N 2010, 'Parental invasive and children's defensive behaviors at home and away at college: Mediated communication and privacy boundary management', *Communication Studies*, vol. 61, pp. 184–204.

Lehto, XY, Jang, SC, Achana, FT and O'Leary, JT 2008, 'Exploring tourism experience sought: A cohort comparison of baby boomers and the silent generation', *Journal of Vacation Marketing*, vol. 14, pp. 237–252.

Liu, E, Easthope, H, Judd, B and Burnley, I 2015, 'Housing multigenerational households in Australian cities: Evidence from Sydney and Brisbane at the turn of the twenty-first century', in R Dufty-Jones and D Rogers (eds), *Housing in Twenty-First Century Australia: Contemporary Debates*, Ashgate, Aldershot, pp. 21–37.

Loomis, LS and Booth, A 1995, 'Multigenerational caregiving and well-being: The myth of the beleaguered sandwich generation', *Journal of Family Issues*, vol. 16, pp. 131–148.

McDonald, P 1997, 'Older people and their families: Issues for policy', in A Borowski, S Encel and E Ozanne (eds), *Ageing and Social Policy in Australia*, Cambridge University Press, Cambridge, pp. 194–210.

Neiderhaus, S and Graham, J 2013, *All in the Family: A Practical Guide to Successful Multigenerational Living*, Taylor Trade Publishing, Lanham.

Olsberg, D and Winters, M 2005, *Ageing in Place: Intergenerational and Intrafamilial Housing Transfers and Shifts in Later Life*, Final Report, Australian Housing and Urban Research Institute, Melbourne.

Salt, B 2013, 'Kippers' failure to launch keeps mum and dad in the loop', *The Australian*, 7 February, accessed 11 February 2013, http://www.theaustralian.com.au/business/opinion/kippers-failure-to-launch-keeps-mum-and-dad-in-the-loop/story-e6frg9jx-1226572124793

Saunders, P 1990, *A Nation of Home Owners*, Unwin Hyman, London.

Saunders, P and Williams, P 1988, 'The constitution of the home: Towards a research agenda', *Housing Studies*, vol. 3, pp. 81–93.

Shehan, CL, Berado, DH and Berado, FM 1984, 'The empty nest is filling again: Parent-child relationships', *Parenting Studies*, vol. 1, pp. 67–73.

Storey, K 2010, 'Fly-in/Fly-out: Implications for community sustainability', *Sustainability*, vol. 2, p. 1161.

Sykes, CJ 1999, *The End of Privacy: The Attack on Personal Rights at Home, at Work, On-line, and in Court*, St Martin's Press, New York.

Veevers, JE and Mitchell, BA 1998, 'Intergenerational exchanges and perceptions of support within "boomerang kid" family environments', *International Journal of Aging and Human Development*, vol. 46, pp. 91–108.

Vicente, H and Sousa, L 2009, 'The multigenerational family and the elderly: A mutual or parasitical symbiotic relationship?' in L Sousa (ed.), *Families in Later Life: Emerging Themes and Challenge*, Nova Science Publishers Inc., New York, pp. 27–48.

6 Housework, intergenerational dependency and challenges to traditional gender roles

Lyn Craig and Abigail Powell

Introduction

This chapter investigates predictors of domestic work in two-generation households in which young people aged 15–34 co-reside with their parents. While we know about the gender division of housework among adult couples (e.g. Bianchi and Milkie 2010), the literature on the domestic work of children and teenagers is growing (Evertsson 2006; Salman Rizavi and Sofer 2010; Miller 2012). However, the domestic work of co-resident young adults and their parents is largely unexplored (Mitchell 2004). This significant knowledge gap has occurred despite the number of young people who co-reside with their parents (e.g. Mitchell 2004; ABS 2013a) and divisions of domestic work being a marker of workload and gender equity (Craig and Baxter 2016). Using nationally representative time use data from the Australian Bureau of Statistics (ABS) from 2006, we address this gap by examining the domestic contribution of young adults, together with their parents' domestic work time.

Background

The transition to adulthood is a life stage in which young people are establishing their identity and learning to take control of their life (Erikson 1959). In Western societies, the transition is a loosely defined process, consisting of a number of milestones that reflect aspects of independence and together indicate adult autonomy (Furlong 2009). Over the last century, the markers of the transition to adulthood were generally thought to include completing education, securing stable employment, leaving the family home, marrying or cohabiting and having children (Furstenberg et al. 2004; Mahaffy 2004). In recent decades, the achievement of these milestones has become less predictable and the pace at which they are reached slower (Bell et al. 2007; Raley et al. 2007; Mandic 2008), such that the period during which young people transition to adulthood has lengthened (Swartz et al. 2011; Hendry and Kloep 2012). Whereas during the mid-twentieth century most people transitioned to adulthood by their early to mid-twenties, the contemporary transition is considered by many scholars to encompass the age range 18–34 (Furstenberg et al. 2004; Mahaffy 2004; Furlong 2009), and to be an extended period in which individuals may be independent in some contexts but not fully autonomous in others (Tanner and Arnett 2009).

The reasons the transition to adulthood is taking longer include macro-level social and economic changes such as less stable employment, low youth wages and high housing and education costs (Furstenberg et al. 2004; Bell et al. 2007). School retention and tertiary study rates have gone up, delaying the onset of regular paid work (Flatau et al. 2003). Housing availability and affordability has diminished in many countries. In Australia, for example, national house prices have increased substantially (Richards 2008) and there is a shortage of private rental accommodation (AHURI 2011). The global economic downturn since 2008 has meant young people find it harder to obtain work (Bell and Blanchflower 2011) and young people's jobs are more likely to be casual, part-time and short-term (Woodman 2012; Foundation for Young Australians 2014). At the same time, state support is being reduced through policies such as limited benefit access for those under age 25 and rising costs of higher education (Cash 2012). Such measures not only affect young people's life chances directly but also shift the costs of welfare support for young adults from the state to the family (Cobb-Clark 2008; Buckley 2011).

One manifestation of these trends has been a rise in the number of households in which young people co-reside with their parents beyond the teenage years. In Australia, 21 per cent of young people aged 18–34 lived at home in 1976, increasing to 29 per cent in 2011 (ABS 2013a). Leaving the parental home is also less likely to be a one-way, one-time event. In Australia more than 40 per cent of young Australians who leave home return at least once for financial, emotional or practical reasons (de Vaus 2004).

The lives of family members are intricately linked, and an obvious corollary of young people taking longer to reach full autonomy is their parents continuing to support them beyond their teenage years (Greenfield and Marks 2006; Fingerman et al. 2009; Swartz et al. 2011). Recent US research estimated that nearly a quarter of the financial cost of raising children is incurred when they are between 18 and 34 years of age (Schoeni and Ross 2004). While co-residence is a form of financial subsidy, in that it is likely to save young people living expenses, it does not necessarily involve direct money transfers, and may also bring in-kind support in the form of domestic services. Multigenerational living may be driven by economic or budget considerations, but it is also a form of family solidarity. It may also allow for mutual interdependency with two-way reciprocal exchanges occurring. Thus, the exchange of resources between household members and generations can include emotional or other nonfinancial resources of which domestic labour is only one example, and could be from younger to older as well as vice versa (Vicente and Sousa 2009; Katz and Lowenstein 2010). Family relationships are unlikely to be driven by resource exchange alone, but rather to be affected by the solidarity of relationships between generations, reflected by behavioural, affectual, cognitive and structural dimensions of the family (Katz and Lowenstein 2010).

However, non-financial exchange in the form of domestic labour is relatively unstudied. Although scholars increasingly argue that work-family issues should be approached from a household, rather than an individual, perspective (Bianchi and Milkie 2010; Cooke and Baxter 2010), 'most studies of "household" divisions of labour are actually reporting "conjugal" distribution, since they discuss only the adult partners' participation' (Punch 2001: 803). Yet, research conceptualizing the domestic workload as the combined inputs of couples overlooks that many people live in larger family units. Particularly, patterns of domestic work across co-resident young adult–parent households are largely unknown (Mitchell 2004).

Domestic work in co-resident young adult–parent households

Contributions to domestic labour vary according to the particular circumstances, characteristics and resources of both parents and young people. They also vary across different types of domestic work. Domestic work is highly diverse, encompassing daily activities that need to be done at regular times, as well as activities that can be done on a flexible timetable or when the need arises (Sullivan 1997). Indoor activities including cooking, cleaning and laundry are generally regarded as routine and stereotypically female. Non-routine tasks such as outdoor work, household management and maintenance are more stereotypically male. However, grocery shopping, traditionally a female activity, may now be more gender neutral (Baxter 2002; Bianchi and Milkie 2010).

We expect young people and their parents to participate differently in these forms of domestic work. A qualitative study from the United States found that parents regularly prepared meals and did grocery shopping for adult children living at home, but doing their laundry was less frequent (Veevers and Mitchell 1998). This finding suggests that parents may do more of the regular activities that are essential to the smooth running of the household, and/or which can be done for all household members at once, while young people do domestic activities for self-maintenance. Young people may also do tasks that are more infrequent such as putting out the garbage, sweeping the path or performing car maintenance than routine daily activities. Moreover, they may participate in routine activities but only irregularly, for example cooking or cleaning sometimes but not often. To explore this finding, it is necessary to examine not only the amount of time spent in various domestic activities but the frequency with which they are done.

We expect that a central characteristic explaining young people's housework contribution will be gender, because a large body of research documents gender divisions in domestic work among adults. Women do more domestic work overall, and also more of the routine and indoor tasks; men's time spent on domestic work is lower, and includes proportionally more non-routine tasks such as outdoor work and car maintenance (e.g. Bianchi and Milkie 2010). Research also finds that girls do more housework than boys, and that there are gender differences in the type of housework performed by children and teenagers (Coltrane 2007;

Salman Rizavi and Sofer 2010). Teenage daughters face greater expectations than teenage sons to contribute to domestic chores (Manke et al. 1994; Evertsson 2006), and co-resident adult sons are more likely to report receiving domestic services than daughters (Mitchell 2004). This seems particularly so in families with more traditional attitudes, including those from cultural backgrounds with more tightly defined gender roles (Mahaffy 2004; Mitchell 2004). We expect the influence of gender to be pervasive, with differences in associations between gender, domestic work and factors including young people's age, time availability, household demand and resources. For this reason, we stratify our multivariate analyses by gender.

We are particularly interested in whether and what young people contribute in terms of domestic work, how this may be associated with their mothers' and fathers' amount and composition of domestic work, and how this may challenge traditional gender divisions, if at all. For example, do the same characteristics that predict young people contribute more to domestic work also predict that mothers and/or fathers do less? In other words, do the contributions of mothers and fathers to domestic work decrease if young people contribute?

Method

We analyzed data from the ABS 2006 Time Use Survey (TUS), a nationally representative survey of the population of Australian households, which provides the most recent time use data in Australia. To a detail level of five-minute intervals over two consecutive days, all individuals aged 15 and older in sampled households were required to complete a time-diary. Therefore, we could analyze the time use of both young people and their parents in matched households. We excluded three-generation households and those in which there was more than one family unit. The final analytic sample is 593 households, among which there are diary records for 556 mothers, 465 fathers and 828 young people aged 15–34 years. Most individuals have diary entries for two days, but some completed the diary on only one day, providing a total of 1,624 diaries from young people. A sample description is given in Table 6.1.

Dependent variables

Our interest is in domestic work, which includes food preparation (e.g. cooking, clean-up, setting the table); laundry and cleaning (e.g. washing, ironing, sorting clothes, wet and dry housework); outdoor work (e.g. gardening, animal care, cleaning grounds, pool care); household maintenance (e.g. home improvements, making furniture and furnishings, car care); household management (e.g. paperwork, bills and budgeting, recycling and disposing of rubbish) and communication and travel associated with domestic work as well as the related activity of purchasing consumer goods (buying groceries, food etc.). We separately analyze the routine tasks of i) food preparation, ii) laundry and cleaning, iii) the sum of non-routine activities (outdoor work, household maintenance, and household management), and iv) grocery shopping.

Analysis plan

We used multivariate regression (OLS) models to examine associations between each type of domestic work and young people's, parents' and household characteristics. Because gender is central to the performance of housework (Sayer

Table 6.1 Descriptive statistics (weighted)

Sample descriptives		%
Young person data (*n* = 828)		
Gender	Male	50.9
	Female	49.2
Age group	15–19	58.7
	20–24	28.4
	25–34	12.9
Current main activity	Studying	56.2
	Working	36.0
	Not in employment or education/ training (NEET)	7.9
Fathers' characteristics (*n* = 465)		
Relationship status	Single	8.4
	Partnered	91.7
Employment status	Employed fulltime	85.1
	Not employed fulltime	14.9
Educational level	No tertiary degree	75.5
	Degree	24.5
Mother's characteristics (*n* = 556)		
Relationship status	Single	21.3
	Partnered	78.7
Employment status	Fulltime	38.4
	Part time	38.0
	Not employed	23.6
Educational level	No tertiary degree	75.7
	Degree	24.3
Household data (*n* = 593)		%
Household type	Single parent	22.9
	Couple parents	77.1
Number of children < 15 in household	None	70.3
	One or more	29.7
Number of young persons in household	One	66.1
	Two or more	33.9
Main language spoken at home	English	92.2
	Other language	7.8
Area located	Urban	89.7
	Rural	10.3
Income deciles	Low	18.4
	Medium	43.2
	High	38.4

(*Continued*)

Table 6.1 Continued

Participation and time in activities	Participation (%)	Mean minutes per day	Participation (%)	Mean minutes per day
	Young women		*Young men*	
Total domestic work	68.9	46	51.9	36
Food preparation	49.2	17	33.3	12
Laundry and cleaning	30.8	14	16.4	9
Non-routine tasks	33.3	7	25.3	4
Grocery shopping	29.2	13	19.8	13
Parents	*Mothers*		*Fathers*	
Total domestic work	97.7	219	85.3	121
Food preparation	89.7	83	63.7	31
Laundry and cleaning	81.2	88	32.6	23
Non-routine tasks	35.5	11	29.5	7
Grocery shopping	59.8	38	56.8	55

2005), and implicated in the pace of achieving transition to adulthood (Mahaffy 2004) and the likelihood of being co-resident with parents (Mitchell 2004), we ran our models separately by gender for both generations. Analysis is limited to households where at least one person participated in the domestic work of interest (i.e. household total is greater than zero).

We entered the sex of the young person (*female* = 1) and age of the young person (15–19/20–24/25–34). Young people aged 15–19 years are the base category because it is most age-appropriate for them to be living at home, still be studying and not be self-sufficient (Fingerman et al. 2009). Teenagers are most likely to be recipients of parental domestic services, since co-residence in the teenage years is most usual (Settersten et al. 2005) and older co-residents may be expected to contribute more to the running of the household. The amount of time spent in domestic labour depends, in part, on how much time people have available and what other demands they have on their time (Gager et al. 1999). As indicators of time availability, we entered the young person's current main activity (studying [omitted]/working/neither working nor studying). We also entered parents' employment status (mothers: employed full-time [omitted]/part-time/not employed; fathers: employed [omitted]/not employed or employed part-time), since mothers' employment status is known to be associated with their own time spent on domestic work (Craig and Mullan 2009) and some studies have shown that children and teenagers do more domestic work with stay-at-home, rather than employed, mothers (Salman Rizavi and Sofer 2010). We did not use part-time employment as a separate category for fathers because the overwhelming majority of employed fathers have full-time status. Because family structure may impact on young people's domestic contribution (Gager et al. 1999; Bonke 2010; Miller and Bowd 2010) and indirectly on parents' time availability (Craig 2006; Craig and Mullan 2011) we controled for the relationship status of parents (couple [omitted]/single).

As indicators of household resources, we entered equivalized household income (low/middle [omitted]/high). Higher household income may be associated with more material assistance to grown children (Schoeni and Ross 2004) and less domestic work since it can facilitate domestic outsourcing (Craig and Baxter 2016). Equivalized income takes into account the number of people in the household. Household income groups were based on the full ABS samples across the survey years. The bottom three deciles were classified as low income, the top three as high income and the remainder as middle income. We entered mothers' and fathers' education (no tertiary degree [omitted]/tertiary degree), as it could be related to both household resources and gender attitudes (Baxter 2002; Schoeni and Ross 2004). As indicators of household demand, we entered the number of young people aged 15–34 (1 [omitted]/ 2 or more) and whether there were children younger than age 15 in the household (yes/no [omitted]). To capture ethnicity, we entered whether the household was from a non-English-speaking background (NESB) (yes/no [omitted]) because these households may have more traditional gender ideology and household time allocation (Mitchell 2004; Craig 2007). We also controlled for whether the household was in an urban (omitted) or rural location, because rural households may have greater levels of outdoor work (part of our non-routine activities) in particular.

Results

Descriptive findings

A sample description is presented in Table 6.1. A higher proportion of co-resident young people are male than female, and most who co-reside are teenagers, rather than age 20–24 or 25–34. Over half of the co-resident young people are studying, 36 per cent are working, and 7.9 per cent are not in employment or education/ training (NEET). The proportion of co-resident young people who are NEET is larger in older age groups, supporting research which suggests it is a factor in co-residence beyond the more normative teenage years (Settersten and Ray 2010).

The descriptive findings also show rates of participation in domestic work and the mean number of minutes per day young men, young women, mothers and fathers spend on each domestic activity. Overall, it illustrates that mothers' participation in domestic work is highest; 97.7 per cent of mothers responding to the survey did at least some domestic work on the diary day, compared with 85.3 per cent of fathers, 68.9 per cent of young women and 51.9 per cent of young men. Mothers also spent more time in domestic work on average: 219 minutes per day, compared with 121 minutes per day for fathers, 46 minutes per day for young women, and 36 minutes per day for young men. This result indicates that there are both gender and generational differences in domestic labor, such that the older generation (parents) and women are more likely to carry out domestic work and spend longer on it than the younger generation and men. There are similar patterns across the specific domestic activities we examined. However, it is worth noting that fathers and young women have similar rates of participation in laundry and cleaning activities (although the amount is greater for fathers). The smallest gender and generation differences are for grocery shopping, with similar rates of participation across the board, and for non-routine domestic activities. Although female participation in non-routine activities is slightly higher than for males in both generations, men average longer in these activities than women, with a more substantial gender difference in the older generation. This finding is consistent with previous research that suggests outdoor work and maintenance are more likely to be done by men, in part because these tasks are more time-flexible and sporadic than routine domestic activities (Craig and Baxter 2016).

Multivariate analysis

We now turn to our multivariate analysis to examine factors that are associated with the time spent by parents and young people in domestic activities. These results can be found in Tables 6.2 and 6.3.

We found that young people's gender only mattered for fathers' time. Fathers were predicted to spend 4.9 minutes per day less in food preparation, 10.8 minutes per day less in laundry and cleaning and 4.3 minutes per day less in grocery shopping, if the young person was female. Young people's gender had no association with mothers' time.

Young people's domestic contribution differed slightly by how old they were, but the only differences were between the 15–19 year age group and 25–34 year age group. Young women aged 25–34 did more food preparation (15.6 minutes per day) and non-routine activities (19.2 minutes per day) than young women aged 15–19, and young men aged 25–34 did more food preparation than young men age 15–19. They were estimated to do 10.7 minutes more per day, in addition to the 10.8 minutes estimated for the base category 15–19 year olds. However, young people's age showed little corresponding association with parents' domestic work time, with the exception that fathers of young people aged 25–34 spent 17.4 minutes per day less on laundry and cleaning than fathers of young people aged 15–19.

Young people's time availability was not significantly associated with the time they or their parents spent in most domestic tasks. The only exception was that NEET young men spent longer on food preparation (16.6 minutes per day) and non-routine activities (30.2 minutes per day) than young men who were studying.

Parents' time availability was more related to their own time in domestic work than with their children's, with some exceptions. Fathers who were not employed full-time spent significantly longer than other fathers in food preparation, laundry and cleaning and non-routine activities (16.5, 36.0 and 34.4 minutes per day respectively). Mothers and young people's time was not associated with fathers' employment status, with the exception of mothers' time on grocery shopping. Mothers spent an average 10.4 minutes per day less on grocery shopping if their spouse did not work full-time compared to if they did. Mothers' time availability

Table 6.2 OLS regression of parents' and young people's minutes per day in food preparation and laundry/cleaning

	Mothers		Fathers		Young women		Young men	
	Food prep	Laundry/cleaning	Food prep	Laundry/cleaning	Food prep	Laundry/cleaning	Food prep	Laundry/cleaning
	B	B	B	B	B	B	B	B
Young people's characteristics								
Female	-3.4	1.2	-4.9*	-10.8*				
Age 20–24	-0.6	4.0	3.8	1.3	3.9	3.4	0.8	-1.8
25–34	10.3	-4.0	-5.2	-17.4*	15.6**	5.1	10.7*	10.3
Main activity Paid work	0.2	1.3	-1.3	-3.8	-1.4	-3.8	2.0	5.4
NEET	-2.6	4.4	-5.5	-3.6	5.6	11.1	16.6**	11.7
Parents' characteristics								
Father Has a tertiary degree	5.1	4.5	-0.5	-12.8*	-2.3	6.4	0.3	1.7
Employment status Other than FT	-5.5	5.2	16.5***	36.0***	-6.1	5.9	-2.6	1.4
Mother Has a tertiary degree	-2.6	-8.6	7.4*	5.4	2.2	-1.5	-2.2	-2.4
Employment status Part time	15.9***	16.4**	-4.7	-20.3**	-0.2	-2.8	-4.1	-1.8
Not emp'd	55.0***	48.1***	-9.2**	-11.7	-2.3	-7.7*	-1.5	0.2
Household characteristics								
Single parent	-3.8	-21.3**	8.1	4.2	5.5	2.9	4.2	-6.5
Child aged 0–14	4.7	7.8	-2.2	4.8	2.8	1.0	2.9	1.2
2+ young people	0.8	7.7	-0.9	13.8**	-3.1	-4.	-2.2	-2.7
NESB	16.5*	-7.6	-0.6	-21.1***	0.8	-5.0	2.4	-10.5*
Rural location	18.8*	17.7	0.8	-7.0	5.0	1.4	-3.1	-0.8
Low income	5.8	-6.0	-1.9	-8.5	4.7	-0.9	0.5	6.3
High income	-6.9	-5.9	0.3	-7.0	-0.5	1.2	-2.0	-5.0
Intercept	67.7·***	71.5***	33.4***	34.9***	16.7***	14.1***	10.8***	8.7*
Diary days (n)	1301	1226	1079	1008	684	656	687	621

Note: $*p < 0.05$, $**p < 0.01$, $***p < 0.001$

Table 6.3 OLS regression of parents' and young people's minutes per day in non-routine domestic tasks and grocery shopping

	Mothers		Fathers		Young women		Young men	
	Non-routine	Grocery shopping	Non-routine	Grocery shopping	Non-routine	Grocery shopping	Non-routine	Grocery shopping
	B	B	B	B	B	B	B	B
Young people's characteristics								
Female	5.1	-1.8	2.6	-4.3**	—	—	—	—
Age 20–24	4.3	0.9	6.2	4.4	17.4	-4.5	-8.3	0.8
25–34	-3.4	-2.5	0.1	4.9	19.2*	-6.5	-2.1	1.3
Main activity Paid work	2.4	-2.2	-5.3	-4.4	-8.9	6.8	14.3	2.6
NEET	-6.4	-2.0	-10.1	0.7	2.8	-3.1	30.2**	-0.3
Parents' characteristics								
Father Has a tertiary degree	1.8	-1.4	-15.4	-0.3	5.6	2.2	0.2	5.9**
Employment status Other than FT	-9.9	-10.4***	34.4***	1.3	-12.3	-3.0	-9.5	0.5
Mother Has a tertiary degree	1.4	-2.4	-1.0	2.7	-2.9	1.5	1.6	0.1
Employment status Part time	13.3*	5.8**	-2.3	-2.6	-10.3	3.5	7.3*	0.2
Not emp'd	25.8***	8.0**	-14.4	-3.0	-14.1*	5.1	3.5	-2.5
Household characteristics								
Single parent	-2.1	-10.3***	1.6	-9.6***	1.5	1.2	6.8	0.6
Child aged 0–14	-1.0	-2.6	12.2	-2.8	-4.8	3.8	-4.8	2.1
2+ young people	-5.9	-4.0*	0.3	-3.5*	-10.2*	-2.9	-0.6	-2.2
NESB	-12.7*	-2.9	27.8	-4.9	-10.5**	5.1	-13.8***	-3.7
Rural location	26.7*	-0.5	11.7	-5.8*	36.6	-4.5	8.7	3.1
Low income	3.1	-1.3	-20.1*	-3.5	16.2	0.8	5.2	4.7
High income	7.2	0.0	-12.4	-1.6	-5.7	3.2	-11.1*	0.2
Intercept	28.0***	24.2***	58.4***	17.9***	24.3**	7.2*	12.0	2.2
Diary days (n)	1198	970	965	737	662	546	625	513

Note: *$p < 0.05$, **$p < 0.01$, ***$p < 0.001$

and employment status had a greater association with time use than did fathers'. Part-time employed and not-employed mothers spent significantly more time in food preparation, laundry and cleaning, non-routine activities and grocery shopping than employed mothers. Fathers were found to spend less time on laundry and cleaning if their spouse worked part-time compared with full-time (20.3 minutes per day) and less time on food preparation if their spouse was not employed compared with employed full-time (9.2 minutes per day). Interestingly, young women were found to spend less time on laundry and cleaning and non-routine activities if their mother was not employed (7.7 and 14.1 minutes per day respectively), while young men were found to spend significantly more time on non-routine activities if their mother was employed part-time rather than full-time (7.3 minutes per day).

Rather, associations were concentrated in the older generation. Parents' education was associated with fathers doing less laundry and cleaning work (12.8 minutes per day) if they had a degree than if they did not and more time in food preparation if their spouse had a degree compared than if they did not (7.4 minutes per day). The latter aligns with a recent study showing that higher male childcare is associated with their wives', rather than their own, higher education (Gauthier and DeGusti 2012). With regard to cross-generation effects, sons were found to spend more time on grocery shopping if their father had a degree (5.9 minutes per day). There was no association with daughters' time.

With regard to other household characteristics, these were largely found to have a greater association with parents' domestic work time than young people's. In single- rather than two-parent households, mothers spent less time on laundry and cleaning and grocery shopping (21.3 and 10.3 minutes per day respectively) and fathers spent less time on grocery shopping (9.6 minutes per day). There was no association between having children younger than age 15 in the household and parents and young people's domestic work. Having two or more young people (aged 15 or older) in the household, compared with only one, was associated with more laundry and cleaning time for fathers (13.8 minutes per day), but less time on grocery shopping for both mothers and fathers (4.0 and 3.5 minutes per day respectively). Young women also spent less time on non-routine activities if there were two or more young people in the household.

Being in a NESB household, compared with an English-speaking household, had a number of associations with time spent on domestic work. Specifically, mothers from NESB households spent more time on food preparation (16.5 minutes per day) but less time on non-routine activities (12.7 minutes per day). Fathers from NESB households were associated with spending less time on laundry and cleaning (21.1 minutes per day). Young women and men from NESB households averaged less time on non-routine activities (10.5 and 13.8 minutes per day respectively), and young men averaged less time on laundry and cleaning (10.5 minutes per day). Being from a rural rather than urban location was associated with mothers spending more time in food preparation and non-routine activities (18.8 and 26.7 minutes per day respectively). Finally, being in a low-income household was associated with fathers spending less time on non-routine activities (20.1 minutes per day), compared with those in middle income house-holds. Interestingly, being in a high-income household was associated with young men spending less time on non-routine activities compared with those in middle-income households (11.1 minutes per day).

Conclusion

Housework and its division within families are important indicators of equity and quality of life. This study showed that the time spent by parents and young people on domestic tasks differed in both frequency and duration. Parents did domestic tasks more often, and for longer, than young people of the same gender. Mothers did most tasks more frequently, and for longer, than either fathers or young people, suggesting that 'routine' tasks in particular are regular daily responsibilities for mothers only, with both fathers and young people of both genders more occasional participants. Notwithstanding, young women did domestic work tasks more frequently than did young men. These findings support the extensive literature demonstrating the gendered nature of domestic work.

The focus of this chapter was identifying the factors that predict more or less domestic work among young people and co-resident parents, with a particular interest in identifying characteristics that affected both generations. Since age norms strongly influence parental expectations of young people (Mahaffy 2004; Settersten et al. 2005), we anticipated those co-resident at older ages would contribute most to the running of the household. For both young men and young women, food preparation was higher among 25–34 year olds than 15–19 year olds; and non-routine activities were higher among older young women. However, we found little evidence that this higher time by older young people relieved their parents of domestic work, with *positive* associations between mothers' food preparation and having a 25–34 year old co-resident. It could be that such activities become more pleasurable as children grow older, and all members of families with an interest in food preparation do more of it, perhaps cooking together. Alternatively, when young people are older, household members may be increasingly cooking for themselves but not for others in the family, thus doubling up on household effort. In any event, the implication is that older young peoples' domestic work does not save parents' time. The only indication of young people's domestic work off-setting parents' work was in relation to laundry and cleaning work, with fathers predicted to spend significantly less time in this activity if their child was aged 25–34. However, although young women and men were predicted to spend more time on laundry and cleaning if they were older, this was not statistically significant. Similarly, young people's time availability through their employment/student status had more associations with their own domestic time than with their parents' time.

On the other hand, there were some parental characteristics that were associated with apparent trade-offs between parents and young people. Mothers' time availability was associated with housework variation in the younger generation: sons spent slightly more time on non-routine tasks if their mother was employed part-time rather than full-time. With mothers not in employment, rather than employed full-time, daughters spent less time in non-routine tasks and laundry and cleaning work. Fathers' employment status showed no associations with young peoples' domestic work. Overall, young people's domestic work time was slightly more sensitive to fathers' than to mothers' characteristics. This finding is perhaps because the domestic contributions of both fathers and young people are more contingent than for mothers (McMahon 1999; Bianchi et al. 2000; Connell 2006).

Accordingly, previous research has established that adult women's housework is more responsive to family characteristics than men's (e.g. Sayer 2005). We expected the same would apply to co-resident young women, but found little evidence to support this. Most household or parental characteristics that predicted variation did so for young people of both genders. That is, although gender differences in absolute amount of time were wide, factors associated with divergence from average patterns were broadly similar for young men and young women.

Overall, this study suggests that young people contribute only marginally to domestic labour in co-resident households. This finding may be due to taken-for-granted assumptions about housework, such that it is thought appropriate that domestic services flow down the generations. It may be difficult for parents, particularly mothers, who are predominantly the primary carers, to adjust from doing everything for children to expecting them to take over some net responsibility for domestic tasks (Kloep and Hendry 2010). Similarly, it may be difficult to increase adult children's contribution to the household chores, if this has not been the norm when they were younger. If an indicator of adulthood is taking care of oneself and others in the household, this study suggests that it is not attained by co-resident young people in two-generation households. Rather it suggests that there is continued domestic dependency, even among older co-resident young people. The findings also show that gender continues to be central to the division of domestic labour beyond couple relationships. We conclude that gender and generation are both important and outweigh the power of other explanations of differences in domestic contribution such as time availability and relative resources.

References

ABS 2006, *Time Use Survey: User Guide*, Cat. No. 4150.0. Australian Bureau of Statistics, Canberra.

ABS 2013, *Australian Social Trends 2013*, Cat. No. 4102.0. Australian Bureau of Statistics, Canberra.

AHURI 2011, How great is the shortage of affordable housing in Australia's private rental market? *AHURI Research and Policy Bulletin*, Issue 144, Australian Housing and Urban Research Institute, Melbourne.

Baxter, J 2002, 'Patterns of change and stability in the gender division of household labour in Australia, 1996–1997', *Journal of Sociology*, vol. 38, pp. 399–424.

Bell, D and Blanchflower, D 2011, 'Young people and the great recession', *Oxford Review of Economic Policy*, vol. 27, pp. 241–267.

Bell, L, Burtless, G, Gornick, J and Smeeding, T 2007, 'A cross-national survey of trends in the transition to economic independence', in SH Danziger and C Rouse (eds), *The*

Price of Independence: The Economics of Early Adulthood, Russell Sage Foundation Press, New York, pp. 27–55.

Bianchi, SM and Milkie, MA 2010, 'Work and family research in the first decade of the 21st century', *Journal of Marriage and Family*, vol. 72, pp. 705–725.

Bianchi, SM, Milkie, MA, Sayer, LC and Robinson, JP 2000, 'Is anyone doing the housework? Trends in the gender division of household labor', *Social Forces*, vol. 79, pp. 191–228.

Bonke, J 2010, 'Children's housework – are girls more active than boys?' *Electronic International Journal of Time Use Research*, vol. 7, pp. 1–16.

Buckley, J 2011, *Ageing in the 21st Century – Are Baby Boomers Prepared? A study of Preparation for Later Life in a Context of Social Change*, PhD Thesis, School of Social Science, University of Adelaide, Adelaide.

Cash, J 2012, 'Obedience to authority and its discontents', in G Hage and R Eckersley (eds.), *Responsibility*, chap. 1, Melbourne University Publishing, Carlton.

Cobb-Clark, D 2008, 'Leaving home: What economics has to say about the living arrangements of young Australians', *Australian Economic Review*, vol. 41, pp. 160–176.

Coltrane, S 2007, *Fatherhood, Gender and Work-Family Policies. Real Utopias*, The Havens Center, University of Wisconsin, Madison.

Connell, R 2006, *Masculinities: Knowledge, Power, and Social Change*, Polity, Oxford.

Cooke, L P and Baxter, J 2010, ' "Families" in international context: comparing institutional effects across western societies,' *Journal of Marriage and Family*, vol. 72, pp. 516–536.

Craig, L 2006, 'The money or the care? A comparison of couple and sole parent households' time allocation to work and children', *Australian Journal of Social Issues*, vol. 40, pp. 521–540.

Craig, L 2007, "Is there really a 'second shift', and if so, who does it? A time-diary investigation," *Feminist Review*, vol. 86, pp. 149-170.

Craig, L and Baxter, J 2016, "Domestic outsourcing, housework shares and subjective time pressure: gender differences in the correlates of hiring help," *Social Indicators Research*, vol. 125, pp. 271–288.

Craig, L and Mullan, K 2009, 'The policeman and the part-time sales assistant: household labour supply, family time and subjective time pressure in Australia 1997–2006', *Journal of Comparative Family Studies*, vol. 40, pp. 545–560.

Craig, L and Mullan, K 2011, 'Lone and couple mothers' childcare time within context in four countries', *European Sociological Review*, vol. 28, pp. 512–526.

de Vaus, D 2004, *Diversity and Change in Australian Families: Statistical Profiles*, Australian Institute of Family Studies, Melbourne.

Erikson, EH 1959, 'Identity and the Life Circle', *Psychological Issues Monograph 1*, International University Press, New York.

Evertsson, M 2006. "The reproduction of gender: housework and attitudes towards gender equality in the home among Swedish boys and girls," *The British Journal of Sociology*, vol. 57, pp. 415–436.

Fingerman, K, Miller, L, Birditt, K and Zarit, S 2009, 'Giving to the good and the needy: Parental support of grown children', *Journal of Marriage and Family*, vol. 71, pp. 1220–1233.

Flatau, P, James, I, Watson, R, Wood, G and Hendershott, PH 2003, 'Leaving the Parental Home in Australian over the 20th Century: Evidence from the Household Income and Labour Dynamics in Australia (HILDA) survey', paper presented at the HILDA Survey Research Conference, 13 March 2003, University of Melbourne, Melbourne.

Foundation for Young Australians 2014, *Renewing Australia's Promise*, Foundation for Young Australians, Melbourne.

Furlong, A 2009, 'Changing contexts, changing lives', in A Furlong (ed.), *Handbook of Youth and Young Adulthood: New Perspective and Agendas*, Routledge, New York, pp. 3–24.

Furstenberg, FF, Kennedy, S, McLoyd, VC, Rumbaut, RG and Settersten, RA 2004, 'Growing up is harder to do', *Contexts*, vol. 3, pp. 33–41.

Gager, CT, Cooney, TM and Call, KT 1999, 'The effects of family characteristics and time use on teenagers' household labor', *Journal of Marriage and Family*, vol. 61, pp. 982–994.

Gauthier, A and DeGusti, B 2012. "The time allocation to children by parents in Europe," *International Sociology*, vol. 27, pp. 827–845.

Greenfield, E and Marks, N 2006, 'Linked lives: adult children's problems and their parents' psychological and relational well-being,' *Journal of Marriage and Family*, vol. 68, pp. 442–454.

Hendry, LB and Kloep, M 2012, *Adolescence and Adulthood: Transitions and Transformations*, Palgrave Macmillan, New York.

Katz, R and Lowenstein, A 2010, 'Theoretical perspectives on intergenerational solidarity, conflict and ambivalence', in M Izuhara (ed.), *Ageing and Intergenerational Relations: Family Reciprocity from a Global Perspective*, Policy Press, Bristol, pp. 29–56.

Kloep, M and Hendry, LB 2010, 'Letting go or holding on? Parents' perceptions of their relationships with their children during emerging adulthood', *British Journal of Developmental Psychology*, vol. 28, pp. 817–834.

McMahon, A 1999, *Taking Care of Men: Sexual Politics in the Public Mind*, Cambridge University Press, Cambridge.

Mahaffy, KA 2004, 'Gender, race, class, and the transition to adulthood: A critical review of the literature', *Sociological Studies of Children and Youth*, vol. 9, pp. 15–47.

Mandic, S 2008, 'Home-leaving and its structural determinants in western and eastern Europe: An exploratory study', *Housing Studies*, vol. 23, pp. 615–637.

Manke, B, Seery, BL, Crouter, AC, and McHale, SM 1994, "The three corners of domestic labor: mothers', fathers', and children's weekday and weekend housework," *Journal of Marriage and Family*, vol. 56, pp. 657–668.

Miller, P 2012, 'Do Australian teenagers work? Why we should care', *Feminist Economics*, vol. 18, pp. 1–24.

Miller, P and Bowd, J 2010, 'Do Australian teenagers contribute to household work?' *Family Matters*, vol. 85, pp. 68–76.

Mitchell, B 2004, 'Home, but not alone: Socio-cultural and economic aspects of Canadian young adults sharing parental households', *Atlantis*, vol. 28, pp. 115–125.

Punch, S 2001, "Household division of labour: generation, gender, age, birth order and sibling composition. work," *Employment & Society*, vol. 15, pp. 803–823.

Raley, K, Crissey, S and Muller, C 2007, 'Of sex and romance: Late adolescent relationships and young adult union formation', *Journal of Marriage and Family*, vol. 69, pp. 1210–1226.

Richards, A 2008, 'Some Observations on the Cost of Housing in Australia', paper presented at the Address to the Economic and Social Outlook Conference, The Melbourne Institute, Melbourne.

Salman Rizavi, S and Sofer, C 2010, 'The third partner in the household: An analysis of children's household work', *27th Journées de Microéconomie*, University of Angers, France.

Sayer, L 2005, 'Gender, time and inequality: Trends in women's and men's paid work, unpaid work and free time', *Social Forces*, vol. 84, pp. 285–303.

Settersten, R, Furstenberg, F and Rumbaut, R 2005, *On the Frontier of Adulthood: Theory, Research, and Public Policy*, University of Chicago Press, Chicago.

Settersten, R and Ray, B 2010, 'What's going on with young people today? The long and twisting path to adulthood', *The Future of Children*, vol. 20, pp. 19–41.

Schoeni, R and Ross, K 2004, "Material Assistance Received from Families during the Transition to Adulthood," in R Settersten, F Furstenberg and R Rumbaut (eds.), *On the Frontier of Adulthood: Theory, Research, and Public Policy*, University of Chicago Press, Chicago, pp. 68-82.

Sullivan, O 1997, 'Time waits for no (Wo)Man: An investigation of the gendered experience of domestic time', *Sociology*, vol. 31, pp. 221–239.

Swartz, TT, Kim, M, Uno, M, Mortimer, J and Bengston O'Brien, K 2011, 'Safety nets and scaffolds: Parental support in the transition to adulthood', *Journal of Marriage and Family*, vol. 73, pp. 414–429.

Tanner, J and Arnett, J 2009, 'The emergence of "emerging adulthood"', in A Furlong (ed.), *Handbook of Youth and Young Adulthood*, Routledge, New York, pp. 39–45.

Veevers, JE and Mitchell, BA 1998, 'Intergenerational exchanges and perceptions of support within "boomerang kid" family environments', *The International Journal of Aging and Human Development*, vol. 46, pp. 91–108.

Vicente, H and Sousa, L 2009, 'The multigenerational family and the elderly: A mutual or parasitical symbiotic relationship?' in L Sousa (ed.), *Families in Later Life: Emerging Themes and Challenges*, Nova Science Publishers, New York, pp. 27–48.

Woodman, D 2012, 'Life out of Synch: How new patterns of further education and the rise of precarious employment are reshaping young people's relationships', *Sociology*, vol. 46, pp. 1074–1090.

7 Families and ageing

Intergenerational relations in health and care negotiations

Rodrigo Mariño, Victor Minichiello and Michael I. MacEntee

Introduction

This chapter describes how intergenerational relations and other cultural characteristics influence health care for older people through self-care decisions, negotiations, filial/parental obligations and other living arrangements in Australia. After an overview of notable demographic characteristics of the Australian population, the chapter describes intergenerational relations and different cultural family systems and norms, their contributions and challenges for negotiating care and health and the relationship of families and households characteristics. The second part explores the influence of culture on health beliefs and behaviours, including and contrasting self-care decision and negotiations; filial/parental obligations and independence and independent living; and the implications of such arrangements in health negotiations to provide an overview of what is taking place in the Australian context. The last section presents the results from a case study of older Chinese immigrants living in Melbourne, from which we derive recommendations for health-related culturally appropriate policies suitable to intergenerational relations in health and care negotiations.

Background

Demographic data shows two major trends in the Australian population that have the potential to influence the provision of health care to older people. First, the trend for an increase in life expectancy and a decrease in fertility. For example, in 2011 there were 3.08 million people aged 65 years or older in Australia (Australian Bureau of Statistics 2011). This figure represents an overall rise from 13 per cent of the total population in 2001 to 14 per cent in 2011. On the other hand, in the same period, the proportion of people of working age (15 to 64 years) increased only marginally from 66.9 per cent to 67.3 per cent over this ten-year period.

Second, Australia has one of the most diverse populations in the world. Australia is home to migrants from more than 120 different countries (ABS 2012). Such diversity is reflected in the more than one-quarter (26 per cent) Australian residents who were born overseas, more than half of whom were born in countries where the main languages are not English (ABS 2012).

Migration to Australia has occurred in waves, which has created many migrant communities with different age profiles, some with a relatively young age profile, while other communities are much older. In 2006, Italians and Greeks, together with Vietnamese and Chinese, were the largest culturally and linguistically diverse (CALD[1]) groups in Australia, but, over the past decade, the Asian population has increased more than any other group, with 319,000 migrants from China, followed by 295,000 from India, and 185,000 from Vietnam (ABS 2012). Together, these three countries, plus those from Italy (185,000) provided about 20 per cent of all migrants to Australia in 2011. Most Chinese immigrants live in the suburbs of Sydney, Melbourne or Brisbane in communities with distinctive cultural features but in the midst of the dominant Anglo-Celtic Australian society (ABS 2012; Department of Immigration and Citizenship 2014).

The Australian Bureau of Statistics (ABS) also reported in 2011 that over 1.1 million Australians aged 65 or older were born overseas, a proportion (36 per cent) of the population substantially higher than that of people under 65 who were born overseas (24 per cent). This older CALD population is projected to grow more rapidly in the coming decades to about 1.5 million by 2026 (ABS 2012).

In Australia, the overwhelming majority (79 per cent) of family households consist of only one nuclear family (Baxter et al. 2011). While people born in Australia made up the majority of multigenerational household residents (Millward 1998), people from some migrant groups as well as Aboriginal people are significantly more likely to live in multigenerational households (Thomas 2003; Baxter et al. 2011). For example, a substantial proportion of older immigrants (22 per cent), when compared with mainstream Australian-born (7 per cent), live with their children (Ikels 1990; Paice 2002). Such multigenerational cohabitation may occur because of personal preference (Thomas 2003) or to facilitate health and well-being by creating a sense of belonging, safety and social support (Millward 1998). Nonetheless, many immigrants are less likely to receive the same level of care and support usually accessible to the broad population in the receiving society (MFH Project Group 2004; Johnstone and Kanitsaki 2006; 2007). Consequently, different programs and policies may be required to meet the health and social needs of people from cultural backgrounds that rely heavily on extended family support (Thomas 2003; United Nations 2005).

Intergenerational family systems and norms

The connection between generations is an important social bond in all societies (Bubolz 1999). Families exist in many different forms, in how they are housed, how they live, and how they manage intergenerational bonds and relationships. Some preserve the conservative influence of traditional values and practices by attempting to perpetuate traditional expectations and contributions from their members (Kagitcibasi et al. 2010). Yet, family interactions change over time and across generations and show remarkable diversity. A global survey of the patterns and trends in the living arrangements of older people in more than 130 countries revealed an enormous diversity in living arrangements (United Nations 2005).

Family relationships are influenced by myriad socioeconomic and cultural factors ranging from education to income and social security; they are also influenced by living conditions in urban or rural locations, and these factors are filtered through contemporary societal and family cultures and values.

Contemporary social and economic strategies and policies in Australia have reduced the role of government in sponsoring and delivering services by encouraging private competition in health care and other social services. This shift has influenced the role, expectations and responsibilities of families and their communities. In addition, the current immigration policy favours skilled immigrants at the expense of family reunification involving all age groups (Larsen 2013). In Australia, skilled migration has overtaken the number of arrivals of older members in the 'family' stream, and the latter has seen a reduction from around 70 per cent of all migrant arrivals in 1995–96 to around 32 per cent in 2013–14 (Larsen 2013). These changes are important as the extent of intergenerational exchange is influenced by the proximity and frequency of contact among members (Millward 1998; Kagitcibasi et al. 2010).

Migrants with strong cultural values, beliefs, rules and interpretations that differ markedly from the dominant society can experience difficulties acculturating in the adopted society (Kagitcibasi et al. 2010). These difficulties are likely to be compounded by communication challenges in a new language, pre-migration cultural beliefs, and knowledge of the dominant culture's ways, which will affect every aspect of their lives and may create, for immigrant groups, a unique experience of health care and support. Families are regarded as having an anti-acculturative influence that might counteract influences toward the dominant value system (Tharp 1968). For example, a family's preferences for friends, neighbourhoods and social contacts within the same cultural group limit exposure to the dominant culture to further impede acculturation and can create intergenerational tensions. Maintaining connections with family members overseas is common for families of immigrant background. Information and communication technologies, sponsorship of family members, and financial assistance to those left behind (Millward 1998) facilitate these connections. This continuous contact may also have conservative influences in a family's traditional values and practices.

Although most research on cultural diversity has been carried out in traditional immigrant-receiving countries such as Australia, Canada, New Zealand and the United States, these issues have also become increasingly important in the rest of the world (Berry 2005). Most Western countries are now culturally diverse, composed of numerous ethno-cultural groups (e.g. indigenous people, recent immigrants, established immigrants and their descendants) coexisting within a larger, predominant culture and creating multicultural and multiracial societies.

Conceptually, acculturation can be assessed in any ethno-cultural groups made up of individual members of a minority national group living in a larger society of a modern state, with a different cultural background from the mainstream culture, but who at the same time have a strong co-national support and conform to a substantial proportion of the community. For example, half of the world's population lives in culturally diverse societies in Asia, where people experience daily intercultural encounters (Berry 2005). Thus, most of the world's population lives in places where cultural diversity is a fact of daily life.

Multigenerational cohabitation can provide a supportive environment for new immigrants, especially in the context of psychological support, social interaction and the practical exchange of money, goods and services, and even more so when the dominant culture offers only limited health care and other social services (Millward 1998). On the other hand, cohabitation can be stressful to relationships between parents and their adult children, as Mariño and his collaborators (2010) discovered among Cantonese-speaking immigrants in Melbourne. Interdependence is a core value of many immigrant families whereby aging parents expect financial and welfare support from their adult children in return for babysitting and other domestic assistance (Chiu and Yu 2001; United Nations 2005). Practical applications of this core value, expressed as 'filial piety' in Confucian philosophy, do not necessarily run smoothly when people see themselves as supportive but without reciprocation, and when cultural values clash as acculturation occurs differently among parents, children and grandchildren. Indeed, as affluence improves, the different generations of many immigrant families prefer to live apart, usually after the children marry (Mariño et al. 2010). Still, a substantial proportion of older immigrants live with their children despite growing differences of opinion about food, raising children and entertainment, and persistent fears of burdening their children (Ikels 1990; Paice 2002).

Influence of culture on health beliefs and behaviours

Increases in life expectancy together with falling birth rates will translate to increases in the absolute and relative number of older adults, which in turn is likely accompanied by a significant increase in the number of people living with chronic conditions throughout the world. Continuous good health of older adult populations is a major challenge to society and to healthcare provision in developed and developing countries, which will impact on all aspects of twenty-first century society (Coulson et al. 2005; World Health Organisation 2011; Barnett et al. 2012). Family members are usually the source of community-based care for older persons who have difficulty managing on their own or who need specialized medical services (Millward 1998). When a parent, parent-in-law or grandparent needs assistance because they have health problems or disabilities, those co-residing are more likely to be responsible for being the carer. As already mentioned, the proportion of multi-family households is significantly higher in some cultural groups (e.g. migrants, Aboriginals) living in Australia. Families of those cultural groups are more likely than other families to have a parent, brother, sister or other relative living with them (Millward 1998). Thus, depending on the family configuration, carers may include spouses, sons and daughters, sons- and daughters-in-law, siblings and grandchildren as well as friends and neighbours (Wolf et al. 1997; Stuifbergen and Van Delden 2011). Close neighbourhood support networks traditionally serve to extend family support in some communities (e.g. Millward 1998; Thomas 2003).

While there is no homogeneity in Australia in regard to aspects of family composition, family life, and social networks, interdependence among family members characterizes the Australian family. Nonetheless, a number of demographic trends and values mediate filial expectations or obligations to care for, or provide support to, elderly parents (Stuifbergen and Van Delden 2011). For example, attitudes toward filial obligations are influenced by the age of the children, gender, workforce participation, ethno-cultural background and the marital status of the child and/or the parent in need (Millward 1998). Also, as previously mentioned, this type of intergenerational exchange is influenced by dimensions of family structure and cohesion (Millward 1998). However, these influences may not be the only mediator of family change. For example, falling birth rates and better healthcare education are associated with changes in family relationships, including the roles of women and men, and family obligations (Millward 1998; United Nations 2005).

In any case, in Australia immigrants must interact with a Community Health Centre or other agency, public or private, oriented to mainstream patients. There are substantial differences between ethno-cultural groups that extend beyond ethnic or linguistic characteristics. One cannot understand how a person reacts to illness, pain, death or misfortune without understanding the culture in which he or she has been socialized (Alvarado 2008). A typical Western model for health and social services is based on a set of principles, values and assumptions drawn from the mainstream culture. It encourages individuals to become autonomous and to be in charge of their life and detached from the broader community to define who they are, or could be. It assumes that once the goal has been accepted by the individual, he or she will engage in the appropriate direction and persevere and challenge himself or herself to realize the goal (Erez and Early 1993; Minas et al. 2010). However, conflict may arise for individuals and families from more collectivist-oriented cultures when confronted with the individualism that predominates in many Western societies, including Australia.

A study of similarities and differences in the family structure and function of thirty countries revealed that families are generally more hierarchical, interdependent and conservative in agrarian, low affluence and Orthodox Christian or Islamic societies than in affluent, educated and Protestant societies (Georgas et al. 2006). Western cultures tend to favour family values that promote personal achievements, productive efficiency and interpersonal competition rather than close social interactions where the 'self' is subservient to the more collective needs and expectations of the family and society as a whole. Asian cultures, for example, emphasize authoritarian power and an individual's obligations to the rites and honour of the ancestral family, whereas Western cultures tend more toward personal autonomy and the anticipated needs of the future (Triandis et al. 1986; Leong et al. 1990; Nguyen and Williams 1989; Mak and Chan 1995). Regarding relationships with nature, some cultures tend to harmonize and adapt to their environment, rather than manipulating nature to suit individual concerns (Erez and Early 1993). This distinction is relevant to health and medical care, where an orientation to dominate nature may translate into an individual having high expectations of the health system and therefore to be more demanding on a range of medical care and treatment (Minas et al. 2010).

Family relations, such as child-rearing practices, how to relate with people and couple relationships, are also changing around the world, with collectivist values being replaced by more individualistic, self-oriented ones (Silverstein et al. 2006; Jin 2010; Mariño et al. 2010). Increased exposure (including through acculturation) to Western values such as individualism has produced norms of greater autonomy between generations and social security schemes have contributed to financial independence, both of which have helped to redefine intergenerational dependency. Still, self-health and self-sufficiency are major features of some cultural groups (e.g. Chinese), whether as immigrants (Kwan and Williams 1999; Mariño et al. 2010) or living in their own country (Wan et al. 2008). Social support, self-reliance and social participation were major topics in a study on Cantonese older adults (Mariño et al. 2010). Participants believed that when there is family support there is less need of self-care. On the other hand, it was mentioned that 'the advantage of living in Australia was the possibility of independence and self-reliance' (Mariño et al. 2010).

Cultural and family values fundamentally shape the intergenerational context of chronic illness and end-of-life decisions. The projected demographic profiles together with the prolonged survival of people with chronic disease will see a further increase in the number of people with cognitive impairments in Australia (Australian Institute of Health and Welfare 2014). Thus, the prevention, treatment and rehabilitation of cognitive impairments will continue to be challenged in the twenty-first century. How society views people with dementia is important because it includes the person's ability to organize their lives according to their own will, insights and beliefs, regardless of cognitive impairment (Coulson et al. 2005). The social meaning of dementia is affected by culture, personal values, gender, race, class, age, geography, sexual orientation and ability to make decisions for oneself (Coulson et al. 2005).

As with other chronic conditions, a supportive environment is the cornerstone for care and in assisting a cognitive impaired patient to maintain an acceptable level of functioning (Marcantonio 2003). It is best achieved where a patient is surrounded by familiar environments, such as the patient's home environment, where people with cognitive impairment may keep up their daily routines and regular social and physical activities (Marcantonio 2003; Alzheimer's Association 2009). Families can organize themselves to provide care and support, however, this partnership may not always be available (Harding et al. 2006), so institutional living has become an option in many developed countries (United Nations 2005). However, there are many low-income societies, and even within affluent countries, where institutional care is unavailable or inadequate, and the burden of care falls heavily on spouses, sons and daughters, siblings, grandchildren, friends and neighbours. In many countries, including Australia, the reduction of assistance from government or agencies for these services would decrease standards and increase deinstitutionalization (Browne 2015).

Interdependency can be built and reinforced by policy arrangements. Keeping a patient in his or her home environment and/or intergenerational exchanges when the patient is not capable of participating in the relationship anymore has social and economic implications. For example, looking after someone would require support systems for carers and the provision of information about how to manage different aspects of their condition.

Within this context, different program and policy approaches may be required to address the health and social needs of people living in a multigenerational household. When examining background effects in health and care negotiations, it is relevant to take a multigenerational perspective and to consider the characteristics of the extended family. Saraceno and Kneck (2008) propose a different approach where social policies are categorized along a continuum. In this continuum, familisation refers to a situation where the responsibility to provide care and financial support is assigned to the family, including 'familism by default', where no alternatives are available to family care and support. The alternative is to develop policies that can support families in maintaining their financial and caring responsibility ('supported familism'). On the other end of this continuum is 'defamilisation', where care needs are satisfied through public and paid provisions.

End-of-life decisions are experienced by all families and can be a significant source of intergenerational conflict for some migrant populations. The conflict often evolves from the emphasis on personal autonomy that pervades many industrial societies, when compared with the collectivism of the agrarian societies from which some migrants originate. For example, many Western societies have specific legal directives to ensure that the rights and wishes of the dying person are met even if at odds with the collective wishes of their family (White et al. 2011). Severe conflict occasionally arises from disagreements about whether to comfort dying people by withholding information about the seriousness of their conditions (Braddock 2008). Indeed, most decisions about illness and death are shaped by cultural experiences and can lead to damaging intergenerational conflicts unless managed sensitively by everyone involved, including professional caregivers and others who develop and implement healthcare policies (Braddock 2008).

Case study[2]

In Australia, the China-born population is one of the fastest-growing groups among new arrivals. The census in 2011 recorded 319,000 China-born individuals, which is an increase of 54.5 per cent since 2006 (ABS 2012). Chinese migration to Australia occurred over time in waves, and consequently these waves of migrants are ageing differently. One group of 65–75-year-olds arrived as young adults; another arrived as elders under the family reunion program (Thomas 2003); while a third group who came mostly as entrepreneurs or skilled migrants from Hong Kong and Macau dominated immigration in the early 1990s but diminished substantially shortly before and after the reunification of these territories with China (Lui 2006). In Melbourne, the number of Chinese-born migrants living in Melbourne grew considerably in the past decade, more than doubling between 2001 and 2011 from 36,000 to 90,000 people (ABS 2014a). Of the 90,000, 8.5 per cent were over age 65. Like other migrants, with resident status they can access Medicare, community support, and other welfare benefits.

To examine traditional cultural values of China-born, older migrants living in Melbourne, six focus-group discussions were organized. China-born, Cantonese speakers aged 55 years or older who were living in Melbourne were recruited to participate in the focus-group discussions in 2007. The discussions were facilitated by a bilingual (Cantonese-English) facilitator and the topic of discussion was traditional Chinese ways of caring for older people (MacEntee et al. 2012). Volunteers for the focus-group discussions (FGDs; $n = 50$) were recruited through the elders' network of the Chinese Health Foundation of Australia. Recruits lived in one of two neighbourhoods – Box Hill (an area of relative social advantage) and North Melbourne (an area of relative social disadvantage) – each with large populations from Hong Kong and Guangzhou.

Questions posed by the facilitator were prompted at the beginning of each discussion by a situational vignette that focused attention on the psychosocial impact of oral health problems involving an older couple facing health problems within the context of traditional values and intergenerational interactions (Brondani et al. 2007). The focus group was guided by three main themes, each one having three to four questions to prompt discussion. However, depending on the answer provided, new questions relevant to the main themes were asked to arrive at a clearer understanding of the issue.

Participants characterized the family as an extended unit involving multigenerational living with a strong sense of filial piety (Chiu and Yu 2001). However, most participants (78 per cent) lived alone or with their spouse rather than with their children in Australia. Participants emphasized family harmony and they believed living apart from their children helped to avoid intergenerational confrontation.

> When living together with children/in-laws, there [are] always generation gaps – regardless of how well they treat you. You have to tolerate the behaviour of each other in order to maintain harmony, I think it is hard. Living by yourself has more freedom.
>
> (F-FGD3)

They acknowledged a cultural gap between themselves and their children when discussing music, food, entertainment and child rearing. Nonetheless, participants also acknowledged that living with others had some advantages, especially to allay fears of loneliness and to assist with financial security. Participants described the extended family more as a socioeconomic necessity in China where housing was in short supply (reflecting the findings of Ikels 1990) rather than as a result of traditional norms or values.

> In China, you have no choice but to live with son or daughter, because there is no housing for old people. Therefore, they end up having to stay with their family.
>
> (F-FGD5)

Some participants did not feel that their relationship with their children in their adopted home was reciprocated, and they complained that the financial and domestic support they gave to the family went unnoticed or unappreciated.

Participants generally preferred to live and socialize within the local Chinese community of Melbourne rather than migrate with their children to the more afflu-ent suburbs. Many of those who arrived under family reunion visas lived with their children immediately after arrival, but as they started adjusting to their new environment, they discovered alternative living arrangements. Therefore, among the participants, independent living seemed to be a preferred pattern of settle-ment in the adopted country, and traditional views about family and kinship were discarded where possible. This reflects the findings of other researchers about the living preferences of Chinese migrants (Chen 1996; Fitzgerald et al. 2001; Wan et al. 2008).

There was strong approval among the participants regarding access to health information in Australia, although some participants said that it would be useful if additional information on education and other aspects of life relevant to the needs of a CALD community could be provided (e.g. selecting healthy food and good health products). On the other hand, some participants noted that having informa-tion about health services was a matter of self-initiative.

Still, participants believed that when there is family support there is less need for self-care, although self-help and self-sufficiency are major features of Chinese culture, whether as immigrants (Kwan and Williams 1999) or as residents back in China (Wan et al. 2008). Participants also believed strongly in their own ability to stay healthy and in the virtues of self-reliance.

> The only good thing in Australia is that we have a good welfare system. I don't have to depend on my children, I do what I want. If I still live in Guangzhou, I will be in trouble.
>
> (F-FGD5)

They valued Australia's political democracy and welfare system as a place to achieve growth, social stability and freedom, but they also acknowledged the eco-nomic growth, technology, social change and improvements in living standards happening in China today.

> We are living in a different age. Now we have fewer children than the old time. Resource from the family will not be diluted down. We could concen-trate our family resource with one or two kids. There is racial, cultural and knowledge difference between the old time and now.
>
> (F-FGD3)

They described life in Australia as quiet, peaceful, clean, pleasant and colourful but they were aware of the high taxation required to sustain the social and health services they received in Australia.

Overall, the picture that emerged from the discussions was of older immigrants living not so much in the stereotypical Chinese family composed of multiple generations under the influence of filial piety, but rather living close to their children, but not necessarily in the same household. Nonetheless, the Chinese family would still remain connected strongly to traditional values tempered by the benefits and stresses of intergenerational relationships. This scenario probably reflects acculturation to mainstream Australian society where the benefits of the new society are accepted differently by each generation, young and old, within the comfort of a strong traditional culture (consistent with the findings of Thomas 2003; Chappell 2005; Rao et al. 2006; Wong et al. 2006). Consequently, the heterogeneity of the Chinese community in Melbourne reflects a successful mix of several generations who interact within their own community but also across cultural boundaries to sustain the multicultural fabric of today's Australian society.

Conclusion

This chapter provided a picture not of stereotypes but of the diversity and values of migrant families in Australia today. It explored the influence of culture on health beliefs and behaviours, including and contrasting self-care decisions and negotiations; intergenerational relations; filial-parental obligations and independence and autonomous living; and the implications of such arrangements in healthcare negotiations among older migrants, using the Cantonese-speaking community living in Melbourne as the example. Our overriding finding has been of continuity and change within the rich, diverse and interacting patterns of family life stemming from the stresses and strains of immigration in old age. Another strong view from the participants was that they valued Australia's welfare system and democracy as a place to achieve growth, social stability and new freedom. However, while independent living seems to be a pattern of settlement in our case study sample, traditional family values intergenerational relations still remain. Indeed, family support was not solely from pious children to ageing parents as parents frequently provided financial and other family support. The picture emerged instead of older immigrants' preference to live independently, providing resources for the community and maintaining close intergenerational links and support to their children.

However, considerable differences exist among and within ethno-cultural groups. To assume that all members of a group have the same values and beliefs is stereotyping that can negatively influence the social or health outcomes. Variation in profiles of Australian families is associated with cultural background; however, while some differences are no doubt related to cultural and family values, arrival patterns of immigrants and age distributions of populations also have a significant effect. Economic and generational needs also appear to be associated with multi-generational cohabitation and exchanges. More important, these needs highlight the role of social policies to build interdependency between and within families, and the need to understand individual circumstances. A more in-depth exploration of these interactions is required not only to explore family relations and supports but also the legal, social and economic trends, as they may affect expectations about family and community responsibilities. These must go beyond 'typical' communities' profiles and explore the wider variation within older adult groups.

Future social trends will affect how families and generations interact. Because these trends represent opportunities and challenges, we need to plan for what that will mean now and into the future. From this perspective, it would be imperative to generate new information and make use of the latest information and communications technologies (ICT) to address needs and utilize the economic benefits and significant contributions that older people make as intergenerational carers and economically active members of the community. These ICT technologies need to be accompanied not only by increasing the literacy skills required to maximize their use but also by being sensitive to language and cultural issues. There is also an urgent need to research how different countries are managing intergenerational relations within ethnic migrant groups, and how elderly care policies and programs influence how seniors across a range of cultural backgrounds integrate within those societies. In Australia, we hope that governments will continue to build and implement policies that foster these interdependencies, and that above all continue to recognize the essential contributions that older migrants make to sustain a fair and culturally diverse society.

Notes

1   The term 'culturally and linguistically diverse' (CALD) has been used in Australia since 1996 to designate people born in countries other than Canada, Ireland, New Zealand, South Africa, the United Kingdom and the United States.
2   A more detailed description of this study can be found in the following paper: Mariño, R, Minichiello, V and MacEntee, M 2010, 'Caring for older China-born Australians Immigrants: Issues arising from focus groups', *Health Issues Centre Journal*, vol. 103, pp. 29–32.

References

Alvarado, A 2008, 'Cultural Diversity: Pain Beliefs and Treatment among Mexican-Americans, African-Americans, Chinese-Americans and Japanese-Americans', Senior Honours Theses, Paper 127, Eastern Michigan University.
Alzheimer's Association 2009, *Dementia Care Practice Recommendations for Assisted Living Residences and Nursing Homes*, accessed 9 September 2015, www.alz.org/national/documents/brochure_DCPRphases1n2.pdf
Australian Bureau of Statistics 2011, *Population by Age and Sex, Regions of Australia*, 2011, Cat. no. 3235.0, Australian Bureau of Statistics, Canberra.
Australian Bureau of Statistics 2012, *Reflecting a Nation: Stories from the 2011 Census, 2012–2013*, Cat. no. 2071.0-, Australian Bureau of Statistics, Canberra.
Australian Bureau of Statistics 2014, *Australian Social Trends, 2014*, Cat. no. 4102.0-, Australian Bureau of Statistics, Canberra.
Australian Institute of Health and Welfare 2014, *Australia's Health 2014*, Australia's health Series no. 14, Cat. no. AUS 178, Canberra.
Barnett, K, Mercer, SW, Norbury, M, Watt, G, Wyke, S and Guthrie, B 2012, 'Epidemiology of multimorbidity and implications for health care, research, and medical education: A cross-sectional study', *The Lancet*, vol. 380, pp. 37–43.
Baxter, J, Hayes, A and Gray, M 2011, *Families in Regional, Rural and Remote Australia* (Fact Sheet), Australian Institute of Family Studies, Melbourne.

Berry, J 2005, 'Acculturation: living successfully in two cultures', *International Journal of Intercultural Relations*, vol. 29 pp. 697–712.

Braddock, H 2008, *Truth-telling and Withholding Information*, accessed 28 January 2016, https://depts.washington.edu/bioethx/topics/truth.html

Brondani, MA, Bryant, SR and MacEntee, MI 2007, 'Elders assessment of an evolving model of oral health', *Gerodontology*, vol. 24, pp. 189–195.

Browne, R 2015, *Disability Sector has Grave Concerns about NDIS Roll Out*, accessed 7 December 2015, www.theage.com.au/nsw/disability-sector-has-grave-concerns-about-ndis-roll-out-20151204-glfkny.html#ixzz3taybAg7a

Bubolz, M 1999, 'Intergenerational relationships in today's families', *Michigan Family Review*, vol. 4, pp. 1–3.

Chappell, NL 2005, 'Perceived change in quality of life among Chinese Canadian seniors: The role of involvement in Chinese culture', *Journal of Happiness Studies*, vol. 6, pp. 69–91.

Chen, YL 1996, 'Conformity with nature: A theory of Chinese American elders' health promotion and illness prevention processes', *Advances in Nursing Science*, vol. 19, pp. 17–26.

Chiu, S and Yu, S 2001, 'An excess of culture: The myth of shared care in the Chinese community in Britain', *Ageing & Society*, vol. 21, pp. 681–699.

Coulson, I, Mariño, R and Strang V 2005, 'Dementia and the influence in lifestyle', in V Minichiello and I Coulson (eds), *Contemporary Issues in Gerontology: Promoting Positive Ageing*, Allen and Unwin, Crows Nest, pp. 105–119.

Department of Immigration and Citizenship, 2014, *China-born Community*, Community Information Summary, accessed 8 September 2015, www.dss.gov.au/sites/default/files/documents/02_2014/china.pdf

Erez, M and Early, PC 1993, *Culture, Self-identity and Work*, Oxford University Press Inc, New York.

Fitzgerald, MH, Mullavey-O'Byrne, C and Clemson, L 2001, 'Families and nursing home placements: A cross-cultural study', *Journal of Cross-Cultural Gerontology*, vol. 16, pp. 333–351.

Georgas, J, Berry, J, van de Vijver, F, Kagitcibasi, C and Poortinga, YH 2006, *Families Across Cultures: A 30 Nation Study*, Cambridge University Press, Cambridge.

Harding, E, Wait, S, Siba, N, Pointon, B and Georges, J 2006, *Dementia in my Family Taking an Intergenerational Approach to Dementia*, accessed 9 September 2015, www.ilcuk.org.uk/files/pdf_pdf_24.pdf

Ikels, C 1990, 'The resolution of intergenerational conflict', *Modern China*, vol. 16, pp. 379–406.

Jin, L 2010, 'From mainstream to marginal? Trends in the use of Chinese medicine in China from 1991 to 2004', *Social Science and Medicine*, vol. 71, pp. 1063–1067.

Johnstone, M and Kanitsaki, O 2006, 'Culture, language, and patient safety: Making the link', *International Journal of Quality in Health Care*, vol. 18, no. 5, pp. 383–388.

Johnstone, M and Kanitsaki, O 2007, 'Health service and consumer understandings of cultural safety and cultural competence in health care: An Australian study', *Journal of Cultural Diversity*, vol. 14, no. 2, pp. 96–105.

Kagitcibasi, C, Ataca, B and Diri A 2010, 'Intergenerational relationships in the family: Ethnic, socioeconomic, and country variations in Germany, Israel, Palestine, and Turkey', *Journal of Cross-Cultural Psychology*, vol. 41, pp. 652–670.

Kwan, SYL and Williams, SA 1999, 'Dental beliefs, knowledge and behaviour of Chinese people in the UK', *Community Dental Health*, vol. 16, pp. 33–39.

Larsen, G 2013, *Family Migration to Australia*, Research paper series 2013–14, Commonwealth of Australia, 23 December 2013.

Leong, FTL and Tata, SP 1990, 'Sex and acculturation differences in occupational values among Chinese-American children', *Journal of Counseling Psychology*, vol. 37, pp. 208–212.

Lui, CW 2006, 'Transnational Chinese migration: An Australian profile', in D Ip, R Hibbins and WH Chui (eds), Experiences of Transnational Chinese Migrants in the Asia-Pacific, Nova Science, New York, pp. 17–39.

MacEntee, MI, Mariño, R, Wong, S, Minichiello, V, Chi, I, Lo, E and Lin, H 2012, 'Discussions on oral health care among elderly Chinese immigrants in Melbourne and Vancouver', *Gerodontology*, vol. 29, pp. 822–832.

Mak, AS and Chan, H 1995, 'Chinese family values in Australia', in *Families and Cultural Diversity in Australia*, Australian Institute of Family Studies, Melbourne.

Marcantonio, E 2003, 'Dementia', in M Beers and R Berkow (eds), *The Merck Manual of Geriatrics*, Whitehouse Station, New Jersey.

Mariño, R, Minichiello, V and MacEntee, M 2010, 'Caring for older China-born Australians Immigrants: Issues arising from focus groups', *Health Issues Centre Journal*, vol. 103, pp. 29–32.

MFH Project Group 2004, *The Amsterdam Declaration. Towards Migrant Friendly Hospitals in an Ethno-culturally Diverse Europe*, accessed 7 December 2015, www.mfh-eu. net/public/european_recommendations.htm

Millward, C 1998, *Family Relationships and Intergenerational Exchange in Later Life*, Australian Institute of Family Studies Working Paper No. 15, Australian Institute of Family Studies, Melbourne.

Minas, H, Sullivan, D and Minas, S 2010, 'Culture and expert psychiatric evidence', in I Freckelton and H Selby (eds), *Expert Evidence*, Thomson Reuters, Melbourne, pp. 53–604.

Nguyen, L and Williams, HL 1989, 'Transition from East to West: Vietnamese adolescents and their parents', *Journal of the American Academy of Child and Adolescent Psychiatry*, vol. 28, pp. 505–515.

Paice, J 2002, 'Living arrangements and ethnicity of Australia's older population', *Journal of Population Research*, Special Issue, pp. 159–169.

Rao, V, Warburton J and Bartlett, H 2006, 'Health and Social needs of older Australians from culturally and linguistically diverse backgrounds: Issues and implications', *Australasian Journal on Ageing*, vol. 25, pp. 174–179.

Saraceno, C and Keck, W 2008, *The Institutional Framework of Intergenerational Family Obligations in Europe: A Conceptual and Methodological Overview*, MULTILINKS project, WZB Social Science Research Center, Berlin.

Silverstein, M, Cong, Z and Li, S 2006, 'Intergenerational transfers and living arrangements of older people in rural China: consequences for psychological wellbeing', *The Journals of Gerontology. Series B, Psychological Sciences and Social Sciences*, vol. 61, pp. 256–266.

Stuifbergen, M and Van Delden, JM 2011, 'Filial obligations to elderly parents: A duty to care?' *Medicine, Health Care and Philosophy*, vol. 14, pp. 63–71.

Tharp, RG, Meadow, A, Lennhof, S and Satterfield D 1968, 'Changes in marriage roles accompanying the acculturation of the Mexican-American wife', *Journal of Marriage and Family*, vol. 30, pp. 404–412.

Thomas, T 2003, 'Older migrants and their families in Australia', *Family Matters*, vol. 66, pp. 40–45.

Triandis, HC, Kashima, Y, Shimada, E and Villareal, M 1986, 'Acculturation indices as a means of confirming cultural differences', *International Journal of Psychology*, vol. 21 pp. 43–70.

United Nations 2005, *Living Arrangements of Older Persons around the World*, in United Nations Department of Economic and Social Affairs/Population Division, accessed 9 September 2015, www.un.org/esa/population/publications/livingarrangement/report. htm

Wan, H, Fang, Y and Kolanowski, A 2008, 'Caring for aging Chinese: Lessons learned from the United States', *Journal of Transcultural Nursing*, vol. 19, pp. 114–120.

White, B, Willmott, L, Trowse, P, Parker, M and Cartwright, C 2011, 'The legal role of medical professionals in decisions to withhold or withdraw life-sustaining treatment: Part 1 (New South Wales)', *Journal of Law and Medicine*, vol. 18, pp. 498–522.

Wolf, D, Freedman, V and Soldo, B 1997, 'The division of family labor: Care for elderly parents', *The Journals of Gerontology*, Special Issue, vol. 52, pp. 102–109.

Wong, ST, Yoo, GJ and Stewart, A 2006, 'The changing meaning of family support among older Chinese and Korean immigrants', *Journal of Gerontology: Social Sciences*, vol. 61, pp. 4–9.

World Health Organisation 2011, *Global Status Report on Noncommunicable Diseases 2010: Description of the Global Burden of NCDs, their Risk Factors and Determinants*, World Health Organisation, Geneva, accessed 7 December 2015, www.who.int/nmh/ publications/ncd_report2010/en/

8 Identity, sexuality and stigma in multigenerational households

Perspectives from LGBT household members

Bianca Fileborn, Tiffany Jones and Victor Minichiello

Introduction

This chapter explores some of the emerging issues and challenges facing contemporary lesbian, gay, bisexual and transgender (LGBT) people and their propensity (or not) to live in multigenerational households. Despite extensive research on heteronormative multigenerational families, LGBT multigenerational families represent a significant gap in current knowledge. In this chapter, we seek to address this gap by exploring what little is currently known about multigenerational LGBT families and by drawing on the existing research on LGBT families more generally to provide insight into the potential experiences and unique needs of multigenerational LGBT families. We use the term 'multigenerational LGBT families' broadly throughout this chapter to refer to families with at least two generations of adult family members living together, with at least one member who identifies as LGBT.

In discussing multigenerational LGBT families, it is essential to consider first the historic and contemporary contextual influences on how LGBT families are constructed today. We then move on to consider the current data on the prevalence of LGBT families in Australia, and the experiences of identity, sexuality and stigma for LGBT members of multigenerational families. Finally, we outline key challenges facing these LGBT households and develop an agenda for much needed future inquiry.

Historical trajectories of LGBT families

Until recently, LGBT people were described as, and ascribed to be, outside of the mainstream family unit because they were perceived to be immoral, deviant, criminals or insane. Homosexuality was classified as a mental illness as recently as the 1970s, and up until a few decades ago, conversion therapy was regularly used in Australia in an attempt to 'change' sexual orientation from homosexual to heterosexual (Barrett 2008; Lyons et al. 2015). Within Australia, homosexuality was outlawed in some states as late as the 1990s, although there has undoubtedly been a significant shift in the social acceptance of homosexuality since that time.

Understood from pathology and deviance perspectives, LGBT people were invisible family members, and often sat outside of the sacred and highly protected heterosexual and patriarchal family. This othering and exclusion of LGBT people meant that many disguised or repressed their sexual or gender identity, or risked being ostracized and excluded from the family. Civil and political rights movements throughout the 1960s and 1970s began to challenge dominant discourses on gender and sexuality, and we have slowly witnessed the increased acceptance of LGBT people as valued community and family members.

Despite progress in the acceptance of diverse sexuality and gender, this 'othering' still continues in many respects – and we consider some contemporary examples of this viewpoint later in the chapter. The increased visibility and acceptance of LGBT families is most clearly demonstrated through the legal recognition of same-sex marriage in a number of countries including the Netherlands, the United States, New Zealand and Ireland, with this list continuing to grow. However, same-sex marriage is not legally recognized within Australia at the time of writing, illustrating that LGBT families continue to face state-sanctioned exclusion and marginalization, despite important and significant gains in social acceptance.

The numbers behind same-sex households and families

Until recently, LGBT relationships and families were excluded from government data collection in Australia. Because of this exclusion, the picture that we present here should be considered as partial and emergent. For the first time in 1996, members of same-sex couples were allowed to self-identify as de facto same-sex partners in the Australian census. This allowance was continued in 2006, and by the 2011 census, a new classification was retained that allowed same-sex partners to describe their relationship as husband and wife or de facto partner. However, there are still issues and limitations with the current set of questions asked, or not asked. For example, information on a person's sexual orientation is not collected, and as a result, the census does not provide a complete picture of all LGBT individuals living in Australian households. Furthermore, many gay and lesbian individuals form multigenerational 'families of choice' based on friendship groups rather than biological ties (Smith et al. 2014; Jones et al. 2015). Families of choice are not currently recognized or counted within the census (ABS 2012).

The current official government profile of same-sex households

In Australia in 2011, according to the Australian Bureau of Statistics (ABS), there were 33,714 same-sex couples, the majority of whom (96 per cent) identified their relationship as living with a de facto partner. Despite that at the time of writing Australia had yet to legalize same-sex marriage, 1,338 same-sex couples reported their relationship as husband (gay) or wife (lesbian) (ABS 2011). There were more same-sex male couples (17,600) than same-sex female couples (16,100).

We can now also get a better national profile of how many children live with same-sex couples. The 2011 census reported 6,300 children living in such households, which represents about 12 per cent of same-sex couples having a dependent or adult child living with them (ABS 2012). The majority of these children (89 per cent) lived with female same-sex parents. Approximately 8 per cent of these households had nondependent children; while 14 per cent had dependent students aged 15–24 (ABS 2012). Just over 2 per cent of same-sex couples without children had other relatives living with them, typically a sibling or parent (ABS 2012). These statistics suggest that a significant minority of same-sex couples are living in multigenerational kinship-based households, although not to the same extent as the population more generally where it is suggested that around 20 per cent lived in multigenerational households (Liu et al. 2015). Single gays, lesbians and transgender people are not captured in this dataset, so these figures likely underestimate the true prevalence of LGBT multigenerational households.

Because of the public discussion around gay and lesbian civil rights and changing social attitudes, the census not surprisingly counts more same-sex attracted people. Since 1996, the number of same-sex couples reported in the census has more than tripled, and as stated earlier, the number of children reported to be living in same-sex households is also increasing. These figures are expected to continue to increase over time. However, there is currently no data regarding the number of LGBT multigenerational families living in Australia. This dearth represents a major gap in knowledge. Given that the number of people living in same-sex households has been steadily increasing since the 1996 census, and that this data almost certainly underestimates the true prevalence of LGBT families in Australia, it is reasonable to assume that the number of LGBT multigenerational families is also increasing and deserving of our attention. What, then, are the experiences of Australians living in multigenerational LGBT families?

The voices of LGBT young people

There is, as we have noted, a lack of research that explicitly considers the experiences of multigenerational LGBT families. However, more general Australian studies on LGBT families show that LGBT people engage in multigenerational households in a variety of ways, including when they are living with opposite-sex parents (Smith et al. 2014; Jones 2015; Jones et al. 2015). Of 3,134 same-sex attracted young people aged 14–21 who were asked about their living arrangements in an anonymous online survey, most (71 per cent) were living in the family home (Hillier et al. 2010; Jones 2015). Many found the family home to be an unsupportive environment, but levels of tension among family members fluctuated over time and generally lessened as the young person grew older. For example, Ronan,[1] 20 years old, found his mother and siblings had increasingly accepted his gay sexual orientation over time after initially finding out that he was gay from school and community rumours (Hillier et al. 2010: 16):

> I got scared and told my mum I had shared my secret. She was angry and embarrassed. I had come out to mum in grade eight and nine. I tried to like

girls in between and to find them interesting sexually. It didn't work but I did end up telling people I liked a girl and the rumours ceased till I left town. . . . [A]s I got older I became more comfortable with my sexuality. My mum doesn't like it but she doesn't argue about it like she used to.

A significant proportion of LGBT young adults of these studies, however, reported living outside of their biological family home. Almost one-third of same-sex attracted young people lived outside of their family home (Hillier et al. 2010): a small proportion (4 per cent) lived with relatives and the remainder were living in shared accommodation (12 per cent), on their own (4 per cent), in a boyfriend/ girlfriend's house (4 per cent), in a boarding house (2 per cent), and a small number lived in squats, refuges, streets or caravans (2 per cent). A comparative anonymous online survey of 91 transgender and gender-diverse young people aged 14 to 21 (Jones and Hillier 2013) showed they were less likely to be living at home with the family than same-sex attracted youth (only 51 per cent of gender diverse youth lived at home) and were more likely to be living with relatives (9 per cent) or in shared accommodation (19 per cent). This statistic suggests that, in comparison with their heterosexual counterparts, young LGBT people are perhaps less likely to be living in multigenerational households with their biological families.

Some of the same-sex attracted and transgender young people moved out of the family home at younger ages due to experiences of rejection, homophobic abuse and violence, particularly from parents (Hillier et al. 2010; Jones and Hillier 2013). Ruth, 18 years old, was raised in a Christian family and was made to feel 'constantly embarrassed and disgusted with [herself]' for being gay (Hillier et al. 2010: 93). She was told by her parents that 'it wasn't natural and that it was just a phase that [she] was going through'. She became depressed and suicidal, and moved out after deciding 'that [she] couldn't stay living with [her] parents'. Talon, 20 years old, said, 'I have been beat up numerous times since coming out at 14/15 at school . . . I also got beat and kicked out by my dad when he found out I was gay' (Hillier et al. 2010: 42). Tim, 20 years old, found that being forced to move out of the family home early impacted his work prospects as a young adult significantly (Hillier et al. 2010: 53):

Well my life is bad. I was kicked out of home at 15 when I came out. Because I haven't finished year 10 I cannot be as successful in life as I want to be. After moving out I was poor, had no money. Had no one to go to. I then started drugs, I believe now that I am older I still suffer depression.

For the almost half of transgender and gender-diverse young people in Jones and Hilliers' (2013) study who did not live in the family home, rejection and transphobic violence were common experiences and it had usually not been possible to live out their transgender identities in the presence of family members.

However, families – including multigenerational families – can also provide an important source of support for LGBT young people, and not all LGBT young adults have such negative experiences living with their biological families. For example, an anonymous online survey of 189 gender-diverse and transgender young people aged 14–25 found that parental support was a clear protective factor in their lives (Smith et al. 2014). Overall, 63 per cent of participants had parents or carers who were supportive, and only 33 per cent did not feel that their parents were supportive. Those who had parental support were half as likely to report they had suicidal thoughts (30 per cent compared with 58 per cent of those with no parental/carer support) and twice as likely to see a health professional if they did (32 per cent compared with 16 per cent). Unsurprisingly, they were less likely to have experienced harassment or abuse in the home (15 per cent compared with 40 per cent) and half as likely to report that they had depression (30 per cent compared with 60 per cent). In another study, a few individuals explained that their families were supportive and that living in the family home was enjoyable, such as 18-year-old Al (Hillier et al. 2010: 99):

> I identify as pansexual and genderqueer and refuse to accept that there are only two sexes. My mum is a lesbian and my family is my friends and friends of my mum's who are all queer or queer-friendly. To be honest my sexuality was never really an issue because I was lucky enough to be raised by parents that had many queer friends and relatives.

For those LGBT people who do not enjoy support from their biological family, 'families of choice' are often developed from close friends, partners and community members. Notably, there is virtually no existing data on the number of such 'families of choice' within Australia or, subsequently, the number of multigenerational 'families of choice'. Indeed, this lack raises some questions regarding what constitutes a queer multigenerational family of choice, given that dominant Western constructions of 'family' are typically based heavily on biological kinship (Goldberg and Kuvalanka 2012). For instance, how is a 'generation' defined in families without biological ties? How do LGBT people themselves understand and construct 'generations' within their own families of choice? Clearly, further conceptual and empirical work is required to develop a firmer picture of the queer multigenerational family.

There is some evidence from small-scale survey research, however, to suggest that LGBT people *do* live in multigenerational households. A number of survey respondents in Jones and Hilliers' (2013) study went on to make their own 'queer families' after leaving the biological family home. For example Jo (female-to-male transgender, 21 years old) talked about being kicked out of his home and moving from a rural Victorian town to inner-city Melbourne to live with like-minded people and create his own family-like household (Jones and Hillier 2013: 297):

> I live in a strong and supportive community of queer, trans and feminist people who provide safe spaces for me to live my life and learn how to take care of myself. But this community isn't supported by society at large, it has to support itself.

The practice of 'queer family-creation' among the transgender community in urban areas such as Sydney and Melbourne was also a recurring phenomenon in other recent studies of transgender youth and adults (Smith et al. 2014; Jones et al. 2015). Likewise, an anonymous online survey and facilitated blog discussion board completed by 273 transgender people age 16–64 found 8 per cent described living in multigenerational households with children or grandchildren (Jones et al. 2015). These transgender people became parents in a variety of ways: most commonly through having had their own biological children prior to transition, having children through their partners subsequent to transition, through fostering and adoption or through avoiding sterilizing surgeries during their path to gender affirmation.

Together, the research presented here holds a number of implications for multigenerational LGBT families. First, despite an almost complete absence of research specifically focused on multigenerational LGBT families, there is evidence from LGBT family studies illustrating that LGBT people live in multigenerational households across a number of different contexts. More important, LGBT people's experiences of living in multigenerational households are likely to be distinct from their heterosexual counterparts, notably because of the role of homophobia and transphobia within biological families resulting in these young adults leaving the traditional family home. Homophobia and transphobia, and indeed even the *anticipation of* homophobia and transphobia, often created tensions between different generations living together in the studies examined. However, experiencing homophobia and transphobia was not a universal experience, suggesting that there are also important differences within and between LGBT community members living in multigenerational households.

The challenges facing LGBT families

The following section explores a small number of current issues and challenges that are, in some respects, unique to LGBT families, or are experienced by them in unique or particular ways, and considers the implications of these for multigenerational households. Many of the challenges that LGBT families face are exacerbated, if not caused, by the discrimination and marginalization that these families encounter, rather than being inherent to LGBT families themselves.

Discrimination and marginalization

Despite the increasing acceptance of LGBT communities, these communities continue to face significant levels of discrimination, marginalization and stigma (Crouch et al. 2014). LGBT families are positioned as invisible or as a less 'valid' family structure in the context of a heteronormative society (Lynch 2004; Pennington and Knight 2011; Sasnett 2015). This invisibility can necessitate processes of 'coming out' to other family members, friends, service providers and so forth, and can require constant negotiation and evaluation of whether it is 'safe' to do so (Joos and Broad 2007). Likewise, the reification of heteronormative family structures positions LGBT families as 'other', a positioning that can have conse-quences for the social and emotional well-being of family members – although both Lynch (2004) and Sasnett (2015) note that the impacts of heteronormativity and social exclusion can be buffered by the often strong and supportive bonds formed within LGBT families. Experiences of discrimination and social exclu-sion can also vary significantly for different members of LGBT families, across different family contexts and across different social and political climates (Lynch 2004; Lick et al. 2013). It remains largely unclear how LGBT people in multigen-erational families experience discrimination and social exclusion, and whether or not in which contexts multigenerational families may buffer or compound the impacts of discrimination.

Such experiences of discrimination and marginalization contribute toward LGBT families having higher levels of negative health outcomes, a phenomenon Meyer (2003) terms 'minority stress'. Minority stress is directly associated with poorer mental and physical health outcomes, including higher levels of suicide (Meyer 2003; Crouch et al. 2014). Levels of minority stress and subsequent health outcomes also differ across different family contexts, and not all LGBT families experience minority stress in the same way (Lick et al. 2013). In addition, experi-ences of minority stress and stigma can shift and change across the life course, with members of LGBT families typically learning to cope with or 'manage' this stress over time (Lick et al. 2013). Nonetheless, stigma and discrimination (whether real or perceived) is linked to a range of negative outcomes for mem-bers of LGBT families (Crouch et al. 2014). Given that LGBT multigenerational families of choice are virtually invisible in Australia, this suggests that they may be a particularly marginalized family structure. The extent to which this adds to the effects of stigma and discrimination, or the ways in which multigenerational LGBT families contest and challenge this positioning, remains unexplored.

LGBT families in an ageing society

Populations across a number of Western countries are rapidly aging. In Australia, population projections estimate that by 2061, the proportion of the population aged 60 and over will increase to 22 per cent from the current proportion of 14 per cent (ABS 2013a). The ageing of the population has several implications for LGBT individuals and families, although some of these are also shared with the population more generally.

As the population ages, with it comes an increased number of older LGBT individuals who will require care either within the family home or in residential care facilities. Medical institutions have represented a key site of harm against the LGBT communities, and the medical sector played a significant role in managing and responding to homosexuality (Barrett 2008; Pennington and Knight 2011; Department of Health and Ageing 2012). This undoubtedly shaped the experi-ences that LGBT people had with the medical industry, and likely continues to shape the willingness of some LGBT people to access medical care (Barrett 2008; Price 2012).

LGBT people continue to experience discrimination within healthcare settings, which can include overt discrimination in the form of heterosexist abuse from health professionals, but may also include subtle or covert forms of discrimination, such as the absence of LGBT-appropriate medical advice and policy, or the assumption that clients are cis-gendered and heterosexual (e.g. Willis et al. 2011; Price 2012; Barrett et al. 2015). The fear or perception that they will experience discrimination can also lead to LGBT people avoiding or delaying accessing healthcare service (Cohen and Murray 2006; Price 2012). In turn, this delay may place increased stress or burden on family members providing care for older LGBT people – assuming that they are, in fact, willing to provide this care – within the family home, and negatively affect the health and well-being of these older LGBT people (Blank et al. 2009; Barrett et al. 2015). This situation may be further compounded by the poorer physical and mental health outcomes experienced by LGBT people on account of minority stress, and, particularly for some gay men and transgender people, complications from HIV (Brennan-Ing et al. 2014). It is currently unclear what impact some of these issues may have within multigenerational family households. For example, it seems likely that a lack of appropriate LGBT elderly residential care services could cause difficulties for multigenerational families seeking support for an elder, and that LGBT people may encounter more limited care options as they age (Barrett 2008). To what extent are carers from queer families of choice recognized and supported? These issues remain under-examined in the current literature.

The aging population means that LGBT people may increasingly need to fulfil caring roles for members of their biological or choice families, including within the context of a multigenerational household. As we have seen, families of origin can be a significant source of abuse and hostility toward LGBT individuals (see also Connolly 2005; Blank et al. 2009), or at least may be characterized by strained relationships (Scherrer 2010). Evidence suggests that some LGBT adults take on caring responsibilities for biological family members in later life, such as parents, or must work collaboratively with other family members in providing care to a parent who had been abusive and unaccepting of their sexual orientation (Cohen and Murray 2006; Cronin et al. 2010; Price 2012). LGBT adults without children can face pressure from other siblings to take on caring responsibilities (Cronin et al. 2010; Price 2012). For some LGBT people, taking on a caring role for biological family members can provide an opportunity for 'healing' or renegotiating previously strained or abusive relationships (e.g. Price 2012; Barrett et al. 2015). For others, providing care within such a context can add to the pressures and stressors associated with being a carer (Cohen and Murray 2006).

Although biological family members can provide an important source of support in older age, for LGBT people members of their family of choice frequently fulfil these roles instead (e.g. Fredriksen 1999; Muraco and Fredriksen-Goldsen 2011; 2014; Washington et al. 2015). These caring relationships and family arrangements are not always formally recognized by the state or healthcare organizations, and this can limit the external support and validation of caring roles provided to carers within families of choice. As a result, for example, LGBT people can be denied access to their partner in hospital settings, be unable to make legal and medical decisions on behalf of another family member, excluded from policy and practice guidelines, and be ineligible for government assistance in the face of their partner passing away (e.g. Blank et al. 2009; Westwood 2013; Washington et al. 2015). However, this situation is slowly changing, particularly in countries where same-sex marriage has been legalized. LGBT carers may also be reluctant to access support services due to fear of discrimination and abuse (Cohen and Murray 2006; Blank et al. 2009; Washington et al. 2015).

Together, this suggests that LGBT people providing care in multigenerational households are likely to face a range of challenges and stressors related to their gender identity or sexual orientation not encountered by their heterosexual counterparts (Price 2012). There is a clear need to explore further the unique experiences of LGBT carers in multigenerational families, and to determine the impacts of being a carer (particularly to hostile parents) and the support needs of LGBT carers.

Violence and abuse

There is evidence to suggest that LGBT communities and families experience considerable levels of violence and abuse across a range of different contexts. Heterosexist violence and abuse continues to be a common experience for LGBT communities, which contributes toward and amplifies the marginalization and discrimination faced by these communities. Less commonly acknowledged is the violence that can occur *within* LGBT families. While this can also include forms of heterosexist violence (Smith et al. 2014) – for example, from hostile family members – LGBT people can also experience violence and abuse from their partners, children and members of their families of choice (although almost all existing research focuses on violence between LGBT intimate partners). The research conducted to date illustrates that intimate partner or family violence is experienced by LGBT people at a similar rate to their heterosexual counterparts (Leonard et al. 2008; Duke and Davidson 2009; Fileborn 2012). Yet, their experiences remain largely unacknowledged and excluded from dominant discourses on family violence, and there is virtually no current research explicitly addressing violence within multigenerational LGBT families within Australia – although our earlier discussion illustrated that LGBT young adults commonly experience violence and abuse within the multigenerational biological family home.

It is unclear, however, whether LGBT people in multigenerational families are more likely to experience violence from multiple perpetrators within the family, or whether the invisibility of these families acts as a barrier to seeking help and support. Support services can hold heteronormative understandings of family violence, or may lack an awareness of the specific needs or dynamics of multigenerational LGBT family and relationship structures and dynamics (English 2011; Fileborn 2012). For example, families of choice are often excluded or ignored within current theoretical and conceptual understandings of family violence. LGBT family violence can also be excluded from legislative definitions, although this of course varies dramatically across different jurisdictions (Brown 2008). Such understandings can result in LGBT victims struggling to identify their own experiences as constituting family violence (Bornstein et al. 2006; Baker et al. 2013; Fileborn 2014). Again, there is a need to document and explore experiences of family violence within multigenerational LGBT families, to identify any unique aspects of such experiences and to ensure that relevant and appropriate support services are developed in response.

Conclusion

Throughout this chapter, we have presented an emerging picture of multigenerational LGBT families in Australia. Although the extant literature and research on this issue is currently thin, evidence suggests that LGBT people live in multigenerational families, and we must ensure that these families do not remain hidden in research and policy agendas. Many positive reforms have been introduced over the past few decades in Australia, including the decriminalization of homosexuality, and a range of legislative and equity reforms relating to workplace discrimination, pension, superannuation and better access to health and social services. Yet, Australian multigenerational LGBT families continue to face considerable challenges, and there is an urgent need for research to better understand and document the particular experiences of multigenerational LGBT families. The knowledge landscape has significant gaps in relation to multigenerational families.

As we have argued in this chapter, many more questions require additional and careful investigation. For example, the ways in which sexual orientation and/or gender identity intersects with gender, cultural and religious identities within multigenerational families requires deconstructing. Nor do we have many studies that have delved deeply into how peers, employers, neighbours, teachers, grandparents and other family members interact with and within multigenerational LGBT households, and what, if any, are the differences or impacts of such interactions.

Researchers need to delve more deeply into the intergenerational interactions between older and younger LGBT people, the household arrangements of older LGBT people and those who take on the role of caregiver for a family member or friend within these family structures. Given the recent statistics on the greying of HIV, future studies will also need to closely examine how older LGBT people who are living with HIV manage their household arrangements and access informal care from biological and choice families.

It is equally important to understand the intended and unintended actions and reactions of homophobia and transphobia on multigenerational households, and on their creation, adaption and maintenance. Understanding the stories and narratives of people living in multigenerational LGBT families will be important to developing informed educational and social support programs and reducing some of the negative impacts of the homophobia and transphobia still held by some segments of the population. Likewise, we must work to ensure that family services – such as family violence services, carer-support services and so forth – are responsive to and inclusive of the specific and diverse needs of multigenerational

LGBT families. Researchers should not study LGBT families and households as a homogeneous group. Rather they need to tease out the life experiences and specific social, economic and cultural context of LGBT households living with adult children, LGBT younger adult children living with parents, LGBT older adult children living with and providing care to parents and all of the above in families of choice as well as biological and legally adopted families.

Note

1   The names used to discuss research participants' stories in this chapter are pseudonyms allocated to the participants within the studies cited.

References

ABS 2011, *Counts of Same-sex Couples in the 2011 Census*, Australian Bureau of Statistics, Canberra, accessed 10 June 2015, www.abs.gov.au/websitedbs/censushome.nsf/home/factssheetsssc?opendocument&navpos=450

ABS 2012, *Same-sex Couple Relationships Reflecting a Nation: Stories from the 2011 Census, 2012–2013*, Cat. no. 2071.0, Australian Bureau of Statistics, Canberra.

ABS 2013a, *Population Projections Australia*, Cat. no. 3222.0, Australian Bureau of Statistics, Canberra.

ABS 2013b, *Same-sex Couples*, Cat. No. 4102.0, Australian Bureau of Statistics, Canberra.

Baker, NL, Buick, JD, Kim, SR, Moniz, S and Nava, KL 2013, 'Lessons from examining same-sex intimate partner violence', *Sex Roles*, vol. 69, pp. 182–192.

Barrett, C 2008, *My People: A Project Exploring the Experiences of Gay, Lesbian, Bisexual, Transgender and Intersex Seniors in Aged-care Services*, Matrix Guild Victoria Inc., Melbourne.

Barrett, C, Whyte, C, Comfort, J, Lyons, A and Crameri, P 2015, 'Social connection, relationships and older lesbian and gay people', *Sexual and Relationship Therapy*, vol. 30, no. 1, pp. 131–142

Blank, TO, Asencio, M, Descartes, L and Griggs, J 2009, 'Intersection of older GLBT health issues: Aging, health, and GLBTQ family and community life', *Journal of GLBT Family Studies*, vol. 5, pp. 9–34.

Bornstein, DR, Fawcett, J, Sullivan, M, Senturia, KD and Shiu-Thornton, S 2006, 'Understanding the experiences of lesbian, bisexual and trans survivors of domestic violence: A qualitative study', *Journal of Homosexuality*, vol. 51, no. 1, pp. 159–181.

Brennan-Ing, M, Seidel, L, Larson, B and Karpiak, SE 2014, 'Social care networks and older LGBT adults: Challenges for the future', *Journal of Homosexuality*, vol. 61, no. 1, pp. 21–52.

Brown, C 2008, 'Gender-role implications on same-sex intimate partner abuse', *Journal of Family Violence*, vol. 23, pp. 457–462.

Cohen, HL and Murray, Y 2006, 'Older lesbian and gay caregivers: Caring for families of choice and caring for families of origin', *Journal of Human Behavior in the Social Environment*, vol. 14, no. 1, pp. 275–298.

Connolly, CM 2005, 'A process of change: The intersection of the GLBT individual and their family of origin', *Journal of GLBT Family Studies*, vol. 1, no. 1, pp. 5–20.

Cronin, A, Ward, R, Pugh, S, King, A and Price, E 2010, 'Categories and their consequences: Understanding and supporting the caring relationships of older lesbian, gay and bisexual people', *International Social Work*, vol. 54, no. 2, pp. 421–435.

Crouch, SR, Waters, E, McNair, R, Power, J and Davis, E 2014, 'Parent-reported measures of child health and wellbeing in same-sex parent families: A cross-sectional survey', *BMC Public Health*, vol. 14, pp. 635–646.

Department of Health and Ageing 2012, *National Lesbian, Gay, Bisexual, Transgender and Intersex Ageing and Aged Care Strategy*, Department of Health and Ageing, Canberra.

Duke, A and Davidson, MM 2009, 'Same-sex intimate partner violence: Lesbian, gay, and bisexual affirmative outreach advocacy', *Journal of Aggression, Maltreatment and Trauma*, vol. 18, pp. 795–816.

English, P 2011, 'Words matter: Defining victims in state domestic violence statutes', *International Perspectives in Victimology*, vol. 6, no. 1, pp. 1–8.

Fileborn, B 2012, *Sexual Violence and Gay, Lesbian, Bisexual, Trans, Intersex and Queer Communities*, ACSSA Resource Sheet, Australian Institute of Family Studies, Melbourne.

Fileborn, B 2014, 'Accounting for space, place and identity: GLBTIQ young adults' experiences and understandings of unwanted sexual attention in clubs and pubs', *Critical Criminology*, vol. 22, pp. 81–97.

Fredriksen, KI 1999, 'Family caregiving responsibilities among lesbians and gay men', *Social Work*, vol. 44, no. 2, pp. 142–155.

Goldberg, AE and Kuvalanka, KA 2012, 'Marriage (in)equality: The perspectives of adolescents and emerging adults with lesbian, gay, and bisexual parents', *Journal of Marriage and Family*, vol. 74, pp. 34–52.

Hillier, L, Jones, T, Monagle, M, Overton, N, Gahan, L, Blackman, J and Mitchell, A 2010, *Writing Themselves in 3: The Third National Study on the Sexual Health and Wellbeing of Same-sex Attracted and Gender Questioning Young People*, Australian Research Centre in Sex, Health and Society, Melbourne.

Jones, T 2015, *Policy and Gay, Lesbian, Bisexual, Transgender and Intersex Students*, Springer, London.

Jones, T, del Pozo de Bolger, A, Dunne, T, Lykins, A and Hawkes, G 2015, *Female-to-Male (FtM) Transgender People's Experiences in Australia*, Springer, London.

Jones, T and Hillier, L 2013, 'Comparing trans-spectrum and same-sex attracted youth: Increased risks, increased activisms', *LGBT Youth*, vol. 10, no. 4, pp. 287–307.

Joos, KE and Broad, KL 2007, 'Coming out of the family closet: Stories of adult women with LGBTQ parent(s)', *Qualitative Sociology*, vol. 30, pp. 275–295.

Leonard, W, Mitchell, A, Pitts, M, Patel, S, and Fox, C 2008, *Coming Forward: The Underreporting of Heterosexist Violence and Same Sex Partner Abuse in Victoria*, Australian Research Centre in Sex, Health and Society, Melbourne.

Lick, DJ, Patterson, CJ and Schmidt, KM 2013, 'Recalled social experiences and current psychological adjustment among adults reared by gay and lesbian parents', *Journal of GLBT Family Studies*, vol. 9, pp. 230–253.

Liu, E, Easthope, H, Judd, B and Burnley, I 2015, 'Housing multigenerational households in Australian cities: Evidence from Sydney and Brisbane at the turn of the twenty-first century', in R Dufty-Jones and D Rogers (eds), *Housing in Twenty-first Century Australia: Contemporary Debates*, Ashgate, Aldershot, pp. 21–37.

Lynch, JM 2004, 'Becoming a stepparent in gay/lesbian stepfamilies: Integrating identities', *Journal of Homosexuality*, vol. 48, no. 2, pp. 45–60.

Lyons, A, Croy, S, Barrett, C and Whyte, C 2015, 'Growing old as a gay man: How life has changed for the gay liberation generation', *Ageing and Society*, vol. 35, no. 10, pp. 2229–2250.

Meyer, IH 2003, 'Prejudice, social stress, and mental health in lesbian, gay, and bisexual populations: Conceptual issues and research evidence', *Psychological Bulletin*, vol. 129, no. 5, pp. 674–697.

Muraco, A and Fredriksen-Goldsen, KI 2011, '"That's what friends do": Informal caregiving for chronically ill midlife and older lesbian, gay, and bisexual adults', *Journal of Social and Personal Relationships*, vol. 28, no. 8, pp. 1073–1092.

Muraco, A and Fredriksen-Goldsen, KI 2014, 'The highs and lows of caregiving for chronically ill lesbian, gay, and bisexual elders', *Journal of Gerontological Social Work*, vol. 57, no. 2–4, pp. 251–272.

Sasnett, S 2015, 'Are the kids all right? A qualitative study of adults with gay and lesbian parents', *Journal of Contemporary Ethnography*, vol. 44, no.2, pp. 196–222.

Scherrer, KS 2010, 'The intergenerational family relationships of grandparents and GLBQ grandchildren', *Journal of GLBT Family Studies*, vol. 6, pp. 229–264.

Smith, E, Jones, T, Ward, R, Dixon, J, Mitchell, A and Hillier, L 2014, *From Blues to Rainbows: The Mental Health and Well-being of Gender Diverse and Transgender Young People in Australia*, Australian Research Centre in Sex, Health and Society, Melbourne.

Pennington, J and Knight, T 2011, 'Through the lens of hetero-normative assumptions: Re-thinking attitudes towards gay parenting', *Culture, Health and Sexuality*, vol. 13, no. 1, pp. 59–72.

Price, E 2012, 'Gay and lesbian carers: Ageing in the shadow of dementia', *Ageing and Society*, vol. 32, pp. 516–532.

Washington, KT, McElroy, J, Albright, D, Paker Oliver, D, Lewis, A, Meadows, S and Elliott, S 2015, 'Experiences of sexual and gender minorities caring for adults with non-AIDS-related chronic illnesses', *Social Work Research*, vol. 39, no. 2, pp. 71–81.

Westwood, S 2013, ' "My friends are my family": An argument about the limitations of contemporary law's recognition of relationships in later life', *Journal of Social Welfare and Family Law*, vol. 35, no. 3, pp. 347–363.

Willis, P, Ward, N and Fish, J 2011, 'Searching for LGBT carers: Mapping a research agenda in social work and social care', *British Journal of Social Work*, vol. 41, pp. 1304–1320.

9 Housing design for multigenerational living

Bruce Judd

Introduction

Multigenerational households have two or more adult generations of a family occupying the same dwelling. The *Oxford Dictionary of Sociology* defines a household as 'a group of persons sharing a home or living space, who aggregate and share their income, as evidenced by the fact that they regularly take meals together' (Scott and Marshall 2009). A household is thus a socio-spatial entity where the social and physical components are interdependent, so change in one component will inevitably affect the other. While the social component (the family) changes over time and with circumstances, the physical environment (the dwelling) is relatively fixed in space and time, and its adaptation more difficult. Given the extent of multigenerational living in Australia and its likely future growth, the design of the dwelling and how well or not it supports such households is an important issue. Do these families simply adapt to an existing dwelling design, make modifications, or move to more suitable housing, and what responses to the needs of multigenerational households are forthcoming from housing policy, designers and the housing industry?

This chapter examines housing design for multigenerational living. It draws on an online survey of 392 residents from multigenerational households, 21 solicited diaries and 21 in-depth interviews in metropolitan Sydney and Brisbane as part of the Australian Research Council Discovery Project *Living Together: The Rise of Multigenerational Households in Australian Cities* in addition to an examination of local and international multigenerational housing prototypes and industry products. Participants were recruited via university staff and student online portals and local newspaper advertisements in local government areas with high concentrations of multigenerational household residents. Although households with tertiary students were slightly overrepresented, participants were broadly representative of the Australian population in terms of household make-up, dwelling structure and tenure. For more detailed descriptions of these methods, see Liu et al. (2015) and also Chapters 3 and 5 of this book.

In this study, a multigenerational household was defined as '. . . any household in which more than one generation of lineally related adults (i.e. of parental-offspring relations co-residing in the same household), with the oldest of the youngest generation being 18 years or older' (Liu et al. 2015: 24). This is not to be confused with different (unrelated) generations living in separate dwellings in a multiunit complex, which in Europe is also known as multigenerational living or housing.

Theoretical perspectives

Environment-behaviour theory, which emerged in the 1960s–70s, has provided a useful lens for understanding the relationship between housing design and human behaviour discussed in this chapter. It stressed the interdependency of human behaviour and the physical environment as opposed to physical determinism, which purports that environmental design has a direct and causal influence on human behaviour (Rapoport 1969). Rather, the physical environment is seen as typically neutral, supportive or inhibitive of human behaviour (Barker 1963). The household as socio-spatial entity reflects Barker's (1968) seminal concept of a 'behaviour setting' which he observed as comprising both social and physical components that were interdependent or symbiotic, the survival of which depended on the degree of fit, or congruence, between the social and physical components. Environment-behaviour theory also explains the dynamics of human spatial behaviour in terms of privacy, personal space, territory and crowding – issues all relevant to multigenerational living.

Westin's (1970: 7) foundational work on privacy conceptualized it as 'the claim of individuals, groups or institutions to determine for themselves when, how, and to what extent information about them is communicated to others involving 'the voluntary and temporary withdrawal of a person from the general society through physical or psychological means, either in a state of solitude or small group intimacy, or, when among large groups, in a condition of anonymity or reserve'. He proposed that privacy served four main functions: the need for 'personal autonomy', 'emotional release', 'self-evaluation' and 'limited and protected communication'.

Drawing on Westin's understanding of privacy, Altman (1975: 18) defined privacy as 'selective control of access to the self or one's group', but also considered its relationship to other forms of human spatial behaviour, such as personal space, territory and crowding. He argued that privacy was the central regulatory process of human spatial behaviour, with personal space, verbal and nonverbal behaviours and territorial behaviour as physical environmental mechanisms used to regulate privacy. Crowding, on the other hand, he proposed, was a psychological state where such mechanisms fail to enable control over privacy. More important, he noted that privacy cannot be regarded simply as a state of isolation from others, 'but as a changing, self/other boundary regulation process in which a person or a group sometimes wants to be separated from others and sometimes wants to be in contact with others' (Altman 1975: 207). In other words, it is a dialectic process that is dynamic, varying in time, circumstances and the nature of relationships with others in the situation as well as with the nature of the physical environment. Therefore, he argued that 'environmental designers should create environments that permit different degrees of control over contact with others' (Altman 1975:

207). Both Westin's and Altman's theories of privacy have been largely supported and built on by numerous scholars (e.g. Margulis 1979; Sundstrum and Sundstrum 1986; Kupris 2000) and have thus stood up well to examination over time (Margulis 2003). Altman's theory has also been used to study desired and achieved privacy in multigenerational homes in the United States by Gale and Park (2010).

More recent theories from human geography have also provided insights into the complex relationships between people and the environments they inhabit that are also relevant to multigenerational living. Assemblage theory (Deleuze and Guattari 1987; De Landa 2006), which has been applied to housing by many scholars (e.g. Jacobs et al. 2007; McFarlane 2011; Jacobs 2012), views housing as complex assemblages of human and nonhuman elements. For example, Klocker and Gibson's recent ethnographic study of ten extended family households in Wollongong, Australia, regarded such households as 'assemblages of people, spaces and things of which they are comprised' (2012: 2241) and also observed that 'many extended family households are not intended to be permanent – fragmentation is part of their lifestyle' (2012: 2246). Dwelling type, size, design and the objects of the household were considered important for regulating privacy and maintaining independence.

Multigenerational households and their dwellings

From customized census tables (ABS 2013), the *Living Together* study found that in 2011 around one-fifth of all Australians lived in multigenerational households, representing one-quarter of all households and one-third of all family households. The highest proportion of any age group living in multigenerational households was 18–19 year olds (72 per cent), followed by 20–24 year olds (44 per cent) and 45–54 year olds (33 per cent). Over half (59 per cent) of these households included at least one resident aged 55 and older. Multigenerational households were more commonly found in the middle- and outer-suburban areas of Australia, with the majority (89 per cent) living in detached rather than semi-detached (6 per cent) or apartment (5 per cent) dwellings. Most owned their homes, although the proportion of outright owners had gradually declined between 1986 (53 per cent) and 2011 (38 per cent). For a more detailed description of the demographic characteristics of multigenerational households in Australia, see Liu et al. (2015) and Chapter 2 of this book.

The increasing propensity for young adults in Australia to live with their parents is reflected in the 2012–13 *Living Together* online survey findings, where participating multigenerational households most typically were composed of middle-aged parents and their adult offspring (58 per cent) some of whom (19 per cent) had previously left home but returned (known as 'boomeranging'). The survey respondents also included three-generation multigenerational households (15 per cent), and households where older adults (aged 35 or older) lived in the same dwelling as their parents (8 per cent), including a mix of adult offspring boomeranging to the parental home and older parents moving in with their adult offspring.

The pros and cons of multigenerational living

The reasons the *Living Together* survey respondents live together in multigenerational households are discussed in detail in Chapter 3 of this book. These included a range of (predominantly) financial and care reasons, and to a lesser extent the younger adults not having left the family home or having boomeranged due to relationship breakdown or returning from working and/or studying overseas. Survey respondents were mostly positive about multigenerational living, with over three-quarters (78 per cent) citing companionship and support in the home as a positive aspect of this living arrangement. Financial benefits, while an important reason given for living in a multigenerational family, were stated as a positive aspect by only 14 per cent of respondents, practicality and convenience by 12 per cent, intergenerational solidarity or opportunity to uphold generational contract by 11 per cent and care arrangements by 5 per cent. These are primarily economic and psychosocial reasons without direct reference to the dwelling.

However, in terms of the negative aspects of multigenerational living, dwelling design-related issues became more evident. Concerns about lack of privacy and interference were by far the most commonly cited by more than half (59 per cent) of respondents. Second was the negative impact of multigenerational living on intra- and interfamilial relationships (19 per cent), and third was tension over sharing of chores and family members not 'pitching in' (14 per cent). These concerns were followed by (inadequate) space (9 per cent), lack of flexibility and having to make compromises (7 per cent) and noise (3 per cent). While only space and noise may appear to be specifically dwelling-related concerns, in reviewing the subsequent interviews and diary entries it became apparent that inappropriate housing design also has contributed to problems of privacy, intra- and intergenerational tensions and compromises arising from inflexibility.

Privacy and dwelling design

What the interviews and diaries revealed was that privacy regulation in a multi-generational household has both social and spatial dimensions influenced by the design of the dwelling. Sometimes conflicts arose predominantly from the social demands of living together when generations have different lifestyles and preferences. For example, one university student interviewed who had never left home stated:

> I feel like – well if you lived alone you could just invite whoever you want to your house and have whatever parties you want, whatever social affairs and they wouldn't know about it. So maybe that's the privacy I'm getting at, not so much, oh they're invading my personal space but just being able to have parties or see people without the questioning. Sometimes . . . I go, "oh okay I'm going out for lunch now". "Who are you going with? Oh I don't know that name, who's that?" Whereas if I lived alone no one would be asking me "where are you going who are you going with". So that might be the privacy thing.

This reflects the aspect of privacy as control over information about oneself. Yet, this may also have a spatial dimension through territorial behaviour as a privacy regulatory mechanism involving components of the physical environment (spaces, walls, doors, etc.), as evidenced in her continuing comments:

> I mean now I actually have a lock on my bedroom door, I didn't use to at my old house . . . but the privacy without a lock on your door was [laughs] like – because they just barge in whenever and they're just like: "oh, hi" [laughs].

She concluded that self-contained accommodation, either on-site or next door, would be preferable:

> Yeah, I think the self-containment, or even I've heard of people who live next door or their parents live behind them – the house behind. So I don't know if it'd be like actually living in the same house after you get married because you kind of want to go and make your own family and live somewhere else . . . but I wouldn't mind living very close [laughs].

In some participating multigenerational families, while differences in lifestyle flourished, this did not result in conflict, but did underline the importance of being able to retreat into an individual territory. In one case where two sons of parents in their sixties had 'boomeranged' following separation, the busyness and diversity was not seen as a problem as individuals' bedrooms acted as personal territories, while family members came together for meals:

> Eldest son returned home for his week off. Also, second son returned home from the Sunshine Coast. So now there are 3 adult children in the house and suddenly the house has become busier – for example, the television is turned on more frequently, the phone rings more frequently. Everyone does their own thing during this time, like visiting friends/family, going to the gym, and they also spend a lot of time in their own space in their respective bedrooms, but everyone usually comes together for meals.
>
> [Diary]

Others used avoidance behaviour to optimize privacy. When asked if she could hide away in her room without being bothered, this daughter in her twenties who lived with her divorced mother in her fifties and younger half-siblings, explained how she used time as a means of controlling privacy. This could represent a way of coping with an unsupportive dwelling design.

> Not always. I mean sometimes I can but then to be fair the times that I do that, it's probably when people are at school or at work and I don't have to go to uni that day or something like that. Or my time is after everyone else has gone to bed, it tends to be the case. So I think that's why a lot of people my

age tend to stay up really late because they need time to do their own thing without having siblings come and bug them.

[Interview]

A number of participants, however, from both older and younger generations saw the design of the dwelling as directly contributing to interference and lack of privacy. For this woman in her thirties living with her husband, infant child and parents, a lack of individual space (territory) for socializing with her partner or friends made multigenerational living difficult.

It can be difficult to find any alone time when you live in a multigenerational household. It can be hard to find time or space for personal discussions with friends or my husband without either [of] the older generation present. You never get the opportunity to watch TV or read a book by yourself as there are always other people around wanting to do things with you or talk to you.

[Diary]

An older woman in her sixties living with her daughter and husband also found the design of the house contributed to privacy violations by her son-in-law.

My only real problem is privacy. [My daughter] is all right but [my son-in-law] walks through without a knock or hesitation. Their store room is in the middle of my flat and as far as he is concerned, it's his house. The same with my property. He never asks to use anything of mine and mostly doesn't put it back, sometimes [leaves it] out in the weather to be ruined.

[Interview]

These responses indicate the complexity of privacy problems in multigenerational households, not always directly resulting from, but often contributed to, by an unsupportive dwelling design. They also suggest the possible benefit of better territory-defining design to create greater self-containment within the dwelling by zoning of the house through the creation of alternative living areas with associated bathrooms and storage for each generation, as well as territorial definition for individuals within each generation.

Inadequate space

For some interviewees, inadequate space in the home contributed to dissatisfaction with multigenerational living. This was particularly the case where adult children had boomeranged after leaving home, in some cases having returned with children and/or a partner. According to one woman in her sixties whose two sons had moved in following relationship breakdowns:

Our house is kind of small and built before the Second World War so it was not designed for today's modern way of using space, so it doesn't really accommodate a lot of adults being in the house at any one time, let alone all of the grandchildren! We never really did any major renovations to our house because my husband and I never envisaged that our children would be living with us when they were adults . . . and married . . . and with children.

[Diary]

She went on to explain how they coped with the inconvenience of not having enough space, and the additional burden of household duties, especially when grandchildren came for the weekend:

So we have to make do with using the space that we have and using it inventively! This situation actually generates a lot of physical work for me and my husband because we need to ensure that stuff is picked up/put away/tidied/cleaned, etc. on a very regular basis – otherwise the house can degenerate into an untidy/unappealing/unhealthy state of chaos in a very short time. There are only three bedrooms, so when my youngest son is here he sleeps in the sun room which is an enclosed veranda that we have converted into a bedroom (with two single beds and a double bed). When any of our six grandchildren spend the weekend with us they also sleep in this room. So, resources are strained at the times when everyone is home at the same time.

[Diary]

Boomeranging often happens unexpectedly and can place great strain on space in the home as another woman in her sixties and her husband found when their divorced daughter moved in with two small children. When discussing what was most difficult for both of them, she stated: 'well, loss of space, fitting everything in physically'. She went on to explain the circumstances:

Our living together began three years ago when my daughter and her husband separated unexpectedly, and my daughter had to move from her home to enable it to be sold. On very short notice we had to find room for all her household possessions, and those of her children. So the beginning was sudden and traumatic – for her emotionally and for all of us having to adjust to a lack of space.

[Diary]

This negatively affected more than one generation. Her daughter did not find adjusting to living with her parents again easy:

[Daughter] had left home at 18. She had a husband and two children and had built two houses, both on acreage. So she felt very constrained and frustrated living back with her parents, and irritated to have to say where she was going and when she would be back. We did not want to monitor her movements, but wanted to know whether to expect her for meals or not. Being a full-time mum at that time she didn't have a job to go to, she had to spend much time in the house. . . . We only have one lounge room and she spent a lot of time in her bedroom.

[Diary]

For the woman's elderly husband, sharing space and facilities was also difficult.

Lack of space was the initial problem. [My husband] had to take all his computer paraphernalia out of our spare bedroom to give it (the room) to one of the girls. We all love our computers and a hasty re-wiring of the house had to be done with new power points and Wifi connections being essential and urgent. [My husband] now shares his bathroom with 3 females – all have a lot of stuff, medications etc. I have the en-suite to myself because there is little storage. Two new bathroom cabinets had to be installed in the main bathroom.

[Diary]

Lack of adequate storage space to accommodate the sudden increase in household size also made it difficult for her to keep the house tidy:

I am a neat freak and no one else is. So I have learnt to let go – up to a point – and accept that we must have things lying around because there is no more room to put things away.

[Diary]

For another couple in their forties, in public housing with three bedrooms, the lack of space was seen as accentuating relationship problems and creating conflict between generations.

It's only a tiny, three bedroom house and we've got a couple and a baby in one room, my husband and myself in one room and my daughter. But the last two days my daughter has moved out. Okay. Well my son and the girlfriend are having relationship trouble and it affects the whole house when they fight. Yeah, it's just . . . it's chaos and you can't escape it. . . . The TV . . . my grandson, he's 15 months old now and he watches his shows and then my husband wants to watch his shows and they're only little things but after a while they get really – I don't know what the word is. You just want to be able to do your own thing.

[Interview]

While having adequate space is clearly important for multigenerational living, dwelling design, especially room layout and articulation, it is equally important for supporting the often different lifestyles, privacy needs and independence of different generations in a multigenerational household.

Noise interference and dwelling design

Dwelling design (room layout, number and articulation of living spaces and room adjacencies) can be a major factor in noise transmission. This is well illustrated in the case of an older couple in their late sixties who had sold their house to live with their daughter, her husband and two small children. Although they lived on separate floors of the same dwelling, an open stairwell made sound isolation between the two living areas difficult.

> When my parents arrived they lived downstairs and I was upstairs. Later my husband moved in too. We learned early on the arrangement, the layout didn't suit. The two lounges were one on top of the other with stairs in-between. Unfortunately the stairwell worked to carry the sound from one lounge to the other, so you could hear conversations and TV programs from one lounge clearly in the other lounge.
>
> [Interview]

Her father's hearing loss made it more problematic.

> **Daughter:**   My father is very hard of hearing but he won't admit it and he won't get a hearing aid, and you can imagine how all this, the TV, the kids, us talking, how difficult that would be for someone who's got that more difficulty hearing with that ambient noise. So for him, that's really challenging. . . . But because he has difficulty hearing, should he go downstairs and turn on the TV, he needs it louder.
>
> **Son-in-law:**   Then we hear it up here, so then people talk louder.
>
> **Daughter:**   Yeah, it just gets worse and worse.
>
> [Interview]

Eventually they addressed this problem by adding doors to the stairwell.

A single mother in her thirties with two young children living with her retired and widowed father explained how the layout of the house and differences in routine contributed to noise interference.

> I'm starting to see that the design of the house is kind of adding to the stress of living together. I don't think he's stressed out with living with me, but I feel very like I don't have privacy and I don't have enough space to myself. So I think – and I can see we did have problems where my bedroom is right next to the kitchen. So his routine is completely different to mine, because I'm more getting up in the daytime, and because he's not working, he sort of eats at night-time and gets up and uses the fridge and makes himself – boils the kettle and kind of wakes me up at 1:00 in the morning, and things like that, but I think that's because my bedroom, just because of the house design, there's no choice for me to be in any other bedroom but the front of the house,

which is usually the media room, but I'm using that as my bedroom, because the other two bedrooms are too small for me to fit a double bed in there.

[Interview]

In addition to the house design, the fabric of the house, particularly the absence of proper insulation, also exacerbated the problem this household was experiencing. Noise as a source of privacy concerns can therefore be strongly influenced by the design of the dwelling in terms of adjacency of room functions, spatial compartmentalization, surface reflectivity, impact noise of surfaces and the sound insulation properties of walls and doors.

Addressing the layout problem

An inappropriate housing layout that is not supportive of multigenerational living can be frustrating and contribute to intergenerational tensions through privacy violations. There were a number of strategies employed by our participants in addressing these design issues, and these can be broadly grouped into two main categories: modifying the home or relocating.

Modifying the home

The emergence (often sudden) of a multigenerational household can soon highlight the inadequacies of the design of a dwelling to accommodate an expanded family, requiring some time to think through how the home might be modified before being ready to proceed. A separated woman in her forties living with two young children who had moved in with her elderly mother considered how their four-bedroom house might be reconfigured to better suit their needs.

I've tried to rework the layouts of this house in my head many times. I would convert the garage if Mum was open to that, because the garage is right there. This house is throughout the whole suburb and it's being converted in many different ways. You can see sort of five versions just in the street, all multiplied a bit. They've all used the garage as a rumpus room or an extra bedroom. So I'd have that as my space and I've had a kitchenette in there and a door to the exterior so that if I came home one night and just wanted to walk in . . .

[Interview]

A number of participants had modified their homes to better accommodate their multigenerational family. For some, the modifications were extensive; in one case expanding space and creating separated living zones by raising the original house and building rooms underneath.

When my parents moved to Australia they lived in my house. I was renovating – making the house big enough for the three of us. I lifted the house up and added three bedrooms, two bathrooms, a lounge room and a double garage and laundry (all downstairs). Upstairs is (and was) two bedrooms, one lounge, one kitchen with two large decks – one front and one back.

[Diary]

Another example of extending the home to cater for a younger couple and child living with elderly parents involved additional kitchens, bathrooms and living areas.

Well we extended the house and put on this big family kitchen so that we can all sit in the kitchen and we can all sit at the table. . . . But we also have space downstairs so that Dad has a lounge downstairs and a bathroom and a bedroom, toilet and a kitchen downstairs, not that he would ever use the kitchen.

[Interview]

For others the changes were modest, within the existing building envelope, and incremental in response to changing family dynamics.

We had three of our adult children living here, all here. So we had to modify our home, which is only a small home, to accommodate – changing the front sun room into a bedroom to accommodate children sleeping over, their children coming here, changing another bedroom into our eldest son's room that we used before for an office, sewing room sort of thing. . . . We've had to modify the space all the time. So that's a big thing, that nothing is static here. It keeps my husband and I very busy, with all these changes.

[Interview]

Some found the cost of modifications a barrier, such as this single, divorced woman in her fifties living with two adult daughters who had not left home.

I've never thought about it because I can't afford it so there's no point in thinking about it. I couldn't afford to extend, I couldn't afford to move to something bigger so it's just not something I've ever considered.

[Interview]

For others, limitations of the size or configuration of the existing dwelling made modifications difficult. Temporary modifications were made by some multigenerational households, especially when they considered their living arrangement to be more temporary. Some families used tall bookcases to create an additional 'bedroom' out of a living area; others converted their garage into bedrooms and additional living spaces by simply choosing to not open the garage door from the street side. As some participants recalled, however, they have been living with these temporary modifications for much longer than they intended – in some cases for over a year – and had they known of the longevity of their arrangement beforehand, they would have opted for more permanent solutions.

Moving house

Some of our participants had moved to or built a more suitable dwelling for their multigenerational household; others had contemplated doing so. For some, the ideal was a detached house with separate 'granny flat' accommodation, as expressed by this woman in her sixties living with her husband, adult daughter and two granddaughters in a four-bedroom outer-suburban house:

> My idea of it would be what I've always thought of – buy a nice block of land, four bedroom house, granny flat up the back. It's close enough that we're there to help without being under the foot or anything like that. I suppose that's the way I see it.
>
> [Interview]

A multigenerational apartment dweller in her forties, with a husband and young family, had considered a number of options including moving to a detached house, or to two adjacent apartments, when her older mother-in-law moved in. In the end, however, they decided to stay and share their three-bedroom apartment.

> We thought about moving to a house, we thought about moving to two apartments within the same complex and lots of other iterations. But eventually we just thought well if we sold this and bought a two bedroom apartment and bought her a one bedroom apartment well really we could, as we've done, semi sort of divide our current apartment into a two bedroom and a one bedroom and share the living space. That would be just as easy and then we don't have to go anywhere or do any trouble of bank loans and selling and buying and going through all the paperwork.
>
> [Interview]

Others had moved into larger houses by necessity, in this case because their previous small rental unit was simply inadequate for this woman's older parents to move into with her young family when in difficult financial circumstances.

> Because they couldn't find permanent stable work I guess it was quite stressful on us knowing that they were here but they were not really coping financially and managing. It was causing them a lot of stress but they were doing it because they wanted to be here closer to us. So in the end I think it was just easier for us to buy a bigger house because where we lived [a rented apartment] was very small and it wasn't suitable for them to come and live with us at all. So we bought a bigger house that enabled them to come and live with us.
>
> [Interview]

For one older woman who had moved in with her daughter and son-in-law, their ideal dwelling with a granny flat proved difficult to find. Eventually they purchased a single dwelling and she used her savings to create the granny flat downstairs.

> Yeah we were definitely looking for something that suited separate arrange-ments as far as that went. We didn't want to be in each other's pockets and we didn't want for us to go through her home and for her to go through our home as far as comings and goings for our own day to day things. . . . When we started to look for houses, there was very little available that actually had a granny flat. I don't think we found one. This was the closest we came to hav-ing the makings of one that was quite feasible with . . . that bit of money . . .
>
> [Interview]

Since many larger houses have two stories, stairs could be a barrier where multi-generational households included older parents.

> One of the biggest considerations for us is the stairs. Making it harder for my husband and I for getting up the stairs, but also we found the dual living meant refrigerator up, refrigerator down. Microwave up, microwave down.
>
> [Interview]

The costs associated with moving house could also be a barrier to relocating to more appropriately designed accommodation.

> We've gone to many display homes with the inten[tion] of seeing what sort of a house we could all fit in together. It came up but it's expensive. By the time you've paid your commission and your stamp duty and your legal fees it's not worth it. None of us have that money spare to do that with. Then you've got to pay rent in the interim if you're building.
>
> [Interview]

The interviews and diaries demonstrate that there can be many frustrations with housing size and design that contribute to negative aspects of multigenerational living. Prominent among the concerns are those related to lack of privacy and poor territorial demarcation. They also reveal that where housing is found to be unsuitable, modifying an existing dwelling or moving to a more suitable dwell-ing is not necessarily straightforward or affordable. Even in the case of the lat-ter – moving to a different home – some kind of modification was often needed to accommodate multigenerational needs. With budgetary constraints, this often meant that multigenerational households would purchase their new homes at lower cost, often in suburban areas farther away from services.

Housing prototypes for multigenerational living

Although the literature on design and planning for multigenerational dwellings is sparse, it has been growing over recent decades. In Australia, as early as the 1980s, Johnson et al. (1984a) undertook a research project entitled *The Integrated*

House, funded by the then Builders Licensing Board of NSW, to consider the impact of likely social, technological and environmental change on future housing design. Using the Delphi Method as a way of predicting likely social and techno-logical futures, a workshop of experts anticipated greater diversity in household types (including multigenerational families). As a result, a flexible 'tri-zonal' pro-totype dwelling was developed (see Figures 9.1 and 9.2). Referred to as The Inte-grated House, it could also be constructed in stages as household configurations changed throughout the life cycle. Examples of how conventional dwellings could be modified to achieve similar zoning were also developed.

Internationally, contemporary housing prototypes have also been developed for multigenerational living over the last few decades. In view of substantial growth in multigenerational households over the last three decades in the United States, accelerated by the 2007–2009 recession (Fry and Passel 2014), there has been a growing interest among planners and architects in multigenerational housing design. Universal housing design advocate, architect Emory Baldwin (2008: 1) wrote about the need for 'a flexible, supportive and nondiscriminatory environ-ment' for a wider range of household types (including multigenerational house-holds) and proposed the following design principles for what he called 'lifespan housing' (Baldwin 2008: 7–11):

- location near amenities
- distinction between primary and accessory function – separation of core and accessory areas to facilitate privacy
- varying amounts of accessory space – allowing changes over time
- private outdoor space for both the primary and accessory parts of the dwelling
- private entrance for the accessory area
- central vertical circulation core – with stairway and dedicated vertical eleva-tor space
- areas for future expansion
- flexible layout to facilitate change in dwelling layout
- minimization of load-bearing walls to maximize flexibility
- zones of building services to allow simpler future renovation

He illustrated the last nine of these principles in the series of diagrams shown in Figure 9.3.

More recently, the American Planning Association with Cornell University published a briefing paper on multigenerational planning that included a discus-sion of various housing options (Hodgson 2011), and a later paper on multigen-erational housing types citing a number of large housing developers offering such housing products (Spivac 2012). Interior design academics Nichols and Adams (2013) also published on various design approaches for 'complex living arrange-ments' including multigenerational families, identifying a number of housing options including 'shared housing', 'doubling up', and 'accessory dwellings', with illustrated examples of conversions of large suburban houses to provide more affordable and accessible housing options in the context of population ageing.

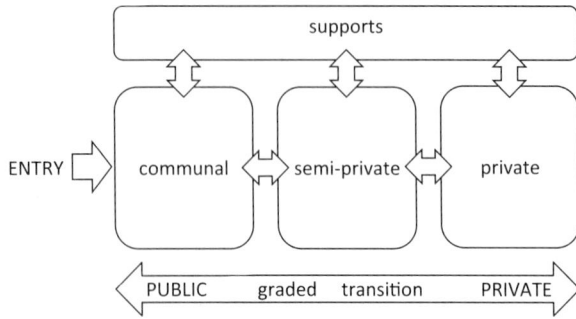

Figure 9.1 The Integrated House: tri-zonal diagram
Source: Johnson et al. (1984b)

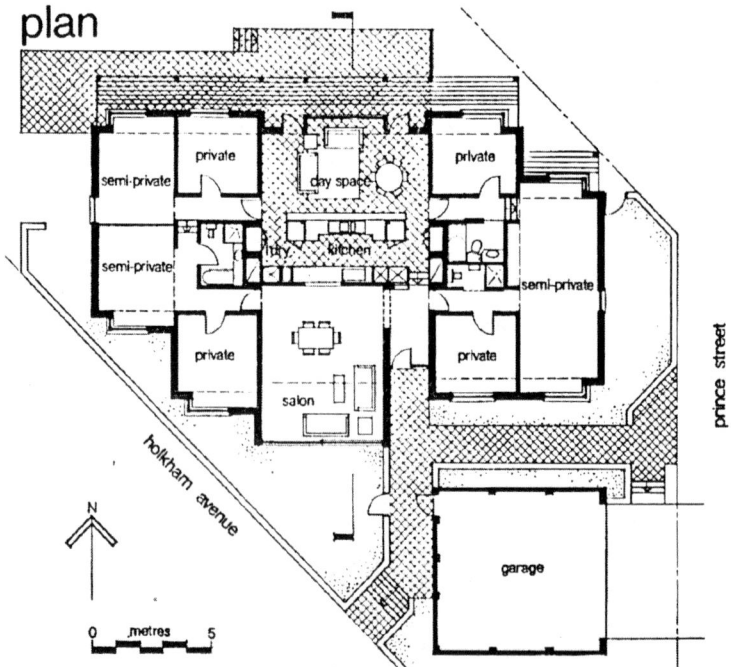

Figure 9.2 The Integrated House prototype: floor plan
Source: Johnson et al. (1984b)

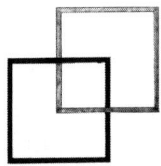

(a) Distinction between primary and accessory functions

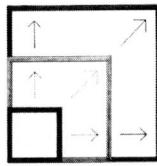

(b) Varying amounts of accessory space

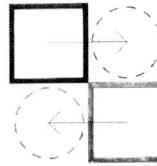

(c) Private outdoor space

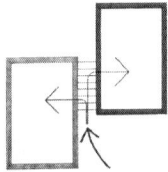

(d) Private entrance for accessory area

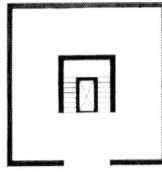

(e) Central vertical circulation core

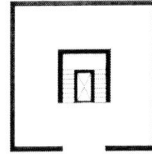

(f) Areas for future expansion

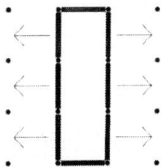

(g) Flexible layouts

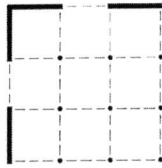

(h) Minimisation of load bearing walls

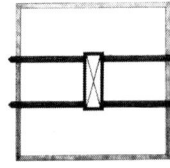

(i) Zones of building services

Figure 9.3 Baldwin's diagrams of lifespan housing design principles

Source: Baldwin (2008)

In Belgium, Gerards et al. (2015) recently wrote about the need for new multi-generational dwelling design in Flanders and utilized a design research approach with five leading architects to develop prototypes of multigenerational dwelling designs based on the typical Flemish terraced house. In the United Kingdom, the journal *Architectural Design* recently dedicated a special edition on 'Designing for the Third Age', which included discussion on multigenerational living and housing design, with Chobham Manor in East London designed by PRP Architects for the London Legacy Development Corporation highlighted as an example (Firth and Patel 2014). These three-storey row houses incorporate a self-contained smaller occupancy separate from the principal dwelling by a courtyard – a variation on the traditional 'granny flat'.

With many Australian cities now promoting a compact city agenda, there are also important lessons to learn from our Asian counterparts. Not only has multigenerational living traditionally been more common among many Asian societies, but many of these societies are densely populated, with apartment dwellings successfully accommodating multigenerational needs.

In a study of housing for the elderly in Taiwan in 1997, Hwang reported that because of traditional multigenerational living arrangements and the shift toward smaller urban apartments, 'an analysis of daily activities showed that sleeping, eating, entertainment, social activities and storage were major areas of disagreement in multigenerational families' (1997: 135). Different sleeping times and nighttime toilet use by older people was disruptive for children; differences in food preferences and cooking caused conflict in kitchens and at meal time; different television viewing habits and program preferences were difficult to accommodate in one living space; different friends and socializing patterns and conversation topics were also not easily accommodated in one living room; and storage was inadequate for the different items of value and furniture tastes between generations. As a result, Hwang (1997: 137) proposed 'that the solution is to provide separate spaces and additional facilities for elderly people in the dwelling. At the very least, an additional living room, bathroom and entrance are required to allow elderly people to have their own entertainment, social activity and privacy' and 'in addition, the need for a barrier free environment'. A design for a prototype apartment design was also developed (Figure 9.4).

Housing industry responses

There are well-established international examples on the housing market of both detached houses and apartments specifically designed for multigenerational living. As reported by the American Planning Association, for many years housing designers and builders have been specializing in multigenerational home designs, including Alan Mascord Home Designs in Portland, Oregon, (2015) and, in California, The New Home Company's (2015) Life Space range and Lennar Corporation's (2013) Nextgen© suite of homes to name a few. In 1987, Singapore's housing authority, the Housing and Development Board (HDB) introduced the concept of Granny Flats (Mehta 2006) now known as '3Gen Flats' (HDB 2014), a concept that was later picked up by the private sector and marketed as 'dual key' apartments. Their popularity in the private sector, however, may be more about savings in stamp duty tax and additional rental returns from two occupancies within the same dwelling. More recently, the concept has also spread to Malaysia (Chan 2014).

In recent years, Australian companies specializing in multigenerational housing design and construction have also begun to emerge, some focusing on the custom-designed home market (e.g. Harper Group 2013) and others on the project home and housing investment market (e.g. Alworth Homes 2015; AusHomes 2015; TR Homes

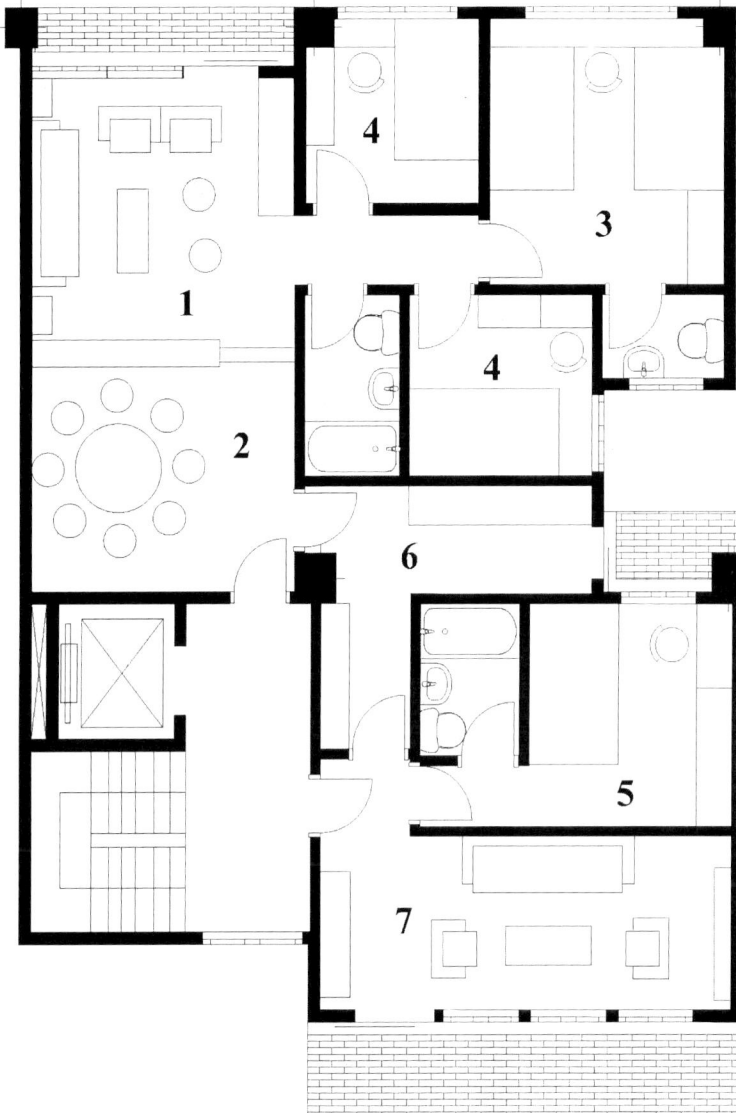

Figure 9.4 Apartment design for multigenerational households in Taiwan

1   main living room
2   common dining room
3   master en suite
4   children's rooms
5   elderly room
6   common kitchen
7   secondary living room

Source: Copy of original drawing provided by Professor Y. R. Hwang, Department of Design, National Yunlin University of Science and Technology, Taiwan, ROC, in 2015.

Figure 9.5 Tri-generational home design (The 3G) by TR Homes Pty Ltd, Western Australia (separate independent living area shown in grey)

Source: TR Homes (2015)

2015). Not unlike the principles embodied in the Integrated House and other prototypes described earlier, these products are typically characterized by a separate
independent living area with its own entrance, bedroom, living area, bathroom
and in some cases a kitchenette (see Figure 9.5). These additional rooms are pro-
moted as ideal for accommodating an elderly parent, a teenage or adult child or a
paying boarder or tenant.

Accessory dwelling units (ADUs) are not new in Australian housing, although
historically these have been in the form of unsanctioned 'granny flats' or 'garden
apartments'. More recently, however, ADUs (also referred to as 'ancillary dwellings' and 'granny flats') are increasingly being legitimized by state and local
governments as an affordable housing option. In some cases (e.g. NSW Government 2009), this option is supported by state government planning policies,
but in others it is more the prerogative of local government (e.g. Brisbane City
Council 2014). These units can be a division of, addition to, or separate from the
principal dwelling and are usually subject to minimum allotment sizes, site cov-
erage, access and setback requirements. While in some jurisdictions occupancy
had been restricted to family members or relatives, the new generation of accessory dwellings are generally not subject to such restrictions and are marketed as
suitable for elderly parents, adult children or an income-generating tenant. There
are now many specialist granny flat companies offering designs in the housing
market (e.g. Granny Flats Australia 2013; Master Granny Flats 2015).

There are also developments in apartment design in Australia that can facilitate
multigenerational living. 'Dual key' apartments are beginning to be developed
in inner- and mid-suburban areas. Property developer Meriton introduced twelve
dual key apartments in its 2002 Trafalgar project in inner Sydney (Schlesinger
2011). Singapore-based Frasers Group, drawing on the Singaporean dual key
model, have also incorporated dual key apartments into a development in mid-
suburban Camperdown (See Figure 9.6) as well as into their recent, inner-Sydney,

Figure 9.6 Floor plan of TRIO dual key apartment in Camperdown, Sydney (separate
independent living area shown in grey)

Source: Image provided by Frasers Property Australia, 2015.

high-density Central Park residential project (Schlesinger 2011), although the latter appear to be directed more toward investors and the international student market than multigenerational households.

Conclusion

It is clear from the survey, interview and diary findings of this study that while many residents of multigenerational households enjoy the companionship and support that this living arrangement encourages, housing design can be a key factor contributing to dissatisfaction with multigenerational living. When asked what they disliked about multigenerational living, privacy/interference was the major reason identified. Other common concerns that have design implications are problems with inadequate space and excessive noise. As indicated by a number of participants, inappropriate dwelling design can also affect other areas of dissatisfaction such as intra- and interfamilial relationships and lack of flexibility and compromise. Conversely, appropriate design should help to ameliorate some of these negative aspects of multigenerational living.

Altman's (1975) model of human spatial behaviour, with privacy as the central regulatory process and personal space and territory as control mechanisms, is useful in understanding housing design for multigenerational living. It is also illuminating to view multigenerational housing as assemblages of human and nonhuman components that are not necessarily permanent but typically fragile and transitory. With privacy needs being individually, socio-culturally and situationally variable, people living in multigenerational households will have different needs at different times and under different circumstances. Therefore, housing design needs to provide spatial options to accommodate these varying needs in the form of alternative areas within the dwelling and associated private open space, or provide the flexibility for easy adaptation. Territorial behaviour, as an important mechanism for regulating social interaction within a multigenerational household, is also evident from the interviews and diaries, particularly the desire of different generations to have their own space, over which they have a sense of 'ownership' and control (Easthope et al. 2015) while also having the opportunity to engage with the other generations in shared spaces when desired.

Having adequate space is an important starting point for multigenerational living, but not one that is always easy to achieve, especially in situations of the often sudden and unexpected influx of 'boomeranging' family members with their children in the wake of relationship breakdowns. Space alone, however, is not enough. As a number of the interviewees have stated, the layout and sizes of rooms are also important. Key strategies for the design of dwellings for multigenerational families that arise from this study include:

- territorial zoning of the dwelling to enable alternative or subsidiary living areas (both indoor and outdoor) associated with related bedrooms and bathrooms

- separate entrances for different generations
- generous or separate kitchens to enable different generations to prepare food concurrently
- careful acoustic design to minimize sound transmission between zones
- adoption of adaptable or universal design principles
- flexibility in design and construction to allow for future spatial reconfigurations
- adequate parking for additional vehicles

These strategies are consistent with the principles of earlier local and international prototypes (Johnson et al. 1984b; Hwang 1997; Baldwin 2008) examined earlier, with the findings of Klocker and colleagues (2012; 2013) and with products currently emerging in the Australian detached housing and apartment market.

With housing affordability problems for younger generations, the growth in the older population ageing in place, and migration from cultures with multigenerational living traditions, it is likely that this market sector will continue to grow. The challenge for the housing industry is to supply a diversity of innovative products from larger spatially zoned single dwellings to independent accessory dwellings (granny flats) and dual key apartments. Planning and housing policy will also need to respond to this demand with supportive planning controls and building regulations that enable a variety of housing options suitable for multigenerational living that are supported by appropriate legal and financial products.

References

Alan Mascord Home Designs 2015, *Dual Living, Multi-Generational, and Extended Families*, accessed 6 June 2015, houseplans.co/house-plans/collections/multigenerational-houseplans/

Altman, I 1975, *The Environment and Social Behavior: Privacy, Personal Space, Territory, Crowding*, Brooks/Cole, Monterey, CA.

Alworth Homes 2015, *Building for 'Extended Family' Living*, accessed 31 May 2015, allworthhomes.com.au/building- per centE2 per cent80 per cent98extended-family per centE2 per cent80 per cent99-living

AusHomes 2015, *Dual Key Homes Advertising Brochure*, accessed 31 May 2015, www.dualkeyhomes.com.au/uploads/1/2/6/8/12680532/special_report_64_pages_—-_dual_key_homes_v5–03–2015.pdf

Australian Bureau of Statistics 2013, *Australian Census of Population and Housing, 1986, 1996, 2006, 2011*, Australian Bureau of Statistics, Canberra.

Baldwin, E 2008, 'Housing in response to the human life cycle', in WC Mann (ed.), *Aging, Disability and Independence*, IOS Press, Amsterdam, pp. 1–17.

Barker, R 1963, 'On the nature of the environment', *Journal of Social Issues*, vol. 19, pp. 17–38.

Barker, R 1968, *Ecological Psychology: Concepts and Methods for Studying the Environment of Human Behaviour*, Stanford University Press, Stanford.

Brisbane City Council 2014, *Houses, Brisbane City Plan 2014*, Development Assessment Fact Sheet 4, accessed 8 September 2015, www.brisbane.qld.gov.au/sites/default/files/20140606_-_brisbane_city_plan_2014_-_houses.pdf

158   *Bruce Judd*

Chan, L 2014, 'Dual key apartments offer flexibility and privacy', *The Star*, 23 August, accessed 31 May 2015, www.thestar.com.my/News/Community/2014/08/23/For-multigeneration-families-Dualkey-apartments-offer-flexibility-and-privacy/

De Landa, M 2006, *A New Philosophy of Society: Assemblage Theory and Social Complexity*, Continuum, London.

Deleuze, G and Guattari, F 1987, *A Thousand Plateaus: Capitalism and Schizophrenia*, University of Minnesota Press, Minneapolis.

Easthope, H, Liu, E, Judd, B and Burnley, I 2015, 'Feeling at home in a multigenerational household: The importance of control', *Housing, Theory and Society*, vol. 32, no. 2, pp. 151–170.

Firth, K and Patel, M 2014, 'Regeneration for all generations: The queen Elizabeth Olympic Park', in L Farrelly (ed.), 'Designing for the third age: Architecture "redefined for a generation of 'active agers"'', *Architectural Design*, vol. 2, pp. 88–93.

Fry, R and Passel, JS 2014, *In Post-Recession Era, Young Adults Drive Continuing Rise in Multi-generational Living*, Pew Research Center's Social and Demographic Trends Project, Washington, DC.

Gale, A and Park, NK 2010, 'Desired and achieved privacy in multigenerational homes', *Housing and Society*, vol. 37, no. 1, pp. 25–41.

Gerards, S, Ridde, R and De Bleeckere, S 2015, 'Designing multigenerational dwelling: A workshop with four Flemish architecture firms', *International Journal of Architectural Research*, vol. 9, no. 2, pp. 20–30.

Granny Flats Australia 2013, *Granny Flats Australia*, accessed 8 September 2015, grannyflatsaustralia.com.au/

Harper Group 2013, *GenLiving – Sydney's First Multi-Generational Home Builder*, accessed 30 July 2013, harpergroup.net.au/103/genliving-sydneys-first-multi-generational-home-builder/

Hodgson, K 2011, 'Multigenerational planning: Using smart growth and universal design to link the needs of children and the aging population,' *Family-friendly communities briefing papers*, American Planning Association.

Housing and Development Board 2014, *HDB InfoWeb: Buying a New Flat, 3-Generation Family (3GEN)*, accessed 6 June 2015, www.hdb.gov.sg/fi10/fi10321p.nsf/w/BuyingNewFlat3Gen?OpenDocument

Hwang, YR 1997, 'Housing for the Elderly in Taiwan', *Ageing International*, Winter/Spring 1997, pp. 133–147.

Jacobs, J 2012, 'Urban geographies 1: Still thinking cities rationally', *Progress in Human Geography*, vol. 36, no. 3, pp. 412–422.

Jacobs, J, Cairns, S and Strebel, I 2007, '"A tall story . . . but, a fact just the same": The red road high-rise as a black box', *Urban Studies*, vol. 44, no. 3, pp. 609–629.

Johnson, P, Judd, B and LeSueur, G 1984a, *The Integrated House: Prototype Experimental Dwelling for the Future*, Res.Arch Residential Research Unit, School of Architecture, University of New South Wales, Kensington.

Johnson, P, Judd, B and LeSueur, G 1984b, *The Integrated House: An Overview*, Res. Arch Residential Research Unit, School of Architecture University of New South Wales, Kensington.

Klocker, N and Gibson, C 2013, 'Looking inwards: Extended family living as an urban consolidation alternative', *Planning Theory and Practice*, vol. 14, no. 4, pp. 555–559.

Klocker, N, Gibson, C and Borger, E 2012, 'Living together but apart: Material geographies of everyday sustainability in extended family households', *Environment and Planning A*, vol. 44, pp. 2240–2259.

Kupritz, V 2000, 'Privacy management at work: A conceptual model', *Journal of Architectural and Planning Research*, vol. 17, no. 1, pp. 47–63.

Lennar Corporation 2013, *Corporate website*, accessed 31 May 2015, nextgen.lennar.com/

Liu, E, Easthope, H, Judd, B and Burnley, I 2015, 'Housing multigenerational households in Australian cities: Evidence from Sydney and brisbane at the turn of the 21st century', in R Dufty-Jones and D Rogers (eds), *Housing in 21st-Century Australia: People, Practices and Policies*, Ashgate, Farnham, 21–37.

Margulis, S 1979, *Privacy as Information Management: A Social Psychological and Environmental Framework* (NBSIR 79–1793), US Department of Commerce, National Bureau of Standards, Washington, DC.

Margulis, S 2003, 'On the status and contribution of Westin's and Altman's theories of privacy', *Journal of Social Issues*, vol. 59, no. 2, pp. 411–30.

Master Granny Flats 2015, *Corporate website*, accessed 8 September 2015, mastergrannyflats.com.au/granny-flats-australia/

McFarlane, C 2011, 'The city as assemblage: Dwelling and urban space', *Environment and Planning D: Society and Space*, vol. 29, pp. 649–671.

Mehta, K 2006, 'A critical review of Singapore's policies aimed at supporting families for older members', in F Caro (ed.), *Family and Aging Policy*, Hayworth Press, Birmingham, pp. 43–58.

The New Home Company 2015, *Corporate website*, accessed 31 May 2015, thenewhomecompany.com/

New South Wales Government 2009, *State Environmental Planning Policy (Affordable Rental Housing) 2009*, accessed 31 May 2015, www5.austlii.edu.au/au/legis/nsw/consol_reg/sepprh2009572/s19.html

Nichols, JN and Adams, N 2013, 'The flexi-nest: The accessory dwelling unit as adaptable housing for the life span', *Interiors*, vol. 4, no. 1, pp. 31–52.

Rapoport, A 1969, *House Form and Culture*, Prentice-Hall, Englewood Cliffs.

Schlesinger, L 2011, 'Some investors find dual-key apartments twice as nice', *Property Observer*, accessed 1 May 2015, www.propertyobserver.com.au/finding/residential-investment/new-developments/13227-some-investors-find-dual-key-apartments-twice-as-nice.html

Scott, J and Marshall, G (eds) 2009, *A Dictionary of Sociology*, (3 rev. ed.), Oxford University Press, Oxford.

Spivac, J 2012, 'Making room for Mom and Dad: Multigenerational families are seeking new housing types', *Planning*, October, pp. 8–12.

Sundstrum, E and Sundstrum, M. 1986, *Work Places. The psychology of the physical environment in offices and factories*, Cambridge University Press, Cambridge.

TR Homes 2015, *The 3G*, accessed 6 June 2015, www.trhomes.com.au/homes/3g

Westin, A 1970, *Privacy and Freedom*, Athenaeum, New York.

10 The environmental implications of multigenerational living

Are larger households also greener households?

Natascha Klocker, Chris Gibson and Erin Borger

Introduction

Multigenerational family households rarely form out of environmental concern – or an intentional desire to be 'green'. More typically, they form because of financial pressures, caring responsibilities or to accommodate disruptions in extended families such as divorce or unemployment (Klocker et al. 2012). Yet, they offer important, innate opportunities to reduce resource consumption. On a per capita basis, household size is inversely related to resource consumption and waste production (Liu et al. 2003). By housing more family members under one roof, multigenerational family living presents unheralded opportunities to save energy, water, building materials and land. Our ethnographic research with multigenerational family households in Wollongong, in the Illawarra region of southeastern Australia, explored the ways in which resources are consumed and shared in their rhythms of everyday life. These families inadvertently reduced their consumption of material resources by sharing space and everyday objects: white goods, furniture, cooking equipment, electronics, clothing, books, food, swimming pools and more. Although these sharing practices were not intentionally 'green', they nonetheless obviated the need for additional purchases to be made.

At the same time, these households were sites of environmental debate and intergenerational learning. Older generations – while not identifying as environmentalists – sought to instil values of thrift among their younger relatives. They wanted to pass their inadvertent – or unintentional – sustainabilities onto their children and grandchildren. The term 'inadvertent sustainabilities' refers to practices not conceived with sustainability in mind, but which are environmentally beneficial nonetheless (Krueger and Agyeman 2005; Klocker et al. 2012). Some younger household members, for their part, made persistent attempts to counter their parents' and grandparents' climate change skepticism, and to promote intentionally sustainable practices and purchases. Multigenerational family households thus provide fertile ground for the frugal (inadvertently 'green') practices and skills of older generations, and the intentional environmentalism of younger generations, to collide and coalesce – with profound implications for everyday domestic life.

Throughout this chapter, we follow Blunt (2005) and Reid et al. (2010) in defining a household as a social unit occupying a single place or space of residence (the dwelling). Our definition of multigenerational family households is expansive. It includes adult children who have remained in – or returned to – the parental home (with or without their own spouse and children), and elderly parents living with one or more adult children. Additional relatives (whether aunts, uncles, grandparents or cousins) may be 'added on' to an existing nuclear family unit. Each of these household configurations brings together *related* individuals in a manner distinct from single-parent or nuclear family living arrangements that involve one or more parents and their dependent child(ren) (see also Klocker et al. 2012). In so doing, they decrease the overall number of dwellings required to house an equivalent number of people.

In the remainder of this chapter, we provide detail around the innate environmental benefits of larger households, before positioning our study within a broad body of cultural environmental research at the household scale. After outlining our research methods, we present empirical evidence of two types of sharing that take place in multigenerational family households – of space and material objects *and* more important, of ideas, skills and knowledge. Multigenerational family households engender opportunities to be inadvertently and deliberately 'green'. We conclude by taking our research findings to a further, speculative, step: in a climate-changing world, these households also hold important and unexplored potential for coping with environmental calamities.

The innate environmental benefits of larger households

Taken at an aggregate level, larger households – those with more members – consume more resources (e.g. energy, water, food); they also produce more waste. Yet, on a per capita basis, the inverse is true. Economics of scale are at work, meaning that households with more members typically consume fewer resources – and generate less waste – *per person* (e.g. Keilman 2003; Lenzen et al. 2004; Yu and Liu 2007). Individuals' ecological footprints decrease with increasing household size (Lenzen and Murray 2001). The multigenerational family households in our study contained an average of 4.3 occupants, well above the national average of 2.6 persons per household in 2011 (Australian Bureau of Statistics 2012).

A range of quantitative studies has demonstrated the significance of the previously mentioned inversion. In a provocative paper entitled *The threat of small households*, Keilman (2003) raised concern about declining household sizes globally. Between 1970 and 2000, the average number of occupants per household decreased from 5.5 to 4.4 people in the Majority World (developing countries) and from 3.2 to 2.5 in the Minority World (developed countries). This trend compounds the demand for additional resources generated by population growth because opportunities to 'share space, home furnishings, transportation and energy' are reduced (Keilman 2003: 489; see also Liu et al. 2003). The magnitude of resource savings generated by cohabitation is not trivial. An early study conducted in the United States found that two-person households consumed 17 per cent less energy per person than single-person households, while three-person households used one-third less energy per capita (O'Neill and Chen 2002). Yu and Liu (2007) found that divorced households in the United States (which had fewer occupants than married households) spent 46 per cent and 56 per cent more on electricity and water per capita. This usage resulted in 73 billion kilowatt hours of additional electricity use and 627 billion gallons of additional water use in the United States in 2005 alone (Yu and Liu 2007). In Sydney, Australia, the Independent Pricing and Regulatory Tribunal (IPART 2010) found that households with five occupants consumed 2.1 megawatt hours of electricity per person, per year. This usage was *less than half* the amount used (per capita) in single-person households (5.6 megawatt hours per year). Similarly, households containing five or more people used around 54 kilolitres of water per person per annum, compared with 135 kilolitres in single-person households (IPART 2010; see also Lenzen et al. 2004). Similar economies of scale in relation to water use were reported in Zaragoza, Spain: single-person households consumed 0.1845 m^3 (around 185 L) of water per person, per day – but four-person households used just over half that amount (0.0999 m^3 or 100 L per person, per day; Arbués et al. 2010). And in an iconic case, in the area around the Wolong Nature Reserve in China, Liu et al. (2001) linked shrinking household sizes to increased fuel wood consumption, increased deforestation and thus habitat loss for giant pandas.

By reducing the aggregate number of dwellings needed, larger multigenerational family households can also contribute to reduced demand for land and building materials. In relation to the first issue, Liu et al. (2003) argued that biodiversity conservation is threatened by the dual trend of increasing population *and* shrinking household sizes – which is causing the aggregate number of households to grow rapidly. The significance of these trends is particularly apparent in China. The Chinese population is projected to approach 1.5 billion by 2030, over which time the average household size is projected to drop to 2.2 people (from 3.5 in 2000, and 4.5 in 1985; Liu and Diamond 2005). Liu and Diamond (2005) found that declining household sizes alone would create 250 million additional households by 2030, even if the overall population size were to remain constant.

While on a lesser scale, these trends also matter in Australia. Here, one-quarter of households contain only one person (ABS 2012). Following current trends in living arrangements, and aggregate population growth, the number of households in Australia is projected to grow from 7.8 million in 2006 to 11.4 million in 2031 (ABS 2010). In Sydney, 770,000 more homes will be added over the next twenty-five years (Nicholls and Moore 2011), at least half of which are predicted to be built on greenfield sites (O'Neill and James 2014). Urban expansion threatens peri-urban farmland (Han 2013) and biodiversity (Smith 2015). In addition to reducing demand for space, multigenerational family households can also generate savings in building materials, as fewer dwellings are needed. This reduction is significant due to the sizeable carbon emissions associated with construction. The steel, glass, concrete, wood, tiles and bricks (among others) that go into constructing a new dwelling carry the baggage of embodied energy consumption associated with their extraction, manufacture and transportation. According to Berners-Lee

(2010), each new two-storey, two-bedroom cottage produces 80 tonnes of carbon dioxide equivalent (CO_2e) emissions due to the embodied energy encapsulated in building materials[1]. Wright et al. (2009) provide a means of visualizing these emissions – one tonne of CO_2e can be imagined as 10,000 garbage bags filled with carbon dioxide. Construction of the previously mentioned cottage thus generates the equivalent of 800,000 garbage bags. Based on these calculations, the 770,000 new homes needed in Sydney will produce 616 billion garbage bags filled with carbon dioxide through embedded emissions alone. Efforts to mitigate the cumulative environmental impacts of these trends – both in terms of carbon emissions and habitat loss, should factor in the possibility of larger household sizes. Policymakers and planners could do more to promote the benefits of – and support the formation of – multigenerational family households.

Cultural environmental research at the household scale

Our own study – while inspired by the evidence outlined earlier – did not seek to replicate a quantitative investigation of carbon emissions in multigenerational family households. Instead, it was informed by a growing body of cultural environmental research undertaken at the household scale. We asked *why* multigenerational family households form, and for these families, what kinds of sustainability benefits stem from practices of sharing (objects and resources) among the exigencies of everyday life. The economies of scale that operate in these typically larger households relate to the sharing of resources, but how such sharing occurs remains opaque in large quantitative datasets. Our research provides an opportunity to explore sharing in currently existing larger-than-average households. Here, we consider how multigenerational family living arrangements provide fertile ground for sharing, thus obviating the need for additional resource consumption.

In recent years, households – particularly those in the Minority World – have become a focal point for environmental policymaking. Policymakers expect householders – as self-regulating and purportedly rational consumers – to take responsibility for reducing their resource consumption and waste production (Hobson 2006; Gibson et al. 2011; Lane and Gorman-Murray 2011). Governments have provided funding and subsidies for home solar panels, insulation, smart meters, rainwater tanks, energy efficient lightbulbs and shower timers; and householders have been encouraged to reduce their waste (for instance, by recycling and using 'green' shopping bags) and to take public transport. Cultural environmental research has acknowledged the importance of households as logical sites for understanding the consumption of resources, and as a crucial scale of social organization for pro-environmental behaviour (Reid et al. 2010; Gibson et al. 2013; Head et al. 2013). However, such research has also troubled the often simplistic ways in which policymakers have conceived of households.

A number of researchers have argued that environmental policies have failed to have their desired effect at the household scale, because they have not adequately considered 'what happens inside the home' (Horne et al. 2011: 89; see also Hobson 2008; Gibson et al. 2013). Households are increasingly diverse – demographically, culturally, socioeconomically – and everyday life within households is composed of complex internal politics, practices, social relations and attributes. The ways in which we consume water, energy and other resources is shaped by the rituals, rhythms, emotions, habits and routines of everyday life (Shove 2003; Maller 2011).

Dominant policy approaches to household sustainability have also come under scrutiny for limiting their focus to so-called pro-environmental behaviours – explicitly and intentionally 'green' practices (Hobson 2006; Klocker et al. 2012). However, day-to-day domestic life is motivated by diverse sets of concerns, values, priorities, demands and pressures beyond being 'green' (Gibson et al. 2013). This helps to explain why householders' stated environmental concerns do not always translate into action, widely referred to as the 'value-action gap' (Kollmuss and Agyeman 2002). Cultural environmental research has shown that environmentally beneficial actions regularly emerge without an explicit desire to be 'green'. Inadvertent environmentalisms arise when actions that are undertaken for other reasons (such as saving money) generate positive environmental spin-offs. Hitchings et al. (2015) refer to the 'action-value opportunity' of inadvertent environmentalisms – such as frugal heating practices that are intended to save money, not the environment (see also Evans 2011). With these results in mind, our research on multigenerational family households was open to a diverse range of environmentally beneficial practices, whether or not they were conceived with sustainability in mind. We sought to explore how multigenerational family households function on a day-to-day basis, and how their internal dynamics – the diverse assemblages of people, spaces and things of which they are composed – build on (or at times constrain) the innate environmental benefits of their living arrangements.

Methods

Our research was conducted in Wollongong, a medium-sized coastal city in Australia, located around 60 kilometres south of Sydney. Two key methods were used: semi-structured in-depth interviews with seventeen participants from ten multigenerational family households and home tours. Participants were initially recruited through a quantitative survey conducted by researchers at the University of Wollongong's Australian Centre for Cultural Environmental Research (AUSC-CER)[2] and then via snowballing (see Klocker et al. 2012 for further detail). Home tours are an increasingly common method used by human geographers to learn about the rhythms of everyday life – offering deeper insights into participants' ways of living (Tolia-Kelly 2004). Together with semi-structured interviews, they provided insights into how material resources and spaces in the home were used and shared. Participants showed the interviewer around their homes to provide insights into their ways of living. Interviewees were also asked to discuss their motivations for living in a multigenerational family household, and about the highlights and challenges of so doing. Although none of the study participants nominated environmental concern as a reason for their living arrangement, toward the end of interviews they were asked to consider whether they could see any environmental benefits related to their household structure. Relevant information about the households involved in the study is provided in Table 10.1.

Our interviewees were primarily female (13 of 17), but offered a multigenerational perspective, being between 18 and 70 years old. Our sample did not aim to be representative of Australia's socioeconomic and cultural diversity, but instead sought to provide insights into the nuances of everyday life in multigenerational

Table 10.1 Description of households involved in this study

Interviewees (name[a], age)	No. of people	Family relationships	Anticipated duration	Housing tenure
Living together				
Leanne (~40), Jodi (30), Brooke (23)	3	Adult daughter (Jodi) and partner (Brooke) moved in with Jodi's mother (Leanne)	Short-term	Owner-occupied (Leanne)
Nathan (~40)	5	Adult son (Nathan), his wife and young son, moved in with his mother and father	Short-term	Owner-occupied (Nathan's parents)
Neil (~70), Anne (~70)	3	Adult son moved in with mother and father (Anne and Neil)	Short-term	Owner-occupied (Neil and Anne)
Alex (18)	3	Adult granddaughter (Alex) continued living with grandparents after her own mother moved out	Long-term	Owner-occupied (Alex's grandparents)
Michael (~20)	6	Adult son (Michael) moved in with mother and father, plus his adult sister, her husband and her young child	Short-term	Owner-occupied (Michael's parents)
Living together but apart				
Gail (~70), Gabrielle (~30)	4	Grandmother (Gail) moved in with adult daughter (Gabrielle), son-in-law and granddaughter	Long-term	Owner-occupied (Gabrielle and husband)
Wendy (~40), Wes (40)	3	Mother moved in with adult daughter (Wendy) and son-in-law (Wes)	Long-term	Owner-occupied (Wendy and Wes)

(Continued)

Table 10.1 Continued

Interviewees (name[a], age)	No. of people	Family relationships	Anticipated duration	Housing tenure
Pauline (~50), Melissa (23)	5	Adult daughter (Melissa) with young child moved in with mother (Pauline) and two adult sisters	Long-term	Renting
Marion (~60)	6	Adult daughter, her husband and two young children moved in with mother (Marion) and father	Long-term	Owner-occupied (Marion and husband)
Theresa (23), Marissa (20)	5	Two adult daughters (Theresa and Marissa) living with mother and grandparents	Long-term	Owner-occupied (grandparents)

[a] Pseudonyms have been adopted where requested. Table adapted from Klocker et al. (2012).

family households in ways that could shed further light on the environmental implications of these living arrangements. Some of the families involved in our study were low income and others comfortably middle income; five had migrant (Italian or Filipino) backgrounds. All but one of the dwellings was owner-occupied. The households involved in the study varied in size, from three to six occupants (with an average of 4.3). All exceeded the national average of 2.6 persons per household (ABS 2012).

The ten multigenerational family households broadly fell into two (partially overlapping) categories: elderly parents who could not (or did not want to) live alone and therefore moved in with their adult children; and parents of young children who struggled to balance paid work and caring responsibilities. The latter typically moved in with their own parents to 'get back on their feet' financially or emotionally following marriage breakdown, a period of study or overseas travel, and/or due to the pressures of single parenting. In both scenarios, family members made an intentional decision to live together. Bringing family members together under one roof provided invaluable support and opportunities to care for one another without needing to jump in the car.

Two different *modes* of multigenerational living were associated with these two categories. When an adult child moved in with his or her parents, the living arrangement was generally intended to be short in duration. These multigenerational families tended to live in standard dwellings, where they shared communal living spaces and activities. In Klocker et al. (2012), and in Table 10.1, we have referred to these families as 'living together'. When elderly parents moved in with their adult children, the multigenerational living arrangement was generally understood as a longer-term scenario. Under such circumstances, multigenerational living was made manageable by dividing the dwelling into separate living spaces. This mode of living was influenced by a culturally driven predilection for privacy and independence afforded by space. These families ostensibly lived under one roof, but they occupied self-contained areas and were able to live relatively independently. We have referred to them as 'living together but apart'. Five of the participating households fell into each mode.

Inadvertent environmentalisms: sharing space, sharing stuff

On the surface, those families that we classified as 'living together' might be expected to be more sustainable because they shared household spaces to a greater extent, especially kitchens and living rooms (bathrooms and bedrooms were rarely shared across family units, irrespective of the mode of living adopted). However, as explained next, sharing was a common feature of everyday life in both household types. More important, the separation of spaces in households that were 'living together but apart' made multigenerational living palatable as a longer-term arrangement, because it allowed the household members involved to fulfil a culturally ingrained need for privacy and independence. This way of living may have (in some respects) reduced the environmental gains of multigenerational family living – but by making it durable, the gains that were realized would extend over many more years.

Households that were 'living together' typically shopped and cooked communally – and thus saved on transportation costs and fuel consumption, as well as on the energy used by cooking (Berners-Lee 2011). Shared living spaces also raise the attendant benefit of reducing electricity use – for instance, by lighting and heating/cooling one living room instead of two. However, some family members who had separate living spaces made an effort to share heating and cooling anyway. Gabrielle noted that her mother (Gail's) separate living space did not get heated during the day because, 'Mum can come up here if it's a particularly cold day, and in summer if it's one of those really boiling hot days then Mum sits up here with us with the aircon on'. While household spaces (and attendant activities) were typically shared to a greater extent in households that were 'living together', material objects – the stuff of everyday life – were shared abundantly in both household types. Sandwich toasters, pasta cookers, spices and sauces, Pyrex dishes, books, DVDs, furniture, clothing, vacuum cleaners, washing machines and clothes dryers were all widely shared.

Leanne noted that she purchased clothes less regularly, after her adult daughter Jodi moved in: 'I'll come and try Jodi's on and then I'll go back to the shop if I can't find anything'. The women living in Pauline's household also regularly shared clothing: 'Melissa and I would often share clothes. Megan and Patricia [sisters] share. So it does the rounds . . . The girls can't see the point in buying something that they will only wear once or twice'. Leftover food was also passed within and across both household types, thus reducing food waste. Gardens and swimming pools (where present) were shared irrespective of the mode of living adopted – thus reducing water use, a particularly important outcome given recurrent water shortages in southeastern Australia (Askew and McGuirk 2004). All of these seemingly minor and trivial acts of sharing contribute to a cumulative reduction in material consumption. While sharing also occurs among family members who live in separate dwellings – the ease of sharing in multigenerational family households is enhanced by proximity (being able to run upstairs or downstairs just before dinner to grab a bottle of soy sauce, or a dress before heading out for the night). Household members in these settings are able to share items, without needing to get in the car (and use fuel) to do so.

Amid all of this sharing, it is worth noting that cars, televisions and computers were rarely shared – irrespective of the mode of living adopted. The cultural value placed on independence and freedom (of viewing choices and movement), made replication of these items non-negotiable. As noted by Michael in relation to television and computer use: 'I think that it is a crucial thing when it comes to your personal space, is having that thing you can watch where you can switch your mind off from everything that's happening'. While our households owned multiple cars, multigenerational living meant that they had to drive them less – they no longer needed to travel by car to care for or visit family members who were under the same roof. Wendy cared for her elderly mother and noted: 'before we moved in together . . . I spent a big chunk of time driving up and down . . . that doesn't happen now'. When it was convenient, family members also shared trips – as noted by Gabrielle: 'If Mum was in a house on her own, she would quite often take her car to go to the beach . . . whereas we go together now'. Theresa and Marissa reported combining their grocery shopping trips with those of their grandparents.

Several study participants initially appeared to be taken by surprise when asked whether multigenerational family living offered opportunities to be more environmentally sustainable – they had not given this possibility prior thought. However, they were quickly able to identify important gains made through this living arrangement. Nathan (whose own multigenerational family household was recently disbanded) commented:

> [W]e are using more energy in separate houses than when we were in one house . . . If we were still living at my parents' house, that's one less T.V., that's one less light that's on, that's one less heater that's on, because we'd be sharing theirs.

For Wendy, fuel savings were 'probably the biggest thing', while Gabrielle was able to identify a variety of ways in which multigenerational family living reduces consumption:

> Just because there's not a whole other house operating . . . if you're running your own whole house, it's a lot less sustainable than living in part of someone else's house. And we'll quite often do stuff together [saving fuel] . . . Even your garden, if you were looking after your own garden you would be watering that . . . we just have the one garden . . . [also] the heating and

electricity and the lights. You've got to do your washing . . . you would be doing half loads . . . it just seems intuitive.

In the following section, we consider how sets of knowledge, skills and values can also be shared across generations in multigenerational family households, in ways that may generate environmentally beneficial outcomes.

Multigenerational households: sharing ideas, skills and knowledge

Generations 'represent a distinct, temporally located cultural field' characterized by taste, values and dispositions shaped by popular culture, social norms and the socioeconomic and political circumstances of individuals' formative years (Jones et al. 2009: 101; see also Vanderbeck 2007; Stanes et al. 2015). Individuals who were born within the same broad time period often share important experiences 'in their maturation and socialization' (Büttner and Grübler 1995: 116). The silent generation (aged 65 or older) grew up during the Great Depression, and also the rationing of World War II. They are widely identified as a thrifty and frugal generation (Stanes et al. 2015). Among our householders, Nathan spent a great deal of time discussing his father's thrifty nature:

> Because they're on a fixed income, they're pensioners and so they can't get everything they want. That's partly why he is so thrifty, then again he's always been thrifty . . . he comes from a family of nine brothers and sisters and his mother never worked so his father worked at the Steelworks. . . . When he was growing up, when it came to bath time . . . they would say, you would have a bath in the *Sydney Morning Herald* [newspaper]. You know, the Sydney Morning Herald is large, and the time it took for the Sydney Morning Herald to burn was how long the hot water lasted, and the bathtub was heated underneath. They all shared the same water. He left school at 15, because his family didn't have the money to send him on.

Nathan acknowledged his parents' frugality as a form of environmentalism:

> Probably what motivates them more for shorter showers is the cost. Although they are probably *old school environmental* actually. Having long showers is a waste of water so they wouldn't be doing it purely out of being environmentally friendly, but they would be doing it because they don't like waste.
>
> [emphasis added]

At the opposite end of the generational spectrum, generation Y (around age 18 to early thirties) has been typecast as a consumer generation. Despite evidence that young adults are environmentally informed and concerned, they have been widely criticized for extravagance and throw-away consumerism, with attendant implications for resource consumption (Bentley et al. 2004; Autio et al.

2009; Percy-Smith and Burns 2013). While these stark generational stereotypes demand scrutiny (Stanes et al. 2015), the presence of multiple generations under one roof provides important opportunities for intergenerational learning (c.f. Strengers and Maller 2012). These opportunities were certainly evident in the households that participated in our study. On the one hand, older generations sought to instil their inadvertently 'green' behaviours upon younger generations, by being critical of waste and excess consumption. On the other hand, some younger household members actively sought to convince their co-habiting older relatives of their environmental values and knowledge. Either way, multigenerational family households provided fertile ground for the exchange of diverse sets of knowledge, values and skills. Green domestic practices can be fostered via intergenerational effort and flows of encouragement: different generations bring 'diverse environmental skills to the table' (Stanes and Klocker 2016).

Evidence of parents and grandparents exerting influence over their children and grandchildren's consumption practices was abundant in the households involved in our study. In all cases, interviewees asserted that such efforts were motivated more by thrift and financial imperatives than environmental concern. Gabrielle, who described herself as fairly frugal, felt further compelled to avoid unnecessary purchases with her mother living in the same house:

> I think, through my whole life it's been Mum's influence because we've always shopped at op shops . . . I always have trouble telling people when I've bought something new. I always feel like I shouldn't have bought something new [laughter] . . . I would have felt that . . . coming home to Frank [husband] and saying that I bought something new, I say "but it was on sale, I've needed it for a long time" [laughter]. But quite possibly more with Mum here . . .

Nathan's wife was sensitive to his parents' criticisms when purchasing expensive, out-of-season fruit or vegetables: '[H]e'll [Nathan's father] question her on why she bought it and would say "[O]h you shouldn't have done that. That's too expensive"'. Marissa and Theresa were pressured by their grandmother to avoid throwing out leftover food, and Gabrielle was more careful to avoid food waste with her mother (Gail) in the house:

Gail: If they've got pasta leftover, I just say, "Don't throw the pasta out I'll eat it".

Gabrielle: And that paid off because Frank [husband] was going to chuck out pasta two nights ago and I said, "No mum wants us to keep it". And he's got it for lunch today [laughter].

Leanne dissuaded her daughter Jodi, and Jodi's partner Brooke, from using the air conditioner unless it was absolutely necessary:

> [T]here were a few days that . . . you'd [Jodi and Brooke] come home and it'd be like, "How come you don't have the air conditioning on?", and I was

like, "well it's not really necessary". You know, with like the windows open and stuff like that. And plus we've got the overhead fans so that makes a bit of a difference sometimes.

Lights were a regular point of contention, with older generations typically enforcing more careful standards. Brooke commented: 'Leanne sometimes follows me around the house turning off all the lights', and Marion 'nagged' her grandchildren to do the same:

> The things that we mainly talk about are things like turning out the lights . . . younger people seem to think, turn on a light in a room and then walk out of the room and leave it on. Whereas when I grew up, you turned the light off.

By living in the same dwelling as her grandchildren, Marion felt that 'we've got a lot of influence over the things that they do and the way that they think . . . They do get nagged a bit.' Wendy's mother exerted a similar influence:

Wendy:	When we go downstairs, Mum is like, "Turn that light off".
Wes [Wendy's husband]:	Yeah and, "Can you turn the front porch light off?"
Wendy:	Yeah, and 'Go turn that light off'. If I leave a light on she'll say something, so she's always been aware of that, but I think that would be more from a financial perspective, because she was a single mum for a long time. But it has the spin-off of being environmental as well.

Wendy also noted that her mother would be annoyed if they used the clothes dryer: 'Mum likes to hang things out on the line, just from a money perspective, not using electricity'. Opportunities for the intergenerational transfer of skills were also apparent, as in Brooke and Leanne's conversation about a vegetable garden:

Leanne:	I've often thought about putting a veggie patch . . . but it's a lot of hard work . . . the old knees are not as good as they used to be, you know with bending over . . . I've done it before so I could do it again.
Brooke:	Yeah that's the difference, I wouldn't know how to start a vegie patch.
Leanne:	I could show you . . .
Brooke:	Yeah definitely . . . I work at Bunnings [home depot store] so we could go get all the stuff from there . . . I'm always curious to how they get things to grow at different times of the year . . . but I've never gone out and read about it to grow my own one [veggie garden].

Previous studies have also identified the potential for children and young people to transfer environmental values and knowledge within the home – to act as 'Trojan horses' for more environmentally sustainable lifestyles (Collins and Hitchings 2012: 195; see also Ballantyne et al. 2001; Larsson et al. 2010). Hadfield-Hill (2013: 356) noted that young people, armed with environmental knowledge, 'are in the ideal position to extend the environmental agenda beyond the confines of the classroom, to homes and the wider community'. Yet, there was limited evidence of upward knowledge transfer among our multigenerational family households. In Nathan's instance, this was because he and his wife did not feel comfortable criticizing his parents. He and his wife discussed the folly of his parents' decision to use two old and inefficient fridges, but did not pass on this knowledge:

Nathan: The fridge . . . is close to thirty years old . . . the freezer is in the garage, and they've also got a bar fridge for the drinks. My wife thought it was silly because they were using up all that electricity when you could just buy a big one . . .

Interviewer: Did she ever say anything or question that when you were living there?

Nathan: No . . . although their electricity bill could probably be halved. . . . If they said, "What do you think?", she would probably tell them that having one fridge would be better, but she would never offer her opinion unsolicited . . . It's just a matter of respect for somebody. She wouldn't walk into a room and say, "No you've got too many fridges, get rid of them" . . . I don't do it either. If my parents were complaining about their electricity bill, I would say, "Well you know you've got a fridge here, do you really need it, because it is just Dad's beers, you don't need 20 bottles of cold beer all at once, you only need one cold beer . . ."

Michael was the most obvious example of a 'Trojan horse' among our sample of interviewees. He reported trying (mostly unsuccessfully) to convince his parents of anthropogenic climate change. He also tried to encourage them to replace their lawn with a food garden, to purchase furniture from op shops and to install an 'environmental toilet'.

It's hard to teach an old dog new tricks. It takes persistence, I had a massive argument with my dad the other day about climate change and whether it was happening or not, and so I brought all this information that I had from the University . . . he's refusing to read little articles that I bring back . . . So I'm going to keep leaving things around. I think it's important because there is a lot of information out there that he needs to know. He's very environmentally conscious, he knows to recycle . . . and cut down water use. He's installing solar panels, but he thinks that this climate change thing is a natural occurrence . . . I think he needs to know [about anthropogenic climate change], and it's my little goal to convert him across to this . . . It will take time.

Michael also took his parents to visit an environmentally sustainable house in Port Kembla, south of Wollongong:

[M]y mum loved it, being from a Filipino background where they grew everything, like this whole backyard was overgrown with fruit and vegetables . . .

These people are awesome and there is another one in Unanderra, similar size to my parents' backyard, with fruit in one section and veggies in another section . . . one of the guys that takes you around there, picked up some grass off the ground and said, "Can you eat this? Why have grass then?" Grass is like this manicured little thing, so instead of having grass that you have to cut every fortnight you could just plant veggies and trees and these are things you can reuse and eat. *And my dad has actually really considered it*, because he understands that cutting the grass is an absolute mission and having little dirt paths that go around fruit trees and veggie gardens in the backyard, like a maze of stuff, is just a more wonderful thing than having manicured grass.

[emphasis added]

Michael conceded that he had not yet won such battles: 'There's a lot more education that needs to go through my parents', but he was admirably persistent.

Multigenerational family households: mitigating environmental harm, coping with environmental calamity

In this chapter, we have drawn attention to multigenerational family households as sites with the potential to foster a range of environmental benefits: innate, inadvertent and intentional. These larger-than-average households reduce per capita resource consumption through economies of scale, and through reduced demand for new dwellings and land for development. Multigenerational family households can achieve such sustainability gains without even trying to be 'green'. Our own research has added insights on the types of sharing (of space, stuff and knowledge) that occur in the everyday lives of multigenerational family households. The households involved in our study enacted a range of environmentally beneficial practices – oftentimes inadvertently, through decisions, behaviours and values which they made based on caring and/or financial imperatives. Multigenerational family living undoubtedly provides opportunities to mitigate environmental harm – to reduce resource consumption and waste. As shown throughout this chapter, such living arrangements also foster intergenerational learning about environmentally beneficial practices.

Such insights are critical to attempts to rethink housing, the fabric of urban living and the shifting nature of families (Klocker and Gibson 2013). In closing, though, we want to also suggest that multigenerational family living provides more than sheer quantitative reductions in resource use and carbon footprints (something that requires further, ongoing monitoring and research). Qualitatively, multigenerational living contributes to everyday resilience, to capacities to care for relatives as they age and to the strengthening of intergenerational knowledge exchanges. In short, it enables families to pool resources and to cope with disruption. In this regard, multigenerational family households also provide an under-explored resource for responding to the kinds of environmental extremity and more frequent disasters that climate scientists now predict as inevitable (Solomon et al. 2009).

Climate change projections for the Illawarra region, where our study took place, anticipate that all temperature variables (average, maximum and minimum temperatures) will increase in the near future (2020–2039) (Office of Environment and Heritage 2014). Studies of heatwave mortality in Europe and the United States have shown that people who live alone, and are socially isolated, are at greater risk of death – with particular attention being drawn to the elderly (Klinenberg 2002; Naughton et al. 2002). Kovats and Ebi (2006) noted the risk of people who live alone dying during a heatwave – before their health status comes to the attention of others. The care within family networks enabled by proximity in multigenerational family households will likely prove useful as societies adjust to a climate-changing world. Furthermore, it is now clear that transformational adaptation – including in the domestic sphere – will be necessary under potentially four degrees of warming (Stafford Smith et al. 2011). As Gibson et al. (2015: 416) have argued, the 'resources for survival are ultimately social and therefore compel greater scrutiny of . . . household life'. Household sustainability practices (including the inadvertent ones) may need to be rethought as survival skills (Gibson et al. 2015). The frugality of Nathan's father, Leanne's food-growing skills and Michael's steady efforts to encourage his family to live differently may have implications beyond identifiable reductions in resource use and carbon footprints. By pooling family members' financial resources, by bringing diverse sets of skills and knowledge under one roof and by ensuring that vulnerable family members – such as the elderly and young – are cared for, multigenerational family households may prove to be an important adaptive resource.

Notes

1   Berners-Lee (2010) based this calculation on a cottage of that size in Scotland. CO_2e refers to the total climate change impact of all the greenhouse gases caused by an activity/thing (expressed in terms of the amount of carbon dioxide that would be needed to have the same impact).
2   The 'Tough times? Green times?' survey was conducted by researchers at AUSCCER in 2009. A sample of 1,443 responses was obtained via a random postal survey.

References

Arbués, F, Villanúa, I and Barberán, R 2010, 'Household size and residential water demand: An empirical approach', *Agricultural and Resource Economics*, vol. 54, no. 1, pp. 61–80.

Askew, L and McGuirk, P 2004, 'Watering the suburbs: Distinction, conformity and the suburban garden', *Australian Geographer*, vol. 35, no. 1, pp. 17–37.

Australian Bureau of Statistics 2010, *Australian Social Trends December 2010. Australian Households: The Future*, Australian Bureau of Statistics, Canberra.

Australian Bureau of Statistics 2012, *2011 Census QuickStats – Australia*, Australian Bureau of Statistics, Canberra.

Autio, M, Heiskanen, E and Heinonen, V 2009, 'Narratives of "green" consumers: The antihero, the environmental hero and the anarchist', *Journal of Consumer Behaviour*, vol. 8, pp. 40–53.

Ballantyne, R, Fien, J and Packer, J 2001, 'Programme effectiveness in facilitating intergenerational influence in environmental education: Lessons from the field', *Journal of Environmental Education*, vol. 32, no. 4, pp. 8–15.

Bentley, M, Fien, J and Neil, C 2004, *Sustainable Consumption: Young Australians as Agents of Change*, Department of Family and Community Services, Canberra.

Berners-Lee, M 2010, *How Bad are Bananas? The Carbon Footprint of Nearly Everything*, Profile Books, London.

Blunt, A 2005, 'Cultural geography: Cultural geographies of home', *Progress in Human Geography*, vol. 29, pp. 505–515.

Büttner, T and Grübler, A 1995, 'The birth of a "green" generation? Generational dynamics of resource consumption patterns', *Technological Forecast and Social Change*, vol. 50, pp. 113–134.

Collins, R and Hitchings, R 2012, 'A tale of two teens: Disciplinary boundaries and geographical opportunities in youth consumption and sustainability research', *Area*, vol. 44, no. 2, pp. 193–199.

Evans, D 2011, 'Thrifty, green or frugal: Reflections on sustainable consumption in a changing economic climate', *Geoforum*, vol. 42, no. 5, pp. 550–557.

Gibson, C, Farbotko, C, Gill, N, Head, L and Waitt, G 2013, *Household Sustainability: Challenges and Dilemmas in Everyday Life*, Edward Elgar, Cheltenham.

Gibson, C, Head, L, and Carr, C 2015, 'From incremental change to radical disjuncture: Rethinking everyday household sustainability practices as survival skills', *Annals of the Association of American Geographers*, vol. 105, no. 2, pp. 416–424.

Gibson, C, Waitt, G, Head, L and Gill, N 2011, 'Is it easy being green? On the dilemmas of material cultures of household sustainability', in R Lane and A Gorman-Murray (eds), *Material Geographies of Household Sustainability*, Ashgate, Aldershot, pp. 19–34.

Hadfield-Hill, S 2013, 'Living in a sustainable community: New spaces, new behaviors?' *Local Environment: The International Journal of Justice and Sustainability*, vol. 18, no. 3, pp. 354–371.

Han, E 2013, 'Urban sprawl eats into Sydney's farmland', *Sydney Morning Herald*, 28 July, online, accessed 18 August 2015, www.smh.com.au/data-point/urban-sprawl-eats-into-sydneys-farmland-20130727–2qr6d.html

Head, L, Farbotko, C, Gibson, C, Gill, N and Waitt, G 2013, 'Zones of friction, zones of traction: The connected household in climate change and sustainability policy', *Australasian Journal of Environmental Management*, vol. 20, no. 4, pp. 351–362.

Hitchings, R, Collins, R and Day, R 2015, 'Inadvertent environmentalism and the action-value opportunity: Reflections from studies at both ends of the generational spectrum', *Local Environment*, vol. 20, no. 3, pp. 369–385.

Hobson, K 2006, 'Bins, bulbs and shower timers: On the "techno-ethics" of sustainable living', *Ethics, Place and Environment*, vol. 9, pp. 317–336.

Hobson, K 2008, 'Reasons to be cheerful: Thinking sustainably in a (climate) changing world', *Geography Compass*, vol. 2, pp. 199–214.

Horne, R, Maller, C and Lane, R 2011, 'Remaking home: The reuse of goods and materials in Australian households', in R Lane and A Gorman-Murray (eds), *Material Geographies of Household Sustainability*, Ashgate, Aldershot, pp. 89–111.

Independent Pricing and Regulatory Tribunal 2010, *Household Survey of Electricity, Water and Gas Usage: Sydney, Blue Mountains and the Illawarra*, Independent Pricing and Regulatory Tribunal, Sydney.

Jones, I, Higgs, P and Ekerdt, D 2009, *Consumption and Generational Change: The Rise of Consumer Lifestyles*, Transactions Publishers, New Jersey.

Keilman, N 2003, 'The threat of small households', *Nature*, vol. 421, pp. 489–490.

Klinenberg, E 2002, *Heat Wave: A Social Autopsy of Disaster in Chicago*, University of Chicago Press, Chicago.

Klocker, N and Gibson, C 2013, 'Looking inwards: Extended family living as an urban consolidation alternative', *Planning Theory and Practice*, vol. 14, no. 4, pp. 555–559.

Klocker, N, Gibson, C and Borger, E 2012, 'Living together, but apart: Material geographies of everyday sustainability in extended family households', *Environment and Planning A*, vol. 44, no. 9, pp. 2240–2259.

Kollmuss, A and Agyeman, J 2002, 'Mind the gap: Why do people act environmentally and what are the barriers to pro-environmental behavior?' *Environmental Education Research*, vol. 8, no. 3, pp. 239–260.

Kovats, R and Ebi, K 2006, 'Heatwaves and public health in Europe', *European Journal of Public Health*, vol. 16, no. 6, pp. 592–599.

Krueger, R and Agyeman, J 2005, 'Sustainability schizophrenia or actually existing sustainabilities? Towards a broader understanding of the politics and promise of local sustainability in the USA', *Geoforum*, vol. 36, no. 4, pp. 410–417.

Lane, R and Gorman-Murray, A (eds) 2011, *Material Geographies of Household Sustainability*, Ashgate, Aldershot.

Larsson, B, Andersson, M and Osbeck, C 2010, 'Bringing environmentalism home: Children's influence on family consumption in the Nordic countries and beyond', *Childhood*, vol. 17, no. 1, pp. 129–147.

Lenzen, M, Dey, C and Foran, B 2004, 'Energy requirements of Sydney households', *Ecological Economics*, vol. 49, pp. 375–399.

Lenzen, M and Murray, S 2001, 'A modified ecological footprint method and its application to Australia', *Ecological Economics*, vol. 37, pp. 229–255.

Liu, J, Daily, G, Ehrlich, P and Luck, G 2003, 'Effects of household dynamics on resource consumption and biodiversity', *Nature*, vol. 421, pp. 530–533.

Liu, J and Diamond, J 2005, 'China's environment in a globalizing world', *Nature*, vol. 435, pp. 1179–1186.

Liu, J, Linderman, M, Ouyang, A, An, L, Yang, J and Zhang, H 2001, 'Ecological degradation in protected areas: The case of Wolong Nature Reserve for giant pandas', *Science*, vol. 292, pp. 98–101.

Maller, C 2011, 'Practices involving energy and water consumption in migrant households', in P Newton (ed.), *Urban Consumption*, CSIRO, Canberra, pp. 237–250.

Naughton, M, Henderson, A and Mirabelli, M 2002, 'Heat related mortality during a 1999 heatwave in Chicago', *American Journal of Preventive Medicine*, vol. 22, pp. 221–227.

Nicholls, S and Moore, M 2011, 'Green light for urban sprawl', *Sydney Morning Herald*, 8 February, accessed 3 December 2015, www.smh.com.au/nsw/green-light-for-urban-sprawl-20110207-1ak8x.html

Office of Environment and Heritage 2014, *Illawarra Climate Change Snapshot*, NSW Office of Environment and Heritage, Sydney.

O'Neill, B and Chen, B 2002, 'Demographic determinants of energy use in the United States', *Population and Development Review*, vol. 28, pp. 53–88.

O'Neill, P and James, S 2014, 'Feeding Sydney: Assessing the importance of the city's peri-urban farms', in B Maheshwari, R Purohit, H Malano, V Singh and P Amerasinghe (eds), *The Security of Water, Food, Energy and Liveability of Cities*, Springer, Chapter 18, pp. 243–256.

Percy-Smith, B and Burns, D 2013, 'Exploring the role of children and young people as agents of change in sustainable development', *Local Environment*, vol. 18, no. 3, pp. 323–339.

Reid, L, Sutton, P and Hunter, C 2010, 'Theorizing the meso level: The household as a crucible of pro-environmental behaviour', *Progress in Human Geography*, vol. 34, no. 3, pp. 309–327.

Shove, E 2003, *Comfort, Cleanliness and Convenience: The Social Organization of Normality*, Berg, Oxford.

Smith, B 2015, 'Biodiversity under threat as Melbourne's grasslands become suburbs', *Sydney Morning Herald*, 27 May, accessed 18 August 2015, www.smh.com.au/technology/sci-tech/biodiversity-under-threat-as-melbournes-grasslands-become-suburbs-20150526-gh9v16.html

Solomon, S, Plattner, GK, Knutti, R and Friedlingstein, P 2009, 'Irreversible climate change due to carbon dioxide emissions', *Proceedings of the National Academy of Sciences*, vol. 106, pp. 1704–1709.

Stafford Smith, M, Horrocks, L, Harvey, A and Hamilton, C 2011, 'Rethinking adaptation for a 4°C world', *Philosophical Transactions of the Royal Society A: Mathematical, Physical and Engineering Sciences*, vol. 369, no. 1934, pp. 196–216.

Stanes, E and Klocker, N 2016, 'Young people in the Global North: Environmental heroes or pleasure-seeking consumers?' in N Ansell and N Klocker (eds), *Global Issues, Change and Threat*, vol. 8 of Skelton, T. (ed.) *Geographies of Children and Young People*, Springer, Singapore, pp. 553–574.

Stanes, E, Klocker, N and Gibson, C 2015, 'Young adult households and domestic sustainabilities', *Geoforum*, vol. 65, pp. 46–58.

Strengers, Y and Maller, C 2012, 'Materialising energy and water resources in everyday practices: Insights for securing supply systems', *Global Environmental Change*, vol. 22, no. 3, pp. 754–763.

Tolia-Kelly, D 2004, 'Materialising post-colonial geographies: Examining the textual landscapes of migration in the South Asian home', *Geoforum*, vol. 35, no. 6, pp. 675–888.

Vanderbeck, R 2007, 'Intergenerational geographies: Age relations, segregation and re-engagements', *Geography Compass*, vol. 1, no. 2, pp. 200–221.

Wright, J, Osman, P and Ashworth, P 2009, *The CSIRO Home Energy Saving Handbook*, Pan Macmillan, Sydney.

Yu, E and Liu, J 2007, 'Environmental impacts of divorce', *Proceedings of the National Academy of Sciences*, vol. 104, no. 51, pp. 20629–20634.

11 Recognizing multigenerational households

Hazel Easthope and Edgar Liu

This book demonstrates the importance of multigenerational households in modern society.

Multigenerational living is commonplace in Australia, as it is in many other societies worldwide. However, the needs and experiences of the people who live in multigenerational households are often overlooked by policymakers, researchers and political representatives. This oversight is reflected in, and perhaps partly the result of, the difficulty of identifying the number and nature of multigenerational households through standardized and widely available statistical data. Yet, analysis of custom census data demonstrates that approximately 20 per cent of all Australians live in a multigenerational household, and that this has been the case for decades (Chapter 2, Burnley).

Some family sociologists might argue that such an oversight is largely irrelevant, as multigenerational households represent just another example of the wide diversity of families in modern society. Research on the 'sociology of the family' is now more likely to speak of the 'sociology of families' or the 'sociology of intimacy' (therefore, the complexity and diversity of families) rather than of 'the family' in a homogenous, singular manner. Such changes are not simply semantic but reflect a trend away from consideration of the family as an institution and toward a focus on reflexivity and 'the open-endedness of intimate relations' (Gilding 2010: 757). Some conservative theorists like Popenoe (1993) have spoken of the decline of the family as a social institution. Critical theorists like Allan (2008) have welcomed the recognition of the diversity and flexibility of these intimate relationships. Despite their ideological differences, both groups of theorists now prioritize reflexivity over institutional understandings of the family (Gilding 2010). This shift has been important for the development of the field of family studies, especially for enabling an increased recognition of the diversity and flexibility of family relationships. However, we share the concern of Gilding (2010) about the disproportionate prioritizing of reflexivity at the expense of a recognition of the ongoing importance of social structure and social institutions in understanding modern-day families. The chapters contained in this book demonstrate the importance of structural changes in society, but also the impacts of public policy, and social and cultural views about the family in influencing people's decisions to live in multigenerational households and their experiences of this living arrangement.

The decision to live in a multigenerational household is complex. It is strongly influenced by structural factors such as housing affordability, as well as changes in the type (increasingly requiring higher education qualifications) and stability (increasingly 'flexible' or casualized) of employment available (Chapter 3, East-hope and Chapter 4, Whelan). It is also influenced by the availability of government support for older people, children, students and others, with many families opting – and sometimes needing – to support those individuals within the household in the absence of government support that is considered sufficient or appropriate for their needs (Chapter 3, Easthope and Chapter 5, Liu). Decisions to live in a multigenerational household also appear to be influenced by cultural and family traditions (Chapter 3, Easthope and Chapter 7, Mariño et al.), a finding supported by the fact that individuals from particular countries of origin are more likely to live in multigenerational households (Chapter 2, Burnley). However, birthplace alone is not sufficient to explain multigenerational living preferences (see also Flatau et al. 2007), and evidence presented in this book (Chapter 3, East-hope and Chapter 4, Whelan) suggests that financial considerations often play a larger role in these decisions than do cultural preferences.

Experiences of multigenerational living vary considerably among families and individuals. In part, this variety reflects the different forms that multigenerational households take – a middle-aged woman living with her husband, elderly mother and adult son will likely have a different experience of multigenerational living than would a young closeted LGBTI adult who has not left the parental home (Chapter 5, Liu and Chapter 8, Fileborn et al.). Yet, the chapters in this book have identified some common themes influencing people's experiences of multigenerational living. Companionship and support and the potential for intergenerational learning were identified as important benefits for many multigenerational households (Chapter 5, Liu and Chapter 10, Klocker et al.), as was the potential to provide care and support to members of the family, especially to older family members (Chapter 7, Mariño et al.). Financial savings, increased housing affordability and being able to afford a better lifestyle were also important benefits for many living in this household type (Chapter 4, Whelan and Chapter 5, Liu). On the other hand, a lack of privacy in the dwelling (Chapter 5, Liu and Chapter 9, Judd) and increased household chores for some family members (Chapter 5, Liu and Chapter 6, Craig and Powell) are oft-cited drawbacks of this living arrangement. Each of these issues is intricately tied up with structural changes in society, the impact of public policy and social and cultural views about the family. In this final chapter, we unpack these issues and consider their implications for the well-being of people living in multigenerational households now and into the future.

Why do multigenerational households matter?

There are three reasons why it is important that we turn our attention to multigenerational households and make up for the dearth of research and understanding of this important group of households over past decades. The first is that this will help to improve the well-being of the individuals and families who live in these households by providing better information and understanding to inform government policy decisions and private sector service provision. The second is that understanding the decisions, actions and experiences of people living in multigenerational households provides us with a valuable window through which to examine economic, social, cultural and small 'p' political processes in contemporary society. The third is because multigenerational living is almost certainly going to continue to be an important way in which families respond to significant structural changes in society.

If we want to understand these changes and their effects on society, we need to understand multigenerational living as an important piece of this story. In the Australian context, multigenerational living has been an important strategy through which families have dealt with housing affordability pressures, the retraction of government support for participation in higher education and welfare retraction. Understanding the motivations and experiences of multigenerational household members also provides us with insights into intergenerational exchange and changing social norms in modern Australian society. Understanding these strategies, and the experiences of multigenerational household members, is essential if we are to provide them with the recognition and support they need in the future. In the following sections, we link these strategies with discussions we had with people who had first-hand experiences in advocating for, and designing policies and housing products that may facilitate better outcomes for, people who live in multigenerational households.

Multigenerational living as a means of combating housing unaffordability

In many Australian cities, the cost of housing (both to rent and to buy) is an important motivator for multigenerational living. As a society that has traditionally favoured homeownership over other forms of tenure (Troy 2012), this main form of tenure continues to be subsidized by state and federal governments through ownership grants, stamp duty exemptions and negative gearing. The high cost of rental housing in Australia affects renters' ability to save for a home deposit (Stone et al. 2013) and renters in Australia have much less security in their housing arrangements than do homeowners (Hulse et al. 2011). Living together can be one means of helping young adults to save money that might otherwise have been spent on rent toward a deposit for a property later in life. Young adults attending university and other higher education institutions make up a significant portion of multigenerational household members in Australia and elsewhere (e.g. the United Kingdom; Marsh 2014). This proportion may continue to increase with a recent push for higher proportions of young Australians to attain tertiary qualifications (Gillard 2009). For many young adults, higher education would be out of the question because of the significant decline in government support for students over the past two decades were it not for the support their parents provide by allowing them to remain in the family home (Chapter 3, Easthope). With further fee deregulation proposed (although rejected by the Australian Senate; The Australian 2015), young people not being able to afford independent living while carrying significant amounts of debt in the form of student loans well into their thirties may be a reality for many Australian families in the future.

Multigenerational living can also be a way of providing financial support to other household members who cannot afford to live independently by way of pooling resources to cover a mortgage and enable property (co)ownership. These family responses to housing affordability, however, are seldom supported by government policies. Most policy efforts have focused on enabling individuals (particularly first homeowners) in purchasing and building their own home (Randolph et al. 2013) or assisting older homeowners to downsize (or 'right' size) in order to free up 'underutilized' stock (Productive Ageing Centre 2015). The relaxation of rules regarding the construction of secondary or ancillary dwelling may be one way of increasing in-fill density while providing the much needed (and wanted) privacy for multigenerational households. A housing developer who specializes in housing products for multigenerational households we interviewed, the building of secondary dwellings have been favoured over house extension since the rules were relaxed in NSW in the early 2010s (NSW DPI 2011). These products, however, may not be affordable to many families, especially not to those who do not own their current home.

Some of the participants in the *Living Together* project spoke of the difficulty (and associated high costs) of making sure that the rights and responsibilities of everyone involved in their co-ownership arrangements were legally protected through specialized contracts. In an interview with a state planner, we subsequently learned that such legal mechanisms already exist in some jurisdictions in Australia. The challenge then becomes connecting those who have such needs with these existing mechanisms.

Multigenerational living in light of welfare retraction

Multigenerational living has already proven to be an important way in which many families have responded to the retraction and privatization of services previously provided by the state. In this neoliberal context in which labour power has been reduced, industry deregulated and finance 'liberated' (Harvey 2005), intergenerational support has filled the gap. With the high costs of both private childcare and elderly care in Australia, multigenerational living can represent a significant cost saving for families. The ageing of the population and government policies promoting ageing in place – older people remaining in the family home rather than moving into institutional care – means that we can expect the importance of multigenerational living for elderly care to increase in the future. These policy changes, however, are often not accompanied by changes in other related policies, such as family care benefits, that may facilitate the provision of care away from institutions. Many of our participants, for example, spoke of the financial burden of caring for an elderly person within the family home with little access to appropriate subsidies. Our interview with a care advocate also noted that some families of disabled people, often in partnership with other families in similar situations, had to contribute large sums in building specialized accommodation for their loved ones once the care institutions had shut down. Sadly, however, not all families have the means to do so, and the well-being of the people who receive such care as well as those who provide them may be compromised.

Furthermore, in the context of social and political arguments about whether it should be the family's responsibility to take care of its own members, there are now movements for the wider recognition of family care providers. The Grandparent Movement, for example, is highlighting the costs (financial and otherwise) borne by some older people when caring for their own family members, which in turn may affect their ability to enjoy their hard-earned retirement, their freedom to achieve long-held ambitions (e.g. overseas travel) or even their ability to spend on essentials. Some advocacy groups are now calling for such carers to be eligible to receive some welfare support (CoTA Australia 2014; Grandparents Australia 2014). Most welfare to families in Australia, however, continues to focus on the nuclear family (such as the Family Tax Benefits).

The continued reform of the disability care sector across Australia sees many people with disabilities being cared for by their family in the family home. The latest reform – the introduction of the National Disability Insurance Scheme (NDIS) in 2012-13 – was lauded by many care providers and disability advocacy groups as an important step in the provision of more tailored care for people with disabilities. The representative of a carers advocacy group whom we interviewed concurred, but also noted that there are drawbacks to this system. Although those eligible for the NDIS would be able to access more professional care through the system, many others will receive little, with only about one in ten people who has a disability being eligible to access NDIS-supported services. The situation may worsen in the future, with some states having announced plans to withdraw their support for state-supported services in view of the federally funded NDIS.

Although the NDIS is seen as a positive step in care provision for some, the withdrawal of state-supported care would have wider implications for the family. For example, the care advocacy group representative we interviewed spoke of the disbanding of respite care for carers. As some of the participants in the *Living Together* project attested, the lack of respite, especially for full-time carers, can have a significant impact on their well-being and relationships with other household members (Chapter 5, Liu). While many home-based carers made an active choice in caring for their own family members, with some believing that they can provide a better level of care than some paid services, many others are constrained by the high financial costs of professional services. As the care advocacy group representative said, 'it shouldn't be an expectation, it should be a choice'. Some of the current welfare reforms in Australia are limiting these families' choices.

Multigenerational living as a form of intergenerational exchange

Most Australian literature has focused on 'downward' economic intergenerational transfers (Olsberg and Winters 2005; Cobb-Clark and Ribar 2009), where assets and other quantifiable aspects of these dependencies are transferred from the parents to their offspring without reciprocation. International research has, however, questioned this understanding of intergenerational dependencies. This is especially the case where the terms 'downward' and 'transfer' imply the relationship is unidirectional. While in Chapter 6 (Craig and Powell) it was clear that in terms of housework the support has mostly been unidirectional and downward, chapters in this book provide examples of upward financial support (Chapter 3, Easthope) and practical and social support in both directions (Chapter 5, Liu and Chapter 10, Klocker et al.). Vicente and Sousa (2009: 35) argued that the multigenerational household can be 'a setting which provides opportunities for mutual help and support' and called for intergenerational dependencies to be examined as intergenerational exchanges. Similarly, Katz and Lowenstein (2010) argue that there is a need for increased recognition of intergenerational or familial reciprocity.

Indeed, multigenerational living can provide support for older household members who are financially insecure (Chapter 5, Liu). It can also enable older members of households to return to study, change their career, set up a business or otherwise take a calculated risk in their working lives (Chapter 3, Easthope and Chapter 5, Liu). With the increasing casualization of the workforce, insecurity of employment and demand among employers for higher education qualifications, multigenerational living provides an important mechanism to enable family members to respond to these demands. This support is also demonstrated in the phenomenon of 'boomeranging' or young adults who have left the family home returning (Veevers and Mitchell 1998), often due to insecurity of employment and job loss (Judd et al. 2010). Multigenerational living is an important way in which many individuals and families deal with the 'flexibility' of modern life, or what Bauman (2001) has called 'liquid modernity' – characterized by endless flows of people, money and ideas.

Some theorists have argued that rapid social change – including a flexible labour market, extended education and training, a shift to service industries, a decline in full-time jobs and an increase in marital breakdowns – has threatened both class and family structures in modern society (e.g. Jones 2000: 154). Yet, the stories of multigenerational households in this book point to the versatility and tenacity of families in responding to these pressures through providing intergenerational practical and emotional support.

As we write this book, the economic outlook for Australia, as in much of the world, is uncertain. In the late 2000s, Australia largely escaped the fate of significant economic downturn as witnessed across the United States and several Western European economies thanks in large part to the mining boom (Cleary 2011). As Perlich (2009) recognized, however, our reliance on the mining boom created a 'dual economy' that significantly depended on the fortunes of (and demands for mined minerals from) China. With fears of a Chinese economic downturn in the mid-2010s (The Economist 2015; 2016), Australia is noted to be particularly susceptible to a less certain economic future (Uren 2016). There is no indication that the volatility of the economy and insecurity of employment will ease any time soon. Between March quarter 2011 and September quarter 2015, the unemployment rate across Australia increased from 5.1 per cent to 6.2 per cent, with some of the sharpest recent increases noted in mining-intensive areas (DoE 2012; 2016). Previous waves of economic turmoil have been linked with a rise in multigenerational living, and especially a delay in the home leaving of young adults in other countries (Fry and Passel 2014; ONS 2014) and it is not a stretch to assume that further economic uncertainty and further cuts to government welfare provisions would result in more reliance on family for economic support, including through multigenerational living arrangements.

Multigenerational living and social change

All of these structural factors that have influenced the formation of multigenerational families, and their experiences of this living arrangement – high house prices, 'flexible' employment, increasing expectations regarding higher education for the workforce, the ageing of the population – both reflect changes in social actions and expectations and act to precipitate them. For example, Mitchell and Lovegreen (2009: 1652) indicate that in Canada the shift toward delayed home leaving is largely the result of structural factors (changed economic conditions) and cultural diversity, both of which have influenced broader societal expectations. Moreover, reporting research on demographic change in Europe, Harper (2006: 165) argues that 'the knowledge of demographic ageing is itself impacting on social, economic and political decisions [taken by] both national and international institutions, and individuals themselves' and that knowledge about what happens in ageing societies can influence individuals in delaying a number of life transitions, including an increase in age at first marriage, first childbirth and first home leaving.

Most previous work on social expectations regarding multigenerational living in Australia, and other immigrant-receiving countries, has focused on the important role that immigration has played in multigenerational living arrangements (ABS 2009; Zorlu and Mulder 2011). In Chapter 2, Burnley demonstrates that country of birth is certainly associated with the likelihood of living in a multigenerational household, with people from countries and regions where multigenerational living is traditional – North Africa, the Middle East, East Asia and Southern Europe – being more likely to live in multigenerational households in Australia. Yet, this is only part of the story, with the majority of people living in multigenerational households having been born in Australia (Chapter 2, Burnley). Such decisions, as demonstrated in Chapter 7 (Mariño et al.), may also be influenced by the social practices of their new home society. Indeed, Flatau et al. (2007) have found that even after controlling for country of birth, education and family background there appears to have been a shift toward later home leaving among young adults in Australia, which they attribute to changing social norms. Local social norms and expectations, may also be dynamically influenced by incoming cultures. In Chapter 3, however, Easthope demonstrates that while there does appear to be a greater acceptance of multigenerational living in Australia, it is qualified by the reasons behind that living arrangement – with households who live together for purposes of economic support or care for children, the elderly, or people with a disability normalized, and those who live together for social support, or because they simply want to, still experiencing some stigma. Multigenerational living, it seems, is tied strongly to ideas of dependence and especially 'appropriate' forms of dependence between family members and between generations.

The importance of multigenerational households

Multigenerational households are important. They are important numerically – they are a common, yet largely overlooked, household type comprising one in five Australians. They are important financially – they provide support to household members in the context of an insecure employment market, expensive housing markets and the retraction of government support for childcare, elderly care and higher education. They are important socially – they provide nonfinancial care and support to their members and facilitate intergenerational information exchange and learning.

In part, the story of multigenerational households is a story of dependence and inter-dependence. It is a story of care provision, financial support and the efficient use of housing and other resources. But it is more than that. It is also a story of meaningful relationships, intergenerational learning, cultural traditions and social norms. Essentially, it is a story of the importance of family in modern society.

Although the experiences of multigenerational living are often positive, they are not universally so, and the decision to live in a multigenerational household always lies somewhere along a spectrum between choice and constraint. Government policies that place increasing emphasis on the role of the family in financial and practical care giving need to recognize these constraints, and the impacts of such policies on the everyday lives of families. A suite of new supporting policy and practice responses is needed to account for these constraints and to mitigate the potentially negative impacts of multigenerational living. These can be provided by government and private sector interests. Examples include clearer legal guidance for families looking to purchase and own property together, the introduction of planning and design guidelines facilitating and enabling better housing design to meet the needs (especially for privacy) of multigenerational households, a recognition of multigenerational living in metropolitan planning guidelines, and recognition of the substantial financial and practical support provided to children, the elderly and differently abled by multigenerational households.

Multigenerational living will continue to be an important way families respond to significant structural changes in society as it has been in the past. Their contribution to our society – in supporting the less independent and in connecting families – must be recognized for and supported by society.

References

ABS 2009, 'Home and away: The living arrangement of young people', *Journal of the Home Economics Institute of Australia*, vol. 16, pp. 29–34.

Allan, G 2008, 'Flexibility, friendship, and family', *Personal Relationships*, vol. 15, pp. 1–16.

The Australian 2015, 'University deregulation is the government's next big test', *The Australian*, 10 August 2015, accessed 15 February 2016, http://www.theaustralian.com.au/opinion/editorials/university-deregulation-is-the-governments-next-big-test/news-story/7799c3124b4eddb9618f955fdc465a30.

Bauman, Z 2001, *The Individualised Society*, Polity Press, Cambridge.

Cleary, P 2011, *Too Much Luck: The Mining Boom and Australia's Future*, Black Inc., Carlton.

Cobb-Clark, DA and Ribar, DC 2009, *Financial Stress, Family Conflict, and Youths' Successful Transition to Adult Roles*, Discussion Paper, Centre for Economic Policy Research, Australian National University, Canberra.

CoTA Australia 2014, *Submission to Inquiry into Grandparents who Take Primary Responsibility for Raising Their Grandchildren*, March, Council of the Ageing Australia.

DoE 2012, *Small Area Labour Markets – March Quarter 2012*, Department of Employment.

DoE 2016, *Small Area Labour Markets – September Quarter 2015*, Department of Employment.

The Economist 2015, 'The great fall of China', *The Economist*, Asia-Pacific Edition, 27 August 2015, accessed 8 February 2016, http://www.economist.com/news/leaders/21662544-fear-about-chinas-economy-can-be-overdone-investors-are-right-be-nervous-great-fall.

The Economist 2016, 'The Yuan and the markets', *The Economist*, Asia-Pacific Edition, 16 January 2015, accessed 8 February 2016, http://www.economist.com/news/leaders/21688396-strains-currency-suggest-something-very-wrong-chinas-politics-yuan-and.

Flatau, P, James, I, Watson, R, Wood, G, and Hendershott PH 2007, 'Leaving the parental home in Australia over the generations: evidence from the Household, Income and Labour Dynamics in Australia (HILDA) Survey', *Journal of Population Research*, vol. 24, pp. 51–71.

Fry, R and Passel, J 2014, *In Post-Recession Era, Young Adults Drive Continuing Rise in Multi-Generational Living*, Pew Research Center, Washington, DC.

Gilding, M 2010, 'Reflexivity over and above convention: the new orthodoxy in the sociology of personal life, formerly sociology of the family', *The British Journal of Sociology*, vol. 61, pp. 757–777.

Gillard, J 2009, 'Opening Address', *Transition, Retention and Progression Forum*, 9 December 2009, accessed 10 March 2010, http://www.deewr.gov.au/Ministers/Gillard/Media/Speeches/Pages/Article_091209_135332.aspx.

Grandparents Australia 2014, *Submission to the Australian Senate on Grandparents as Kinship Carers*, March, accessed 8 February 2016, http://www.aph.gov.au/DocumentStore.ashx?id=df6a3169-d7cf-4c76–94db-924be3a36904&subId=205692.

Harper, S 2006, The ageing of family life transitions," in JA Vincent, C Phillipson and M Downs (eds.), *The Futures of Old Age*, SAGE, London, pp. 164–171.

Harvey, D 2005, *A Brief History of Neoliberalism*, Oxford University Press, Oxford.

Hulse, K, Milligan, V and Easthope, H 2011, *Secure Occupancy in Rental Housing: Conceptual Foundations and Comparative Perspectives*, Final Report No. 170, Australian Housing and Urban Research Institute, Melbourne.

Jones, G 2000, 'Trail-Blazers and path-followers: Social reproduction and geographical mobility in youth', in S Arber and C Attias-Donfut (eds), *The Myth of Generational Conflict*, Routledge, London, pp. 154–173.

Judd, B, Olsberg, D, Quinn, J, Groenhart L and Demirbilek, O 2010, 'Dwelling, land and neighbourhood use by older home owners', Final report No. 144, Australian Housing and Urban Research Institute, Melbourne.

Katz, R and Lowenstein, A 2010, 'Theoretical perspectives on intergenerational solidarity, conflict and ambivalence, in M Izuhara (ed.), *Ageing and Intergenerational Relations: Family Reciprocity from a Global Perspective*, Policy Press, Bristol, pp. 29–56.

Marsh, S 'Rise of the live-at-home student commuter', *The Guardian*, 26 August 2014, accessed 15 February 2016, http://www.theguardian.com/education/2014/aug/26/rise-live-at-home-student-commuter.

Mitchell, BA and Lovegreen, LD 2009, 'The empty nest syndrome in midlife families: a multimethod exploration of parental gender differences and cultural dynamics', *Journal of Family Issues*, vol. 30, pp. 1651–1670.

NSW DPI 2011, 'Supporting secondary dwellings (Granny Flats)', *Fact Sheet*, NSW Department of Planning and Infrastructure.

Olsberg, D and Winters, M 2005, *Ageing in Place: Intergenerational and Intrafamilial Housing Transfers and Shifts in Later Life*, Final Report No. 88, Australian Housing and Urban Research Institute, Melbourne.

ONS 2014, 'Large increase in 20 to 34-year-olds living with parents since 1996', *Population*, UK Office for National Statistics.

Perlich, H 2009, 'The impact of the GFC on Australia as a "dual economy"', *Journal of Australian Political Economy*, vol. 64, pp. 65–90.

Popenoe, D 1988, *Disturbing the Nest: Family Change and Decline in Modern Societies*, Aldine de Gruyter, New York.

Productive Ageing Centre 2015, *Seniors Downsizing on their Own Terms: Overcoming Planning, Legal and Policy Impediments to the Creation of Alternative Retirement Communities*, National Seniors Australia.

Randolph, B, Pinnegar, S and Tice, A 2013, 'The first home owner boost in Australia: A case study of outcomes in the Sydney housing market', *Urban Policy and Research*, vol. 31, pp. 55–73.

Stone, W, Burke, T, Hulse, K and Ralston, L 2013, *Long-Term Private Rental in a Changing Australian Private Rental Sector*, Final Report No. 209, Australian Housing and Urban Research Institute, Melbourne.

Troy, P 2012, *Accommodating Australians: Commonwealth Government Involvement in Housing*, Federation Press, Leichhardt.

Uren, D 2016, 'China economic meltdown sparks sharemarket rout', *The Australian*, 8 January 2015, accessed 8 February 2016, http://www.theaustralian.com.au/business/economics/china-economic-meltdown-sparks-sharemarket-rout/news-story/141d431008064efb90b26142f08c5f37.

Veevers, J and Mitchell, B 1998, 'Intergenerational exchanges and perceptions of support within "Boomerang kid" family environments', *International Journal of Aging and Human Development*, vol. 46, pp. 91–108.

Vincente, H and Sousa, L 2009, 'The multigenerational family and the elderly: A mutual or parasitical symbiotic relationship?' in A Sousa (ed.), *Families in Later Life: Emerging Themes and Challenges*, New Science Publishers, New York, pp. 27–48.

Zorlu, A and Mulder, C 2011, 'Ethnic differences in leaving home: Timing and pathways', *Demography*, vol. 48, pp. 49–72.

Index